The Path
to a
Successful Retirement

A retirement authority shares his insights
in a unique and comprehensible manner.

James F. (Jim) Smith, MBA, CPA, CFP

The information presented in this book was compiled from sources believed to be reliable. Care was taken to provide useful and accurate information. However, the concepts presented are subject to Federal and State laws, which are constantly changing. Furthermore, these laws are subject to differing interpretations. Therefore, the reader is advised to seek professional legal and financial advice for any points regarding law.

This publication is designed to provide accurate and authoritative information in regard to the subject matter covered. It is sold with the understanding that the publisher is not engaged in rendering legal, accounting or other professional service. If legal advice or other expert assistance is required, the services of a competent professional person should be sought.

—From a Declaration of Principles jointly adapted by a Committee of The American Bar Association and a Committee of Publishers and Associations.

Published by: Sligo Publishing Company
               Box #14
               1115 Regents Blvd.
               Tacoma, WA 98466

Cover concept and design : Michael Craft and David Julian—Seattle, WA.
Michael's parents Bud & Gael were kind enough to grace the cover.

Printed in the United States of America

ISBN 0-9646809-3-9 $19.95 Softcover, lay-flat binding

Library of Congress Catalog Card Number 95-069056

Acknowledgments

I often console myself with the fact that my next *original* thought may be my very first original thought. This book has benefited greatly from the many people who helped me by reviewing portions, sharing their experiences, correcting my errors and supporting my endeavors. Without their assistance and encouragement I would still be buried in a morass of unconnected thoughts.

My family provided both encouragement and sage advice as they helped me. A very grateful thanks to my wife Betty for putting up with my moods, and for helping with all the tedious proof-reading. My daughter MaryEileen's degree in English really paid off, but I am particularly grateful for her intuitive sense of phrasing a thought. Thanks also to my son Joe and son-in-law Tom Barr—it was very beneficial to have their banking and accounting skills for the technical portions.

Thanks to my many fellow professionals who reviewed portions of the manuscript: Andy Landis, author of *Social Security, the Inside Story*; Merle Palmer, CLU, CHFC, MSFS, for his 40 years of insurance experience, Dr. Patricia Black, EdD, for her suggestions on the life-style chapters; John Pitts, CFP, and Anne Copeland, CFP, PhD, for their help on the investment and planning chapters; Luke Gjurasic, NALU, for his thoughts on long-term care; Kathleen Miller, CFP, MBA, author of *Fair Share Divorce for Women*, and Patricia Rourke, attorney, for their help on divorce and the single person issues; and Doug Schafer, attorney, for his in-depth review of the estate planning chapters.

Thank you Michael Craft and David Julian for the cover concept and design.

Thank you, Emil Mihelich, author of *Running Clear*, for editing my terrible English composition, and Rick Oldenburg for cleaning up my graphics. Thanks also to the folks at Panorama City, including Marcene Oakley, Phyllis and Jerry Rathburn, and Kay Hirt for sharing their insights on life in a retirement community. I am also indebted to my friends— Betty Frey, a very active senior volunteer, for reviewing the life-style chapters; Len Heritage for sharing his experiences as a divorced and single parent; and Darrel Snyder for taking the time to review the manuscript in its entirety. My final thanks goes to Carol Lindahl for adding that touch of professionalism that this book needed.

Table of Contents

Appendices

Preface

"The future is purchased by the present."
Samuel Johnson (18th century English Author)

Travel with the Meehans and the Keanes as they develop their path to a successful retirement

This book is written for that vast population of people age 50 years and older. Why 50? Because it's at this age that a person finally faces up to the fact that retirement is approaching. Often it's the first time in their lives that most people can even begin thinking about saving money for retirement. Though financial planning is the bedrock of the book, other lifestyle issues are integrated to provide a balanced approach to retirement.

The Meehans and Keanes serve as our surrogates as they plan their futures. You will find your own path as you relate to their concerns as they work to reach their goals. Joe and Betty Meehan are arriving at that magic age of 50. Their in-laws, the Keanes, in their early sixties, have already reached retirement age. The Meehans and Keanes are part of the **sandwich generation.** In addition to having children, they also have a surviving parent. Marie Meehan, in her eighties, lives one hundred miles south of her children. She finds herself addressing the issues of older age.

The two couples make use of their own knowledge and experience. In addition, they engage professionals to assist them. Join them as they visit these professionals in their quest for information.

The couples have made it a practice to get together at least once every couple of weeks. They usually meet over Sunday breakfast, at one house or the other, and discuss their plans, dreams, or just the events of the prior week.

As the story unfolds, Joe and Betty are coming to grips with their failure to plan for a secure and rewarding retirement.

Sunday morning at the home of Jim and Mary Keane

Jim and Mary are entertaining the Meehans on their outside deck, which overlooks beautiful Puget Sound. Joe and Betty marveled at the number of sailboats, off in the distance, as the sun, glistening through the fir trees, began to warm the surroundings. On this morning, the group just wanted to sit and enjoy the scenery.

The couples were finishing their second latté, a flavored coffee which is the current rage in the Northwest, when the conversation turned to the question of, "What happened in work this week?"

Mary began with a description of her week, "On Wednesday, we held a retirement luncheon for an employee who has been with our company for over 40 years. By Friday, we heard that he changed his mind. It seems that after he made his decision and informed management, he had a financial planner look at his affairs. He found out, much to his dismay, that he could not afford to retire just yet. He delayed telling anyone because he was so embarrassed."

"How did management feel about him changing his mind?" Betty asked.

"There really wasn't much they could do," Mary answered. "After all, he was a loyal employee for all those years. Since a replacement was already named, they had to do a quick shuffle to keep everyone happy. Unfortunately, the employee involved ended up with a lower status job."

"That's so sad," Betty commented. "I worry about us being financially able to retire when we want to." She then asked her husband Joe about his thoughts on the subject.

"I really don't know when we will be able to retire," Joe replied, expressing his uncertainty.

"When you think about it," Mary chipped in, "in years past, people were able to plan their retirement date with some degree of certainty. For example, Jim's dad worked until he was almost 75. Today, with all the corporate downsizing, many employees cannot count on long term employment."

"Not only that," her brother Joe added, "look at all the people who job-hop, just to earn a few extra dollars. They often fail to take into account the impact on their retirement. Retirement savings build up very slowly and get their biggest impact only after being in the plan for a long period of time."

The conversation turned to less serious subjects as the couples relaxed in the warmth of the day. Later, after helping clear up the dishes, the Meehans took their leave from the Keanes. During the car ride home, Joe and Betty resolved to get better control of their financial affairs.

Chapter 1

*"To succeed in the future, people need
to get control of their finances during the present."*

What kind of financial shape are we in?

Later that week at the home of Joe and Betty Meehan

Joe and Betty Meehan are still recovering from helping to pay their kids' college costs. They discovered that raising children, combined with purchasing a house, had severely restricted their opportunity to save. Like so many others, they put their financial future on the back burner.

Joe Meehan is turning fifty. He is employed by a medium-sized firm which offers a reasonable retirement package, including a tax-deferred savings plan. Joe, an accountant, has worked his way up in the company to a middle management level. He is currently well paid, but that hasn't always been the case. His professional background includes heavy involvement in statistical analysis and computers. Joe likes to read, and prefers a hands-on approach to problem solving. He is skeptical and does his own research. Joe will press on until he feels his question has been answered. He loves to get involved in details and will go to great length to explain how he reasoned out the answer.

Betty Meehan, also turning fifty, is just returning to the work-force after several decades of raising the children and working as a homemaker. Betty has recently joined a very small business which is looking into providing employee benefits. Though Betty lacks a college education, she is a very practical person and has always handled the family's finances. While Betty pays the bills and worries about the budget, she depends on Joe to handle their long-term finances.

After the children went off to college, Joe made one of their former bedrooms into a home office and furnished it with an old desk for his home computer. It was in this office that Joe and Betty often discussed their financial issues. On this particular evening, they continued the discussion on retirement that began at their in-laws the previous Sunday. Both realized, almost immediately, that neither had ever verbalized their retirement dreams. Consequently, they decided that the recording of those dreams was a good place to start planning their future. The dream of a secure retirement became a major concern to Betty and she wondered, "If they could afford it?"

Like many couples, Joe and Betty discovered that building dreams without a proper foundation frequently leads to poor implementation. After several false starts, they soon realized that first they had to understand their financial position. They needed to answer the question, *"What kind of financial shape are we in?"*

Joe applied his accounting knowledge and structured his personal assets the same way his company did. He understood that companies have been using the **balance sheet** to display their financial condition ever since Alucca Pacioli, an Italian monk, published the first text on the double entry bookkeeping system in 1494. The balance sheet summarizes your **assets** (things that you own) on the left side of the statement and **liabilities** (things that you owe) on the right side. The difference between your assets and your liabilities is your **net worth**. However, Joe made a major change between his company's approach and one that he knew an individual should use. A company's balance sheet is developed using accounting conventions, one of which is to report the values at cost. In computing their net worth, Joe was not interested in what an item originally cost. He was more concerned about the item's current value or fair market value. Simply stated, **fair market value** is

$$\text{assets - liabilities} = \text{net worth}$$

the value that a willing buyer and a willing seller would agree upon. By using fair market value, Joe and Betty can determine their net worth at any given point in time.

Joe thought of the balance sheet as a photograph which captured values at the instant it was taken. He understood that these amounts would change over time. Therefore, he planned to summarize their assets, perhaps once every few years. Summarizing would enable him to chart their progress over time.

To Joe, the balance sheet was more than a listing. It was a summary of his assets and liabilities by category. He ranked the assets and liabilities in the order of their **liquidity**. Liquidity refers to assets that can be exchanged for cash. The assets listed first are those which can be converted to cash most readily, and the liabilities listed first are those which must be paid first. Longer term assets and liabilities, such as mortgages, are listed lower on the statement. By categorizing the assets and liabilities in this manner, Joe could readily understand his financial position.

Assets that can easily be converted into cash are helpful in the event of emergencies, such as the loss of employment or the need for a down payment on a car. For most of Joe's working life, he handled such emergencies by borrowing from the local bank or credit union. But now that he was planning for retirement, he realized that a specific amount should be saved and reserved for emergencies.

Often financial planners have formulas for developing the amount people should carry in their **emergency fund**. Usually this amounts to three to six months of living expenses. Joe took a different view. His simple rule of thumb was to maintain an emergency fund of $10,000 that could cover most low-level emergencies. To preserve this fund for real emergencies, Joe decided to name the fund, "The Meehan Emergency Fund." He hoped this simple gesture would make him and Betty less inclined to dip into it for everyday items. If the emergency were of a greater magnitude or were to continue for a long duration, then he would most probably need to dip into those assets that he had reserved for retirement.

Through his extensive reading, Joe had become aware that Social Security and company retirement plans provide only about two-thirds of a person's retirement needs. Therefore, Joe realizes that their saving must provide one third of their retirement income. Joe further understood that to accumulate the amount needed, he should use **CDs** or money market funds only for short-term parking of their funds. Any excess dollars saved in these low-return investments would hamper the Meehans' ability to earn sufficient growth to meet their retirement income goals.

> # Why sub-optimize your ability to earn a reasonable return just to be ready for an emergency that may never occur?

Joe developed a worksheet (Appendix 1a) to collect the supporting detail of the assets and liabilities and he then summarized this detail into a Balance Sheet.

Balance Sheet				
Joe & Betty Meehan			**January 19XX**	
Assets			**Liabilities**	
Cash:	$	500	Credit Card Debt	$	6,000
Checking Accounts	$	2,000	Other Short Term Debt	$	17,000
Savings Accounts	$	6,000		
Money Market Funds			Loans:	
			Automobile Loans	$	14,000
Investments:				
Retirement Accounts	$	96,000	Mortgages:	
			Home Mortgage	$	35,000
Real Estate:				
Personal Residence	$	156,000		
Personal:				
Automobiles	$	25,000		
Personal Property	$	35,000		
Total Assets	**$**	**320,500**	**Total Liabilities**	**$**	**72,000**
			Net Worth	**$**	**248,500**
Debt-to-equity ratio	**29%**			

> ## Debt-to-equity ratio = total debt / total net worth

To portray how debt relates to net worth, Joe calculated the **debt-to-equity ratio** by dividing the $72,000 debt by the $320,500 total assets. The debt-to-equity ratio is a quick reference for plotting progress. The lower the percentage, the more progress they are making.

"My father used to say people should never owe anyone, yet we seem to always be in debt," Betty observed.

"I recently read an article on the topic of debt that made sense to me," Joe said. "The author explained when it is appropriate to borrow. He described how people should keep the time-frame of their assets and liabilities in balance. According to him, it is appropriate to borrow for 30 years on a house if the borrower intends to use that asset for 30 years, the same is true for a car loan. It is inappropriate to borrow long-term for a short-term benefit, such as paying off credit card debt. In effect, this mismatch of long-term debt means that the person is borrowing from the future to pay for the past. We don't have a mismatch per se, but our short-term debt is something we are going to have to reduce."

The Meehans' investment category represented the sum total of their assets available to consume during retirement. These are the assets that they needed to increase.

> ## Identify those assets available to consume during retirement.

Real estate and personal assets are non-liquid and often non-marketable. In a sense, they make one feel well-off, but often they can't be used to fix the problem of insufficient retirement funds. Joe and Betty decided to count only hard assets. Soft assets, for example, any inheritance anticipated from Joe's parents were ignored. Frequently, parents outlive their money or future medical expenses may eat into their estate.

On the liability side, the Meehans' **short-term debt** consisted of the bills payable within one year. This amount exceeded their liquid (cash) assets and paying off this debt severely drained their current cash flow, leaving them with little **discretionary cash**. This excessive short-term debt was a warning sign that Joe and Betty needed to get their financial house in order.

Looking at their assets and liabilities in this light enabled the Meehans to concentrate on the following action steps:

◆   Significantly reduce their short-term debt.

♦ Establish a Money Market Fund (MMF) as their emergency fund.

♦ Over a period of time, increase the MMF to the $10,000 goal.

♦ Build up their retirement accounts.

Before Joe and Betty could continue their financial quest, Joe received a heart-breaking phone call from his mother Marie. Joe's dad, who had always been the picture of health, died unexpectedly of a heart attack. As with all closely-knit families, this death took precedence over other things. Joe and Betty, their children and their in-laws, the Keanes, attended the funeral.

The day following the funeral at Marie Meehan's home

The sisters-in-law, Betty and Mary, finished cleaning up the debris from the funeral luncheon which, at Marie's insistence to make her friends feel comfortable, was held at her home. Joe, along with his brother-in-law, Jim Keane, talked with Marie about her immediate future. Marie flatly stated that she intended to remain in her home.

"I don't know what I'm going to do in the future, but for the moment I intend to remain in my own home," Marie emphasized.

The sisters-in-law joined the conversation at this point. As a family, they decided that Marie's younger sister Catherine would stay and be a companion for several weeks. Joe and his sister Mary vowed that they would significantly increase their visits to their mother. The conversation then turned to finances.

Marie Meehan, at the age of eighty-one, was faced with handling her own financial affairs for the first time in her life, because Matt, her recently deceased husband, had taken care of their money matters. However, Matt wasn't very open about his financial affairs, and Marie now had the onerous task of trying to understand just where to start. She did not see this as a concern since she was highly independent and in excellent health for her age. Marie had always exhibited a high concern for others and this was returned, in kind, from her many friends.

Neither Joe nor his mother had a clue as to the financial well-being of the senior Meehans. Joe's dad was from the "old school" in that he believed that family finances were the man's job. Joe and his mother began at square one to assemble the data for probate and the filing of the estate taxes. Joe's eyes were opened to the need for good record-keeping. Fortunately, Marie lived in the small town of Centralia in the southern part of Washington, where the Meehans' were well known. This made the job easier, but not simple.

Even Marie's sister Catherine helped with this process. In a letter to a cousin, she explained the predicament.

I am staying with Marie for about two weeks to help her get her life in order. I never realized how much work there is to be done. Affidavits to be sent out, death certificates and signature guarantees by her bank, instruction letters, etc. to be sent out. Telephone calls by the gross to delete Matt's name. Looking for marriage license, insurance policies, etc. It was a nightmare. Please pray for Marie.

One good thing has come out of this. I am going to get my act together.

Love,

Catherine

Joe discovered that even looking for documents cost money and soon learned that, in the State of Washington, attorneys charge by the hour, even when they were just helping the bereaved get their records in order.

To assist the family, Marie and Matt Meehan's attorney supplied a booklet he had prepared, entitled *Thoughtful Suggestions for My Loved Ones* (Appendix 1b). This document enabled Joe to approach the problem in a rational manner and saved the family several hundred dollars of potential attorney fees. With the attorney's permission, Joe supplied his other family members, including Catherine, with copies of this excellent record-keeping tool.

Later, when discussing the awkward situation with his brother-in-law, Joe described the empty feeling of not even knowing where to start.

"Did I feel dumb when the attorney asked us all those questions about Matt's financial affairs. Luckily, his accountant and banker were able to help us, or we would be still at it. In looking back, I now realize that we were afraid to hurt Dad's feelings. If we were to ask about his estate, it would sound like we wanted his money. Whenever we offered to help prepare his income tax return, he got defensive and would say there was nothing wrong with his brain. There is no frustration. "I could make a list of the things that I wish I had asked my dad about."

Jim sympathized with his brother-in-law's predic-ament, and he related how his father used to go down to the basement before paying for something at their door.

"He rattled some cans around, returned and paid the vendor. We never knew whether he hid money in the basement or just did that to throw people off. I remember after his death, Mom and I scoured the basement looking for Dad's cash hoard. We never found it, but I keep wondering," Jim related.

After returning from the funeral, Joe and Betty decided to sit their family down and explain their finances to their adult children. They even walked them through their completed copy of *Thoughtful Suggestions.*

Meanwhile at the home of the Keanes

For several days following the funeral, Mary Keane thought about her father's secrecy regarding his finances. She noticed similarities to the manner in which she and her husband Jim handled their affairs. As she dwelled on the topic, she became aware that her lack of knowledge about their finances really bothered her.

Mary is in her early sixties. She is college-edu-cated with a math degree and an interest in statistics which has provided her with a very rational and logical approach to problems. Mary has worked for many years at a large corporation which offers excellent retirement benefits, including a qualified pension plan and a 401(k) tax deferred savings plan, and she has risen to the middle level of management. Her ability to be a good listener usually enables her to obtain

Joe's wish list:

What adult children should know about their parents' affairs:

♦ Do they have a will or a living trust?

♦ Do they have a durable power of attorney?

♦ Do they have a living will [healthcare directive]?

♦ Where are their important papers kept?

♦ Who is their attorney, accountant, banker, insurance person, financial planner, stock broker?

♦ Have they made funeral arrangements?

♦ Do they have a written list describing to whom they wish to will specific assets, such as jewelry?

consensus from a group. Mary has a genuine interest in preserving family relationships. Even her sibling rivalry with her brother Joe takes second place to family issues. This love of family has intensified following her father's death and has heightened her concern about her mother's well-being.

Jim Keane, also in his early sixties, is a small-business owner whose two sons are ready to take over the business. Jim left college to enter this business with a friend. After several years, he purchased the friend's share, and since then he has built the business into a very successful venture. Jim likes to be in control, is very pragmatic, and is quite willing to take acceptable risks to accomplish his objectives. Jim is a very direct person who frequently employs professionals for their counsel. He is a person who expects immediate answers so that he can move on to the next issue. He has an excellent relationship with his wife and often takes her advice. Jim is an excellent golfer and considers himself to be a gourmet chef. He insists on preparing all of the family's "special meals."

The Keanes are reasonably wealthy and know they can afford a secure retirement. Both Jim and Mary would like to pass on as much of their estate as they can to their children and their grandchildren. They plan to spend their retirement years traveling between their home in Gig Harbor near Puget Sound and their condo in Desert Springs, California.

One evening out of the blue, or so it seemed to Jim, Mary asked, "How much are we worth?"

"Enough, I guess. What brought that up?" Jim replied with a question.

"Ever since the funeral, I have been trying to fill out the booklet that Mom's attorney gave us. I have more blank spaces than I have answers. I'm frustrated. I don't know any more about our finances than Mom knew about their finances. I want you to sit down with me and complete the booklet," Mary insisted.

"If it means that much to you, of course I'll do it," Jim agreed. "It's probably time that we got all our records together in one place."

Sunday morning at the Meehans

Over coffee, the Keanes and Meehans discussed what they learned from their experience with their dad's estate. Joe and Betty brought out a copy of their financial statements and shared the results with Jim and Mary.

"I recently prepared that kind of data to get a bank loan for the company," Jim acknowledged, looking sheepishly at Mary. "I think with just a few changes to a fair market value, we could have our personal assets and liabilities captured as well."

Chapter 2

*"What some people mistake for the high cost-of-living
is really the cost-of-living high."*
Doug Larson

Are we moving in the right direction?

Later that same week at the Meehans residence

Joe and Betty continued with their personal financial planning and dedicated some portion of each evening to accomplishing this task.

Now that they had completed their balance sheet, Joe and Betty tackled their **cash flow** and began to identify their current income needs, spending patterns and savings. They worked to answer the question, **"Can we free up any discretionary funds to invest for our retirement?"**

The **cash flow statement** was very familiar to Joe since it closely resembled the profit and loss statement that his company issued on a monthly basis. It summarizes the money coming in and going out each month. Joe developed a simple worksheet (Appendix 2a).

To save time, Joe and Betty agreed that their figures should only be reasonably accurate rather than absolutely precise. They also decided that the statement should anticipate their future cash flows rather than those of the prior year. They realized, with Betty having recently returned to work, they would have to make some projections as to the impact of this new source of funds.

To begin, Joe used their paycheck stubs to determine their current income. Since Joe's salary had been fairly consistent over the years, they decided to use a 4% annual increase to cover any cost-of-living and incentive raises. They planned a 5% increase in Betty's salary for an anticipated six-month review in her initial year. Then they also used 4% for future years and multiplied the monthly amount by twelve to determine an annual income number.

Their only other source of **income** was interest on their savings. Because it was a minor amount, they projected no growth and used the same amount for all future years.

With these modifications they felt comfortable with the income portion of the statement, and tackled the more difficult portion, the problem of determining their living **expenses**.

To get a quick look at their expenditures, Joe used a single month's figures from their checkbook to represent their cash outflow. He multiplied this by twelve to calculate annual numbers. When he subtracted this amount from the annualized income amount that they had calculated, he knew that additional analysis was warranted. Even adjusting for Betty's income did not bring the numbers even close to being reasonable. Joe understood that they spent every penny of their income so, in his reasoning, there was no way they could have so much money left over. He then chose a three-month period and looked at the numbers in more detail.

Both Joe and Betty had their paychecks directly deposited and used their bank card to withdraw cash when they needed it. They were surprised by how often they used the bank Automatic Teller Machine (ATM).

"Do we really spend that much cash?" Joe wondered.

Like many couples, the Meehans paid cash for the little expenditures and used either checks or credit cards for the major items. Their minor expenditures, covering anything from haircuts, fertilizer, to an occasional trip to the liquor store, were numerous and varied.

"Do we need to account for every nickel to get control of our cash outflow?" Betty asked.

"Let's see if we can determine an easier way," Joe answered.

Using a computerized spreadsheet, Joe quickly reviewed their total cash withdrawals for the past year. The amount had been relatively consistent on a month-to-month basis until Betty returned to work. Then it jumped to a higher level.

With this information, the Meehans decided the difference between the prior average and their current spending level was due to Betty's employment expenses. They developed a similar amount to represent the funds that Joe spent for lunch, etc. They labeled the remainder, which they both agreed was reasonable, a **cash expense**. Thus, they saved themselves the added steps of detailing all the times that they spent cash. It would be easy to keep this under control by simply checking the total amount that they withdrew each month from the ATM. Should it ever increase significantly, then they would do more research to justify the additional spending.

Payroll deductions for income taxes, social security, medical and insurance came from their bi-weekly stubs.

Joe then analyzed their checkbooks and credit card bills for one month to get a flavor for non-cash expenditures. Many of their expenses were easy to recognize, since monthly expenditures, such as the mortgage payments on their residence or cable TV charges, didn't change very often. Other expenses, such as vacation expenses or high utility bills during the cold weather, occurred only periodically. They had to dig into their checkbook and their credit card statements to determine these amounts. Also, they omitted some non-recurring charges, including their daughter's education expenses, from consideration.

The savings included both the amount that they had automatically deposited into their credit union and the amount deducted for Joe's 401(k) retirement savings plan by his employer. To make sure that all the money they spent was accounted for, Joe even included the amount used to increase the emergency fund.

Joe was interested in determining their **discretionary cash**, or the difference between cash inflow and cash outflow. If this really existed, Joe and Betty could add to their savings. The Meehans realized that unanticipated expenses, such as higher-than-planned car expenses, would be part of their future. They were also painfully aware that three of their four children were unmarried and they envisioned some large wedding bills sometime in the future. Joe and Betty planned to put aside some of their discretionary cash to fund these expenditures. Joe included a percentage column with his cash flow statement to enable them to quickly focus on their major expenditures.

> # Cash Inflow - Cash Outflow = Discretionary Cash

The major expenditures, indicated by the percentages, were taxes (24.9%) and recreation (12.5%). The taxes included both income tax and Social Security contributions. The recreation expense included both a winter skiing trip and their normal summer vacation. When they saw how much these were costing in comparison with their other expenses, they agreed to consider a change.

At first, they were surprised at the level of the discretionary cash, then realized that much of it came from Betty's new job. Joe and Betty finally agreed upon a cash flow statement as the most likely one to occur. Joe included an *expense-to-income-ratio*, by dividing the total expenses by the total income, to help them keep track of their progress. Now that they understood their current expenditure level, Betty and Joe began the task of deciding how they wanted to spend their money.

Betty stated how they felt by saying, "I guess our choice is to either spend now or save some money to enable us to spend later."

Both Joe and Betty recognized that some of the expenses were relatively short-term in nature. The clothing expenses were higher because Betty had to rebuild her wardrobe for her new position, and because the automobile loans included Betty's relatively new car.

As they reviewed their efforts to this point, they quickly agreed that reaching the final target in one step would be difficult. Then they worked on some of the short-term solutions.

"Is there any legal way we can reduce our income taxes?" Betty wondered.

Cash Flow Statement Joe & Betty Meehan			
	Monthly	Annually	Percent of Income
Income:			
Salary - Joe	$ 6,000	$ 72,000	
Salary - Betty	$ 2,000	$ 24,000	
Investment Income	$ 20	$ 240	
Total Income	$ 8,020	$ 96,240	
Expenses:			
Cash Expenses	$ 400	$ 4,800	5.0%
Housing	$ 750	$ 9,000	9.4%
Food	$ 400	$ 4,800	5.0%
Clothing	$ 400	$ 4,800	5.0%
Transportation	$ 300	$ 3,600	3.7%
Medical	$ 350	$ 4,200	4.4%
Total Insurance	$ 175	$ 2,100	2.2%
Recreation	$ 1,000	$ 12,000	12.5%
Utilities	$ 175	$ 2,100	2.2%
Automobile Loan	$ 475	$ 5,700	5.9%
Credit Card Loans	$ 125	$ 1,500	1.6%
Joe Work Related	$ 130	$ 1,560	1.6%
Betty Work Related	$ 110	$ 1,320	1.4%
Contributions	$ 50	$ 600	0.6%
Taxes	$ 2,000	$ 24,000	24.9%
Other Expenses	$ 100	$ 1,200	1.2%
			0.0%
Total Expenses	**$ 6,940**	**$ 83,280**	**86.5%**
Savings	$ 500	$ 6,000	
Net Discretionary Cash	**$ 580**	**$ 6,960**	
Expenses to income ratio	**86.5%**		

After giving it some thought, Joe replied. "Right now we are deducting everything that we can, including our contributions, interest on our home mortgage and real estate taxes. However, with almost $600 a month available, I can maximize my 401(k) plan deferral. This will allow us to reduce our current income taxes and save for retirement at the same time."

"How much of a difference would this make?" Betty asked.

"I really don't know, but I'll check with our human resources department. I believe that I can save another 5% in addition to my current deduction. We need to continue to push your company to establish some type of defined contribution plan. At the present time, for the sake of planning, let's assume that we can save an additional $4,000. That will reduce our tax bill by about a $1,000 a year."

"I really think that we should significantly cut down on our recreation costs," Joe speculated. "Let's consider taking a winter vacation one year and a summer one the next. If we don't make major changes in our lifestyle now, I am afraid our dream of retirement won't happen."

"It's OK with me because, with my new job, I can't get all that time off anyway," Betty agreed. She then asked. "Are there other items that we can reduce to increase our savings?"

Cash Flow Statement Joe & Betty Meehan	Current Plan	Interim Plan	Final Plan
Income:			
Salary - Joe	$ 6,000	$ 6,000	$ 6,000
Salary - Betty	$ 2,000	$ 2,000	$ 2,000
Investment Income	$ 20	$ 20	$ 20
Total Income	$ 8,020	$ 8,020	$ 8,020
Expenses:			
Cash Expenses	$ 400	$ 400	$ 400
Housing	$ 750	$ 750	$ 750
Food	$ 400	$ 400	$ 400
Clothing	$ 400	$ 400	$ 300
Transportation	$ 300	$ 350	$ 400
Medical	$ 350	$ 350	$ 350
Total Insurance	$ 175	$ 175	$ 175
Recreation	$ 1,000	$ 700	$ 700
Utilities	$ 175	$ 175	$ 175
Automobile Loan	$ 475	$ 475	$ -
Credit Card Loans	$ 125	$ 125	$ -
Joe Work Related	$ 130	$ 130	$ 130
Betty Work Related	$ 110	$ 110	$ 110
Contributions	$ 50	$ 50	$ 50
Taxes	$ 2,000	$ 1,915	$ 1,915
Other Expenses	$ 100	$ 100	$ 200
Total Expenses	$ 6,940	$ 6,605	$ 6,055
Savings:			
Retirement Savings	$ 500	$ 840	$ 1,390
Emergency Savings		$ 200	$ 200
Future Contingencies		$ 300	$ 300
Net Discretionary Cash	$ 580	$ 75	$ 75
Expenses to income ratio	86.5%	82.4%	75.5%

"There are a number of things," Joe answered. "For instance, we can extend the lives of our cars to reduce monthly expenses. When the car loan is paid off we should save what we are currently spending."

"That's easier said than done," replied Betty. "Remember how often we said that same thing in the past, when we paid off the last car, when we paid off the house remodeling, when..."

"I know, but this time we have a plan, and we will be more disciplined in our savings," Joe promised. "We also need to reduce our use of credit cards," Joe continued. "The interest charges are half again as high as a regular bank loan. A colleague recently told me that it would take over 30 years to pay off a $2,000 credit card balance by only paying the monthly minimum."

Paying the credit card debt when it's due to avoid the interest charge became a goal. The Meehans also resolved to save one-half of every salary increase that either of them received in the future.

"We should identify some of the increases in expenses that will also occur— items such as additional auto maintenance bills," Joe said. "We also need to build up an emergency fund, so if we should list that as a cash outflow as well. And while we are at it, we should specifically identify the monthly amounts that we want to save for future contingencies such as the kids' weddings."

"Let's walk up to our final plan slowly by developing an interim target plan until all the pieces fall into place." Joe said. Based on their agreements, the Meehans revised their cash flow plans.

The revised cash flow plan enabled the Meehans to see the planned improvement from 86.5% expense ratio to 75.5%—over a 10% reduction. All of the increased savings were allocated to retirement, the emergency fund or for future contingencies.

Betty and Joe felt much better about their ability to retire sometime in the future. They hoped their future raises would cover inflation and keep their savings forecasts in line.

"I feel better about our finances," Betty exclaimed. "For years we just seem to drift along, but now I can chart some progress. I am particularly delighted that we recognized our need for emergency savings and for future expenses."

"We did a good job in planning," Joe agreed. "Now we have to live the plan."

Sunday morning at the Meehans' home

At their next coffee klatch, the Meehans proudly explained their plans to the Keanes.

"If we are able to hold the line on future expenses, we figure that we can increase our retirement savings by almost 150%. At the same time we can build up our emergency fund and save for future contingencies like the kids' weddings," Joe said.

They then summarized the changes they would implement in their savings and spending habits.

1. Ensure that their cash spending was under control.

2. Save now in order to have funds available to retire.

3. Increase their tax-deferred savings.

4. Reduce their recreational spending.

5. Save loan payments when the loans are paid off.

6. Reduce their reliance on credit cards and pay off the balance every month to avoid the interest charges.

7. Save for their emergency fund.

8. Save for future contingencies such as new cars and weddings.

Later that evening at the Keanes'

Jim and Mary discussed their need to plan. Mary agreed with her husband that they didn't need to go to the detail level required by their in-laws. They reasoned that retirement for them was coming very soon, and they did not anticipate any large fall-off in income. Therefore, they selected a monthly amount, which approximated their current spending level, as being appropriate. Mary, with Jim's blessing, set an overall monthly target which they could easily monitor to control their cash expenditures.

Mary, like her sister-in-law, was pleased with the path they were taking.

Chapter 3

*"If you knew you were going to live to 105,
you would make different choices."*
Dr. Jennifer James

Quality of life during one's added years

Joe and Mary, driving to Marie's house for their first visit following their father's funeral

As Joe and his sister cruised south on Highway I-5 to visit their mother in Centralia, they drifted into a discussion about the retired life that their mother lived and how it might differ from their retirement.

"Jim and I tried to get Mom to move in with us, but she wants no part of it. I'm a little disappointed and, quite frankly, a little hurt," said Mary as she started off the conversation.

"I am happy that you asked her, but as long as she's in good health, what made you think that she would want to come? We all know that you and Jim want your freedom now that the kids are on their own. What would she do when you guys pop off to Desert Springs? After all, she doesn't golf," Joe replied.

"Yes, Joe, I realize that, but she has to be lonely now that Dad died," Mary responded.

"Do you recall the advice in that booklet that Dad's attorney gave us on *Thoughtful Suggestions for Our Loved Ones* (Appendix 1b). It advised us to avoid making any major financial or life changing decisions for at least six months. It hasn't been six months yet," Joe reminded Mary.

"Remember, dear sister," Joe continued. "There is a big difference between being alone and being lonely. Mom has her old friends, many of them widows, who do things together. They watch out for each other. When you think of it, they are Mom's support group."

Joe continued, "Far too often, widows and widowers chase a dream that doesn't work out. How about that woman that used to work with you.

1. "She sold her house.

2. "She bought a condo, only to sell that.

3. "Then she bought another house down on the ocean only to sell that to repurchase her original house, and all within a year of her husband's death.

4. "In addition, she spent much of her time traveling between her home at Ocean Shores and visiting her doctor, lawyer, and other support people, who were 150 miles away in the Puget Sound area.

"Besides enduring all the heartache and grief involved with her husband's death," Joe continued, "she only succeeded in making real estate agents happy and in running up a lot of mileage on her car. If people only have to stop and think about the consequences before they made major lifestyle changes. I recently came across a housing checklist, *Control of Personal Environment* (Appendix 7a), which could have helped your co-worker," Joe said. "It covers a lot of things that a person should consider before changing locations. I'll fax you over a copy when we get home.

"I think the best thing for Mom, at the moment, is to keep doing what she is doing. We need to help her retain her independence. Don't you agree?" Joe asked.

"I guess you're right, but I keep hoping she will change her mind. In any case, we should be aware of Mom's needs as well as her desires at this stage of her life. Let's pay attention to how she is handling her situation during our visit," Mary answered.

"Come on now, Mary, you don't mean to audit her lifestyle, do you?" Joe asked.

"Now, that's unfair. As you are well aware, Jim and I both admire how well Mom and Dad enjoyed their years of retirement," Mary answered.

"I was surprised that Dad was able to give up the grocery store and actually retire," Joe remarked. "He once confided that this change in life style didn't happen by accident. Did you know that he and Mom developed a plan on how they intended to live in retirement?" Joe asked.

Joe began to answer his own question. "The plan gave them the ability to meet change head-on. How they went about it was quite ingenious. Each of them sat down and drew a picture of what an ideal retirement life looked like, down to the detail of what the living arrangements would be. They then compared the pictures. Dad drew a condo overlooking the ocean. Mom's house on the other hand looked exactly like the one they now live in. Neither of those pictures should surprise us.

"Next they decided how both of them could accomplish their dreams," Joe continued.

At this point, Mary interjected. "The way Jim and I set our goals didn't happen by accident either. We had the living examples of our Mom and Dad from which to draw. You might say that Mom and Dad gave us a gift. Just like them, we want to enjoy the remainder of our lives. I like the way they responded to change, for example. Instead of buying a condo and being faced with the maintenance, they chose a different course," Mary continued. " Mom and Dad decided it would be easier to simply lease a condo in some resort area during the off season. They must have winter-vacationed at their place on Lake Havasu in Arizona for 15 years."

Joe agreed, "Dad got to live his dream for a couple of months a year and Mom was able to keep her roots. And that's just one example of how they were able to compromise to make their dreams come true and still maintain control.

"Did Mom and Dad ever tell you they did more than just plan?" Joe asked, then continued. "Annually, they put together an action program. It consisted of a five-year plan with one-year action steps. Once a year on their wedding anniversary, they reviewed their progress. They then made some changes and decided on the coming year's action steps. For example, that three-month trip to Europe was scheduled and rescheduled at least four times. Finally, Dad put his foot down and said, 'if we don't go soon, we'll be too old to enjoy it.'

"Our parents really had their act together," Joe said.

"They really loved to travel, didn't they?" Mary reminisced.

Mary continued, "Even in their later years, travel was still a priority. Their only change then, instead of driving around themselves, was to go with tour groups. Dad liked the security of knowing the people around them, and Mom appreciated the companionship of other people.

"Remember how she always complained about Dad reading all the time and not talking enough with her? The tour groups worked out best for both of them. They both benefited from the physical activity as well as from the mental stimulation that travel provides. You and Betty ought to create opportunities to travel," Mary said.

"Now that Betty is working and earning a few dollars, we actually plan to travel less, but hope to do more quality travel," Joe replied. "In fact, with the exception of taxes, recreation expense now is the highest amount in our cash flow budget.

"Mom and Dad were more fortunate than many of the people that we know who are about the same age, because they were both in good health. Dad jogged daily until he was about 75. Then he took up walking and Mom joined him. Often, when I would call, they were on some type of volkswalk," continued Joe.

"Like traveling in a group, exercising together also gave them the same feelings of security and congeniality. How many times do we hear people say, 'I'm wearing out?' Then we look at people like Mom and Dad who seemed to get younger each year. The body really does renew itself, if we just let it. I hope when we get to their ages, we can enjoy life as much as they did and as much as Mom still does," Joe said.

"That reminds me of a saying from an old Irish neighbor of mine, 'Live while you can, and die when you can't help it,'" Mary said. "Joe, what do you think life will be like for Jim and me, and, of course, for you and Betty as well, during our retirement years?"

"The major change is going to be technology," Joe answered.

"Think about how far we have come already. Remember when Grandma used to think that the telephone was an invention of the devil and refused to answer it. The technological advancements that are still to come, are mind-boggling. And, like all scientific advances, they will bring both the good and the bad. Think about it. We'll have over 500 TV channels, with movies on demand. It'll be a built-in movie library," Joe continued. "The shopping we see today on television will be archaic in comparison to what will come," Joe went on. "A person will be able to visit a quality store like Nordstrom's, electronically interact with a salesperson about colors, sizes, etc. and complete the purchase without ever leaving the living room. Computers with voice activation already enable us to control the climate in our houses, check for intruders, and operate the sprinkling system—all while we are away on vacation. With the advent of cellular phones, we can even do away with all those overhead telephone wires. It will be quite a sight."

"Joe, you mentioned both the good and the bad. What will be the bad?" asked Mary.

"Less personal communication with other people would be bad. Think about our conversation on Mom and Dad," Joe answered. "They were able to enjoy many of the activities they valued because they did it in groups. The interrelationship with others is essential.

"**Internet**, the so-called information highway, is not just a new computer technology. It will overcome the limitations of travel and space," Joe continued. "People can be anywhere they want to be without ever leaving where they are. For example, even today, people can electronically connect with their library, browse through outlines of books, and have their book request either mailed or delivered. More and more people will either work at home or, if they are employed by a large corporation, they could gather in small sub-units. There will no longer be the need to go to corporate headquarters, which will reduce the highway traffic and potentially increase their productive time and still enable them to be connected with people they have to interface with. Internet will bring change to our culture. It will be a boon to the older generation that has proven it can master new technologies quite effectively."

"Isn't this the dream that all of us have been waiting for?" Mary asked.

"Every cultural change brings both positives and negatives," Joe answered. "Internet will be no different. People, particularly the elderly, will become more isolated. They will first lose the need and then the motivation to mingle with others. Even today, seven out of ten people don't know their neighbors on social terms. In the future, the lonely will become more alone and more depressed."

"Can't the bad dream that you are painting be avoided?" Mary asked.

"Sure, loneliness can be prevented from happening, but it's going to take work. The question is, who is going to do it?" Joe asked. "The government?" he suggested. "Hardly likely!

"We can't look to our churches, because even today they don't have programs. I read somewhere that over 40% of the churches don't have any programs for their elderly parishioners. Look around at how few churches have ramps to enable access for the elderly or hearing aids to enable them to listen to the service and sermon. Churches should really stand up and take notice. Senior citizens tend to desire more spirituality in their lives, so they often return to active church participation. But, as far as I can see, churches aren't prepared to accommodate them. If the prevention of loneliness for senior citizens is to happen, it's going to have to be built neighborhood by neighborhood, family by family," Joe concluded.

The conversation between the siblings concluded as the interstate sign indicated the exit for their Mother's town of Centralia

"I'm surprised how quickly the time flew on the ride down from Tacoma. When I drive with Jim, he just grunts at the other drivers and the trip seems to take forever," Mary commented. "It'll be like old times, you and me at home. Let's leave any serious conversations for another time and just enjoy the time with Mom."

Joe agreed with his sister as he turned the car down the country road toward their mother's house, which was situated on the outskirts of the town.

"Based on the number of cars in Mom's driveway, it doesn't look like she will be one of those who are lonely," Mary remarked as they pulled up close to the house.

"I wouldn't be surprised if we go in and find Mom teaching a computer class to her friends," Joe said, smiling, as he began to unpack the car.

Chapter 4

"Everything starts as someone's daydream."
Larry Niven

Are our goals pragmatic?

One evening, following Mary's visit with her mother, as the Keanes were finishing their dinner

During dinner Jim told Mary about a married couple disagreeing on how to spend their retirement years. As he related the story, Mary realized that they were no better off. She and Jim had never expressed their retirement goals to each other. Each had wrongfully assumed that other would automatically agree with their choice. They brought up the subject that evening, for the first time, and found they weren't even close to agreeing.

"Wow, do we ever need to sit down and talk about our retirement goals!" Mary exclaimed. "It's really imperative, because our retirement is just around the corner. She then related the conversation that she and Joe had regarding the future and the need for planning.

"You and I plan and budget all the time for our business and we track those numbers. I think it's time that we follow Dad's example and use some of our talent to plan around family issues," Mary said.

Jim agreed, "You are right again. Sometimes when I'm sitting in the office watching the kids manage the business, I say to myself, 'My time would be better spent if I gave some thought to what I should be doing next with my life.'"

Jim wanted to transfer his share of the business to their sons and then retire to their condo in Desert Springs, California, but Mary preferred to remain in the Puget Sound area. She had worked for years to establish herself in the community, and she did not want to give up the pleasure she obtained from her friends and volunteer work. Mary is so enthusiastic about the community's needs that she plans to leave a charitable gift—something that will live on beyond her.

"Before we decide how and where we will live out our retirement," Mary declared, "we need to determine our lifestyle goals."

Not because it was high on his agenda, but because it was important to his wife, Jim finally agreed to sit down and thrash it out.

Retirement Questions

♦ **How would I describe my lifestyle in order to be content in retirement? [Draw a picture of my ideal retirement residence]**

♦ **What are my interests and hobbies? [Rank them by importance]**

♦ **How long can I practically pursue these interests/hobbies?**

♦ **How will I take care of my health and nutritional needs? [long-term care considerations]**

♦ **How much income do I think it will take to enable me to live until age 90?**

♦ **What would be a reasonable return on my investments?**

♦ **What is my best guess on the future inflation rate?**

♦ **How do I feel about charitable contributions?**

♦ **How do I feel about leaving an estate to my heirs?**

♦ **How can we help Marie Meehan (Mary's mother) retain her independence?**

♦ **Who will take over should I become incompetent?**

♦ **How do I feel about having my life extended by artificial means?**

♦ **Shall we stay or move? [Draw up a comparison list of the advantages and disadvantages. This should include weather, cost of living, access to shopping, access to medical care, closeness to relatives**

To get started, Mary developed a series of questions for each of them to answer. The questions were to determine points of agreement and points of conflict. The topics covered lifestyles, location, finances and health; and she ranked each topic in importance with one being high and five being low.

It took several weeks and much prodding on Mary's part to get Jim to complete his answers. When they finished answering the questions, the dialogue began.

Mary understood that retirement involved an attitude adjustment. She also recognized that for their retirement to succeed, as well as their marriage, they would both have to work at it. She felt sufficiently secure herself to compromise with Jim on many of his wishes.

Jim, on the other hand, looked at retirement as the same old thing with more time for golf. His first awakening came when he realized that he did not want to give up all association with his business.

Some time later during a discussion with Joe Meehan, he related the change in his attitude to his brother-in-law. "It was at that point I became aware that this planning business may have some real merit."

After long discussions, Mary and Jim finally agreed to participate in some activities as a couple and some independently of each other. Where possible their independent activities would take place concurrently to leave sufficient time for joint activities.

Activities	Mary	Jim
Lifestyle	Continue to be involved in charitable activities, but not more than two days a week on average.	Continue to be involved in the family business, perhaps as a consultant, but not more than two days a week on average.
Location	Agreeable to spending some time at their Desert Springs condo.	After weighing the advantages and disadvantages, Jim came to the conclusion that staying in town was preferable to moving to California.
Hobbies/ Interests	Travel - Mary would like to see more of the world before she gets too old to travel. Education - While Jim golfs, Mary intends to enroll in elderhostel courses, which are education adventures for older adults. Family - Visit, often, with the children and grandchildren.	Travel - Jim enjoys the change of pace and, because of Mary, goes along. Hobby - Golf vacation two weeks each quarter, also wants to take up painting. Family - Take some of the grandchildren when they travel.
Health\ Nutrition	Firmly believes in exercise to reduce stress. Wants to have a structured program for both herself and Jim.	Feels golf will give him all the exercise that he needs, but will go along with Mary. No real concern over long-term care issues.

Activities	Mary	Jim
Finances	Mary agrees with Jim that their current spending level is sufficient. Concerned over their ability to live within their resources.	Jim feels that inflation would remain under control in the 3% range and estimates an average of 15% return on investments. Recognizes need to meet with a financial professional for a review and recommendations.
Estate Planning \ Charitable Contributions	Leave a reasonable estate to all children equally. Concerned that their daughter will not get as large a share as their two sons. Very dedicated to charitable work and wants to make a gift. Thinks both she and Jim need a living will. Has a high level of concern about who would manage their affairs should she and Jim become incompetent.	Believes in a fair share for all their children. However, the business goes to the sons who have worked there. Has no concern about Mary's desire to gift to charity. He looks on it as being her money, so she can do what she wants with it. He wants his estate to ultimately go to the grandkids. Concerned about probate, estate taxes, etc. Sees the need for a good estate attorney to review their wills.

Mary was quite pleased with the outcome. Although they did not agree on everything, they did reach consensus on the major issues. She was most pleased that they talked through the issues together. She now feels that she understands Jim's desires a little better and that will help in their retirement.

Several weeks later during a coffee session with their in-laws, Jim and Mary discussed their success in establishing retirement goals.

Later, when alone, the Meehans continued the discussion on retirement goals

"I feel a little jealous," Betty said. "I'm not envious of their wealth. It just seems they are always ahead of us in planning for the future. This time we even started the process."

"Don't worry about it," Joe replied. "First, we will catch up. Secondly, they did all the legwork on this part which makes our job easier. We'll just use their approach and insert our own goals."

Joe is tired of working for someone else. He would like to retire at age 57 and work part-time, in his own business, until about 62 or 63. Betty, on the other hand, loves her new job and wants to continue working until at least age 62. Because they are compatible as a couple and communicate extremely well, most of their goals were easy to agree upon. The goal that caused the greatest discussion was, "Should we *pay off our mortgage* before retiring?"

"My father worked his entire life with a single goal—to pay off the mortgage," said Betty. "Now, I hear people in work saying that's a dumb idea. They tell me that it's more important to keep getting the tax deduction on the interest."

"It's a dilemma all right," Joe agreed. "It seems to be a conflict between what feels good and what is the best tax decision. But what seems to be apparent may not be the case. Let me illustrate this point." Joe then described a project that the people at his work undertook to help a co-worker answer the question, "Should he pay off his mortgage?" "It seems this co-worker received an inheritance which was sufficient to pay off his mortgage," Joe continued. "The co-worker asked some of us in the accounting department to help him understand his options. We decided there were three ways that he could go.

1. "Invest the inheritance, pay income tax on the earnings and continue paying the mortgage from current income.

2. "Pay off the mortgage and invest the payments now going to the mortgage company in a taxable instrument.

3. "Invest the inheritance in a tax-deferred instrument and continue paying the mortgage from current income."

"What do you mean by *taxable* and *tax-deferred instruments*?" Betty asked.

"Taxable instruments are investments where the income is taxable when earned, whether or not you take a distribution. A tax-deferred instrument is an investment, such as a variable annuity, where income taxes can be deferred *until* you take a distribution," Joe explained.

Joe then described the approach that he and his co-workers took. "First, we used a computer program to separate the interest from the principal for the remaining life of the mortgage. This calculation allowed us to use different tax rates on the interest to determine the amount of tax savings available for investing. We needed to do this calculation first because interest is based on the mortgage balance. As the mortgage is paid off, the tax deductible interest declines."

"I understand that part," Betty said. "Every year, at tax time, you are always complaining about not having enough deductions because we are paying off the mortgage."

"It's the American way to complain about taxes," Joe said with a smile.

Factors involved:

♦ **Marginal income tax rates.**

♦ **Mortgage interest rates.**

♦ **Mortgage duration—to determine if the length of the mortgage influenced the decision.**

♦ **Return on investment and its compounding effect.**

♦ **Insurance cost incurred with variable annuities plus the tax rate applicable at the time of the payout.**

♦ **Sufficient liquidity to take care of the family's living requirements. We didn't want him to become house-rich and income-poor.**

He then continued on with a detailed explanation of the technique used. "Knowing the interest amount enabled us to calculate the total invested tax savings," Joe said. "We used a series of rates to represent some different options available to investors."

The following rates were used:

6% **Return on Investment** (ROI) to represent a long-term investment in fixed income instruments such as CDs or money market funds.

8% ROI which approximates the long-term return for a mix of stocks and bonds.

10.5% ROI equates to the before-tax rate of the 7.25% mortgage interest.

15% ROI just to see the impact of a wonderful investment.

Joe then listed the factors involved. (See chart above)

"The project turned out to be a lot more complex than we had originally thought," Joe said.

"What did you guys finally decide?" Betty asked.

"First, let me tell about what we learned during the process," Joe replied. "The fact that the duration of the mortgage made no difference was the first surprise. A thirty-year mortgage acted similar to a ten-year mortgage. Our next surprise came when we found out that the change in the interest had little impact," Joe explained. "We used two interest rates, 7.25% and 9.00%, to test how each would influence the decision, and neither one did."

"Well, what does make a difference?" Betty questioned.

"The rate of return on the investment proved to be the overriding influence," Joe explained. "We found out that the our co-worker would need an average return to exceed the interest rate on the mortgage before investing the inheritance would make any sense. Unless the return was greater than the interest rate on the mortgage, he was better off paying off the mortgage."

"What is so wonderful about that?" Betty asked.

"It told us that the return on the investment, not the tax savings, was the determining factor in making the decision," Joe answered.

> **Retirees should pay off their mortgage unless they can better the interest rate on an after-tax return basis regardless of their tax bracket.**

"I was surprised," Joe admitted, "Because I had always thought saving taxes drove this decision. We considered three different marginal tax rates—15%, 31% and 39%, which disproved this theory. Surprisingly, it made more sense for those with the lower tax rate to invest when the return was less than the interest rate. Only with a tax-deferred investment earning the 15% return does the highest tax rate predominate."

Joe then illustrated the decision points in the form of a matrix.

"As you can see from the matrix, there is a definite break when the Return On Investment (ROI) rate exceeds the interest rate. Look at the line for the 10.5% ROI, and see how the decision to invest makes sense in *every* instance. If the ROI is less than the interest rate, even by just by a couple of percentage points, paying off the mortgage will earn a greater overall return. Though people should calculate the numbers for each circumstance, the matrix seems to be a good rule of thumb to follow," Joe concluded.

	7.25% Interest			@ 9.00% Interest		
	15% Marginal tax rate	31%	39%	15%	31%	39%
6% ROI	Pay off mortgage	Pay off mortgage	Pay off mortgage	Pay off mortgage	Pay off mortgage	Pay off mortgage
8% ROI	Pay off mortgage	Invest Variable Annuity (VA)	Invest (VA)	Pay off mortgage	Invest (VA)	Invest (VA)
10.5% ROI	Invest Taxable (T)	Invest (VA)	Invest (VA)	Invest (T)	Invest (VA)	Invest (VA)
15% ROI	Invest (T)	Invest (VA)	Invest (VA)	Invest (T)	Invest (VA)	Invest (VA)

"Why does paying off the mortgage make more sense than deducting the interest from our taxes?" Betty asked.

"At a lower ROI, the more you save in tax deductions, the more you pay in taxes on the earnings you receive from investing those deductions," Joe explained. "In fact, at the 6% ROI level, people in the lowest tax rate of 15% end up with a larger overall dollar advantage than those in the 31% or 39% tax brackets. People in the higher rates simply exaggerate this point because they pay a greater proportion of taxes on their earnings than they save from the deduction."

"And from that, you conclude?" Betty asked.

"That people with the ability to pay off their mortgage must be willing to invest in something that will earn a greater return than the rate of interest on the mortgage or they are better off paying down the mortgage," Joe answered. "Regardless of their tax bracket," he added.

"Are you also saying that people shouldn't borrow money on their residence to invest?" Betty asked.

"That's my belief," Joe answered.

"What do all the VAs and Ts in your matrix mean?" Betty asked.

"These serve as a guide to invest in a taxable instrument (T) or a tax deferred instrument (VA)," Joe explained. "Because a variable annuity charges an extra cost for insurance, a taxable investment is often the better choice at the 15% tax bracket. As the tax rates increase, the variable annuity becomes the investment of choice."

"Will the same table work for a person who has been paying a mortgage for a number of years and then wants to pay it off?" Betty wondered.

"Yes, the rule of thumb seems to hold. People should understand that even though more dollars are applied against their principal, the interest paid is based on the current balance. So the numbers work out the same," Joe explained.

After much discussion, Joe and Betty finally settled on their goals. The goals they agreed to were:

1. Set retirement income at 80% of their current income. This, in their view, would be enough to retain their current lifestyle. Their guess at 5% annual inflation was higher than the rate that Jim used in his projection.

2. Pay off their mortgage before retirement.

3. Provide income for life for each spouse.

4. Leave a reasonable estate and divide it equally between their children.

5. Regarding interests, hobbies, travel, Joe and Betty decided to have meaningful leisure time. Both were physically active and planned to remain that way.

6. Be actively involved with their grandchildren.

Joe and Betty decided to spend their years, before retirement, learning how to retire happily. They wanted to talk with current retirees about their experiences. They also decided to use their vacations to test how it would feel to live in different areas of the country. As the Meehans reviewed the results, they were grateful that the Keanes showed them how to set goals.

Chapter 5

*"It only makes sense to protect those assets already
owned before worrying about procuring more. "*

What happens if?

One day during breakfast at the Keanes'

As Jim and Mary conversed over breakfast, Jim mentioned an appointment with Dan Palmer, his company's insurance agent.

"While you are there," Mary interjected, "why don't you ask him about our insurance needs during retirement?"

"You know," Jim complained, "how I hate to talk about insurance."

"Call my brother Joe. He'll be glad to go with you," Mary countered.

Jim called Joe, and asked him to accompany him on a review of insurance policies. "After all, you understand this stuff better than I do and Mary would really appreciate it."

Joe readily accepted. He looked on it as an opportunity to learn more about the complex nature of the insurance world. On the ride over, Jim described Dan Palmer.

Dan Palmer, an insurance professional, took over the Palmer Insurance Agency after his father passed away. The agency handles life, health and accident, as well as property and casualty insurance. Dan has been in the business over 20 years and has an excellent reputation. The Keane Tool and Die Company had been a regular client even before Dan joined the agency.

Jim also told Joe about Mary's request for more information on their insurance needs for retirement. "Suppose we start with our personal insurance issues first and get it out of the way. Then Dan and I can move on to the business related insurance."

At the Palmer Insurance Agency

Dan Palmer was tall and lanky with a quick smile and a ready wit. His natural characteristics complemented his salesmanship requirements, and in Joe's view, Dan seemed to be a typical, glad-handed insurance salesman whose only intention was to sell something. His first impression of the office didn't help either. Papers and files were everywhere. Dan had to clear several clutters of paper off the couch to enable his visitors to sit down.

The initial discussion was very general in nature and concerned questions about Mary's father's death and typical inquiries about the doings of the kids. As Jim's insurance agent, Dan handled both the business insurance and the family policies and he had been prodding Jim to purchase life insurance to pay for estate taxes. However, this day, they just philosophized about the need for protection of assets already owned.

Upon hearing that Joe's wife, Betty, had just returned to work, Dan remarked: "I'm serious when I say this. A fully employed spouse is perhaps a person's best financial asset."

This comment preceded a lengthy discussion on the need for disability insurance, which Dan termed "the living death." "Nothing hurts more than an increase in expenses coming on top of a decrease in income," Dan stated. "This is normally what happens when one spouse becomes disabled even for a short period of time. Income stops and medical and other care expenses climb."

Both of the Keanes, as well as Joe, had disability insurance provided by their employer, but Betty lacked coverage. Dan quickly calculated the cost of having a policy and the cost of being without a policy for the Meehans.

Dan emphasized to Joe, "You and Betty most probably need that income to meet your retirement goal. It would be foolish not to have this type of coverage."

"That's over 2% of Betty's income!" Joe exclaimed, as he became concerned that Dan would try to sell him insurance.

Dan took Joe through the merits of a particular policy that would replace 60% of Betty's income and cover her until age 65 without an increase in premiums. Also, the policy would continue paying until she became able to engage in her profession and not just in any profession. "This means that she must be fully recovered and capable of returning to her present profession," Dan noted. "Without that clause, Betty's income would stop if she were capable of working in any job. That even means working in a fast-food joint."

"I always counsel my clients to pay extra for this protection," Dan advised.

"But what about Social Security. Doesn't that cover disability?" Joe implored.

"Yes," Dan agreed, "Social Security covers disability in a sense."

"The question that needs to be addressed," Dan stated, "is how disabled must you be?"

Social Security Disabilities

♦ **Brain damage resulting in severe loss of memory or judgment.**

♦ **Progressive and uncontrollable cancer or other degenerative diseases.**

♦ **Diseases that result in severe malnutrition.**

♦ **Mental illness.**

♦ **Blindness.**

♦ **Many other conditions similar to the above; which affect your ability to work (call Social Security, 1-800-772-1313, for further definitions).**

Dan went on to explain that disability from Social Security is very narrowly defined. He then listed the types of disabilities covered. (See box)

Dan further explained, "the amount paid depends upon your monthly earnings. Benefits don't begin until after the fifth full month of disability and then only after meeting a 12-month duration test. The disability benefits from Social Security cannot fully replace a disabled worker's wages and they have a strict 'any occupations' definition." In Dan's view, Social Security should be thought of only as a supplement and not as the primary disability income replacement.

Joe promised he would discuss the insurance proposal with Betty and get back to Dan.

"I came to assist Jim and it looks like it's going to cost me money," Joe muttered to himself.

The topic shifted to insurance coverage for automobiles Joe brightened a little when Dan asked if he had dropped his daughter from their automobile insurance.

"That's something I overlooked," Joe admitted.

"It really is worthwhile," Dan advised, "to review your insurance coverage periodically."

Dan illustrated how to offset the cost of higher coverage for bodily injury and uninsured motorist's coverage by increasing the deductible on both collision and comprehensive. "It's a good decision because statistics are on your side," Dan commented. "The potential of a liability claim from an accident will far outweigh the small increase in the deductible." This suggestion will improve both Joe and Jim's coverage without adding to the cost.

Though Joe and Jim had adequate homeowners insurance, only Jim had an "umbrella" policy, to cover catastrophic damages.

Looking at Jim, Dan pointed out, "It's cheap at twice the price. I strongly suggest that you increase your liability coverage and that you, Joe, obtain some." Both Jim and Joe agreed to look into the coverage, because they realized litigation and high liability settlements have become a way of life for many Americans.

Dan emphasized, "Insurance has many uses. It was developed initially as a means of transferring the financial loss associated with premature death to a life insurance company. But unless there are unusual circumstances, most retirees have outlived the need for financial protection for their survivors. At your age, Joe, with about 12 to 15 years to go until retirement, life insurance should still be part of your portfolio.

"Although you, Jim, no longer need the protection for your family and spouse that Joe still requires, there may still be some use for life insurance in your plans," Dan counseled. "As I said to you before," he continued, "life insurance can play a very important and relatively inexpensive part in providing liquidity for your and Mary's estate to provide cash to pay estate taxes."

Dan cautioned, "Before people purchase life insurance, they should understand why they would want to purchase a policy. This early understanding will help determine the type of insurance, who should be the owner and how much insurance is appropriate."

"Let us discuss the basic types of insurance, and you'll see what I mean," Dan assured them.

"**Term insurance** may be appropriate for someone in Joe's position. He has several years to go until his qualified retirement plan can provide adequately for him and Betty. Term insurance

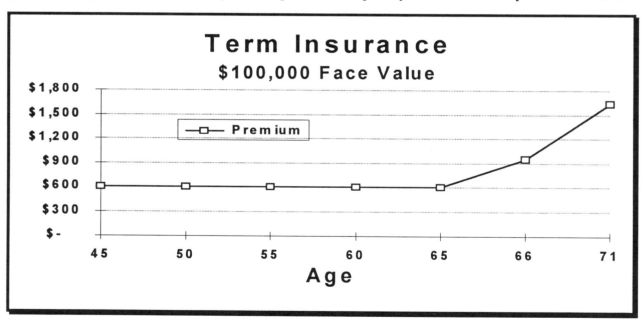

provides protection for specific periods of time. The premiums are level for the initial period, which could be 20 years. However, they increase significantly once this period expires. For example, a 45-year- old-male may pay only $600 annually for the first 20-year initial period, then pay almost $1,000 annually for the next five, and then have the rates jump to over $1,600 annually."

At this point, showing his impatience, Jim piped in, "I understand about term insurance because my company purchases it for its employees, but what about all those other types?"

Dan responded, "The other types of life insurance are called *permanent insurance* because they are usually purchased for life." He explained that permanent insurance provides for a tax-deferred build up of cash values over the life of the policy.

"**Cash value** is the excess premium, after mortality (pure insurance costs) and administrative costs are covered. The original purpose of cash value insurance was to provide a level premium. The level premium coupled with the earnings should be sufficient to pay all debt claims in an age group until the last insured is deceased. Today, in effect, it is a forced savings which can grow income tax free."

"What can we do with the cash value of the policy?" Joe asked.

"Cash values are available for loans at zero or low interest rates," Dan explained. "These loans can even be used to pay the premiums on the policy. However, in the event of an emergency," he continued, "it may be better to reschedule the premium payments than to borrow on the policy. The loan compounds over the years, and under current tax law, the interest is no longer deductible. Furthermore, the amount borrowed is considered cash received, and if it exceeds a person's basis in the policy, there may be a tax issue. The basis, usually, is equal to the cumulative premiums paid plus any accumulated dividend income on which income taxes have been paid. People should consider buying additional paid-up life insurance rather than letting the dividends accumulate."

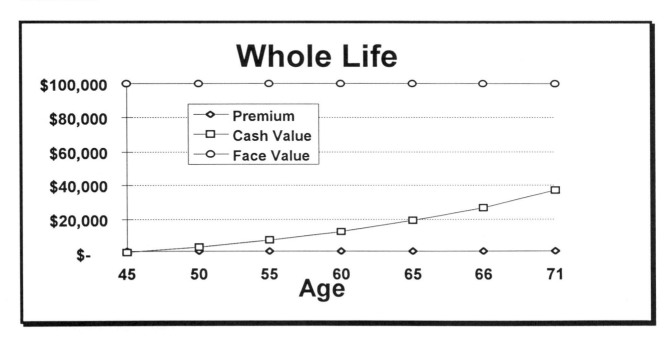

Dan proceeded, "The three basic types of permanent insurance are **whole life**, **universal life** and **variable life**. There are many variations of the above. For example, with a 20-year-pay-life you are simply shortening the period over which the premiums are amortized. In the case of whole life, you pay a lower premium for your entire lifetime.

"Whole Life provides protection at a level premium with the cash values and death benefits typically guaranteed," Dan demonstrated by pointing to the graph. The major benefit of whole life is being assured of the level premium. Once in force, the premium does not change for the life of the policy."

Jim commented. "Both Mary and I have that kind of policy. We bought it a long time ago."

"That's right," acknowledged Dan. "You have owned that policy for a quite a while."

Dan continued, "The other two types allow the policy holder some flexibility.

"With a universal life policy, both the death benefit and the premium can be adjusted. This enables the owner to change the policy as circumstances change. The cash value accumulation is adjusted as the current interest rates change. These rates compete with money market rates," Dan explained.

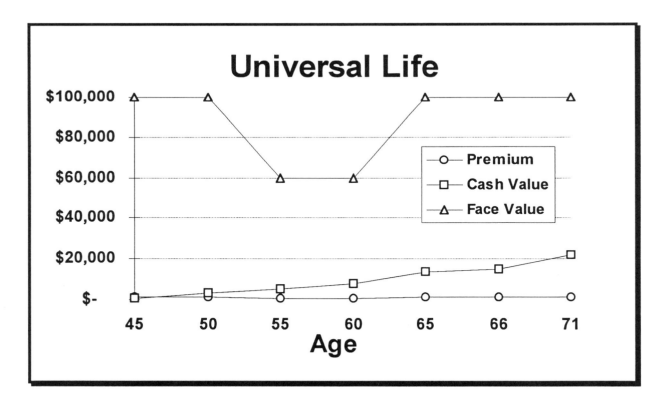

"Universal life is often sold on a 'vanishing premium' basis. This means that high premiums paid early in the life of the policy will accumulate and pay the premiums on the policy. I need to caution you," Dan warned, "about the topic of vanishing premiums. Many times, the illustration used at the time of the insurance sale includes an interest rate that cannot be sustained. Interest rates may fall below the projected target for an extended period of time. Should this occur, then the reserve may be eaten up and premiums restarted—just a reminder to be wary of any gift horses," he cautioned. "Even slight decreases in the interest rate may require additional premiums later on.

"One last point," said Dan. "A Universal Life policy usually provides a modest guaranteed rate which normally will not be sufficient to pay the premiums.

"A variable life policy," Dan continued, "also offers adjustable premiums.

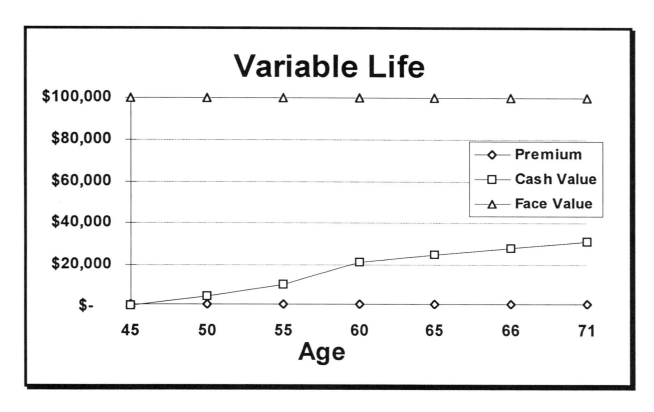

"One way in which variable life differs from universal life is the manner in which the cash value growth is derived. With variable life, the underlying cash values can be invested in equities or bonds similar to a mutual fund."

Jim, just sat there and shook his head. "I'll never understand insurance," he said.

Dan laughed and said, with tongue in cheek, "I agree. It's easier to understand the theory on nuclear energy than it is to understand some insurance policies. Just remember what I said earlier. You have to first decide why you want to buy insurance. If you are *purchasing insurance solely for the death benefit*, then the most direct and effective way to evaluate an insurance policy is to compare it on a cost per thousand basis to other similar policies. The Belth[1] method is often used for this purpose. Most people ask their insurance professional to do the calculations for them," he explained.

"On the other hand," Dan pointed out. "If you are *purchasing insurance as an investment,* as a means of increasing your estate, for example, you may want to purchase a variable life policy in an attempt to provide for an increasing death benefit, one that has the potential to stay up with inflation.

"Keep in mind, your heirs can receive the proceeds of the life insurance policy income tax free. Therefore, the return may be greater than investing the amounts of the premiums in a similar asset portfolio in a mutual fund."

Dan rationalized that the results depend on the circumstances, such as how long the policy is held.

"Often people will tell you to purchase term insurance because it is cheaper. However," Dan warned, "that may not always be the case. Recently, I worked through a number of different policies offered by the same insurance company for a 45-year-old non-smoking male. The calculation demonstrated that his best choice was a small cash-build up policy, one with low premiums, that was offered by the company."

Dan advised, "Use a sharp pencil and work through the numbers, because the results will differ depending upon circumstances."

In wrapping up of their lengthy conversation, Dan asked if the brothers-in-law had taken steps to insure that someone (an attorney-in-fact) was set up to handle their affairs should either they or their spouses become incapacitated.

Dan briefly defined the legal process and expenses involved in having a court-appointed legal guardian. "The court first appoints a guardian, usually another attorney, to investigate and report back. Only then does the court decide who the real guardian will be. The guardian may have to post a bond, obtain court approval for a living expense budget and submit an annual accounting. All this entails visits to the court accompanied by an *attorney.* A complex situation *may even require a CPA* to accompany the individual on his or her court visit. As you can imagine, having a legally appointed guardian is very expensive and time consuming."

"I strongly recommend that *each* family member have a **Durable Power of Attorney (DPA)** drafted by an attorney," Dan stated emphatically. "This legal document will enable a party of your choice to step in and handle your affairs should you become incapacitated. Dollars spent on a DPA," he told them, "may be the best dollars that you ever spend. The alternative is to have the court appoint a guardian, and you don't need that kind of headache."

---

[1]Belth, Joseph M., *Life Insurance, A Consumer Handbook*, Indiana University Press, 1985, p. 79.

Both Joe and Jim left the session with notes of the items that they needed to consider. On the trip home, they discussed how well the session went.

"I take back all the bad thoughts that I had about insurance salespeople," Joe stated to his brother-in-law as he got out of Jim's car.

Later that evening at the Meehan home

Joe described his meeting with Dan to Betty, and explained—using his notes—Dan's recommendations: "We have got to factor some insurance into our financial planning," he emphasized. He then went on to describe their needs.

"Disability insurance should be purchased for you to cover any potential lapses in your income," Joe said. "Should you become disabled, I would have to hire a careworker, causing our expenses to go up," he continued. "Our daughter, MaryEileen, should be dropped from the automobile insurance policy since she now has her own place. This will cut the premium considerably. We need to add higher bodily injury and uninsured motorist's coverage. This only makes common sense. Dan suggested we pay for this additional coverage by increasing our deductible. Catastrophic insurance is a must. We can purchase this liability insurance to cover a major event, such as a tree limb falling on the person delivering the paper. I would hate to lose everything we worked for because of a freak accident.

"We also need some type of term insurance, to cover me until I reach the stage where my retirement kicks in.

"Finally," Joe concluded, "Dan convinced me that we need to look into something called a 'Durable Power of Attorney.' This document enables either of us to handle our financial affairs without court intervention should one of us become incompetent."

With that long explanation, Joe covered all the recommendations expressed at the insurance meeting. He and Betty agreed to set up a meeting with Dan to pursue their needs.

Chapter 6

*"The legal right of a taxpayer to decrease the amount of what
otherwise would be his taxes, or altogether avoid them,
by means which the law permits, cannot be doubted."*
Supreme Court Justice Sutherland

Tax implications for the investment-minded

At the Keane Residence

After dinner one evening, Mary Keane interrupted one of her husband's and brother's favorite discussions—income taxes. Joe was describing the tax-free virtues of municipal bonds.

"Let me tell you about a co-worker's tax experience," Mary interjected.

*"This co-worker had invested in a **mutual fund for municipal bonds (MUNIs)** which seeks current income exempt from federal taxes. After receiving income for a number of years, he belatedly checked up on the fund. His stake had dropped from $50,000 to about $35,000. After checking with a friend in financial planning, he found out that the fund's yield had been lower than its peers'. Consequently, to maintain its payout, this fund was returning some of the principal. Further, he discovered the fund was deducting its high expenses from his principal instead of from the tax-free income. This strategy enabled the fund to report a higher yield."*

"In fact," Mary continued, "the co-worker found out that, with his reasonable tax rate, he would have been far better off just investing in any one of a number of taxable mutual funds. Before you two jump into an investment just to save a few tax dollars, you had better understand the implications," she commented.

"OK," Jim replied, a little peeved by Mary's superior attitude "I'll call my tax accountant and set up a meeting."

Jim invited Joe to join them. Several days later, on their way over to Brian Larkin's office to discuss the tax aspects of investing in municipal bonds, Jim described him.

Brian Larkin is a Certified Public Accountant (CPA) and an expert in taxation. He had been employed by one of the "big six" accounting firms in Seattle for over a decade. He wanted more flexibility in his personal life so he left the firm and ventured out on his own.

At Brian's Office

The Larkin CPA firm was located in a new office building complex adjacent to the residential neighborhood of Fircrest in which the Meehans resided. He shared the office space and the secretary with another CPA. When they first arrived, Brian proudly demonstrated his newly purchased CD ROM tax law retrieval system and then invited the group into the conference room. Joe, who was quick to characterize people, immediately decided that Brian was an introvert, a distinction often associated with accountants.

Mary began the conversation by relating the story of her co-worker.

"Mary, your co-worker may be fortunate that he was not subject to an **alternative minimum tax (AMT)**," Brian commented. "Often MUNI funds have a 31% AMT risk." Brian then briefly explained the interplay of the AMT and individual investors. "Most people believe that all municipal bonds are tax-exempt and purchase these with impunity.

"However, there are two traps that need to be considered," he continued. "The AMT, designed to make everyone pay their *fair-share* of taxes, is the first one to avoid. Taxes are calculated twice, once in the normal manner and a second time using the algorithm for the alternative minimum tax. A comparison is made to determine if the AMT tax exceeds the normal income tax. If so, they have to pay the higher of the two."

"Can you explain briefly the algorithm for the AMT?" Joe asked. "And particularly who it impacts."

"The alternative minimum taxable income is computed by adding back certain tax preference items, one of which is the tax-exempt interest on specified private activity bonds, a type of MUNI," Brian replied. "Income from **private activity municipal securities**, may be subject to the AMT. Private activity municipal securities include bonds issued to finance student loans, housing projects and privately owned treatment facilities. Though this income is exempt from the ordinary income tax," Brian continued, "it may not be exempt from the AMT. I always caution all purchasers of MUNIs to read the contract carefully."

Brian proceeded. "The second trap hits investors when they purchase MUNIs at a discount. This change in the tax law during 1993 isn't very well understood. Today, many MUNIs are purchased in the secondary market. If the current interest rate is greater than the original interest rate of the MUNI, then the MUNI will sell at a discount, at a price lower than its face value. For example, a $1,000 bond paying 4% interest would be discounted to about $925 should the current interest rate rise to 6%. The $75 could be taxed as ordinary income and not capital gains. Depending on the person's tax bracket, the difference could be costly. It may severely impact people who are unaware of the consequences," he said. "The rub may come when these purchasers find out that they need the services of high priced tax advisors to figure out how to account for the gain when the bonds are sold or redeemed."

"Tell me, Brian, do MUNIs have a place in my portfolio?" Jim asked.

"In your case, Jim, at your marginal tax level, I would guess that they do.

"MUNIs are federal-income-tax-free. Had you lived in a state with an income tax, bonds issued by that state are exempt from the state tax as well. The key, Jim, is that MUNIs should be a part of your portfolio, but not your entire portfolio. Most financial experts would advise you not to let taxes drive your investment decisions," Brian answered.

"MUNIs allow you to avoid tax. However, the interest rate paid by the bond is lower than taxable bonds," Brian said as he proceeded. "It's simply a function of supply and demand. Tax avoidance has a value to the high-tax-bracket individuals. This tax avoidance value allows a taxing authority to sell its bonds at a lower interest. To understand whether an 'after-tax interest rate' is a bargain, a taxpayer must relate it to a taxable investment in an 'apples-to-apples' comparison. Such a comparison is done by subtracting your tax rate from the number one (1) and dividing it into the rate offered on the MUNI.

$$\frac{\textbf{MUNI Bond Interest}}{\textbf{1 - Marginal tax rate}} = \textbf{Equivalent Taxable Interest}$$

"For example, if your tax is in the 31% bracket and a MUNI is offering 6% interest, then you would need to purchase a taxable bond paying 8.7% interest to be at a point of equivalency."

Joe left that discussion realizing that MUNIs had a greater benefit for the higher income set. Average people saving for retirement would have to look elsewhere. He also left the meeting with a greater respect for the talents of tax experts. During this and ensuing discussions with other knowledgeable tax professionals, Joe came to understand that the "name-of-the-game" for most people is tax deferral, not tax avoidance.

$$\frac{6\%}{1-(31\%)} = \frac{6\%}{.69} = 8.7\%$$

Joe had been contributing to the **401(k) plan** that his employer had set up. A 401(k) plan allowed Joe to save a portion of his salary in a tax-deferred account. This reduced the tax Joe has to pay currently and defers that tax until he took a distribution of the money.

Later that same week at Joe's home office

"How much better off am I investing in a tax-deferred plan?" he wondered. Inputting values into his computerized spreadsheet, Joe began to calculate the advantage of **tax deferral**. To figure the differential, using the same assumptions, Joe calculated both a tax deferred case investing in a 401(k) and a taxable-investment-case.

He assumed a contribution of $1,000 per month for ten years at an 8% return. The withdrawal phase was also assumed to last ten years with 1/10 with-drawn in year one, 1/9 in year two, 1/8 in year three, etc.

Joe discovered that during the buildup phase, the 401(k) investment would be almost 13% greater than the taxable investment, even if he withdrew all the funds at the end of year 10 and paid all the taxes. The surprise came with an additional 12% increase during the withdrawal phase because the income he was earning on the balance continued to defer taxes. The calculation showed Joe that he was better off, by 25%, because he deferred taxes.

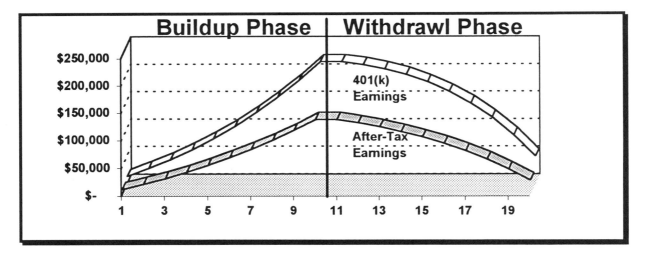

He explained his results to Betty and described them in terms of dollars "available to spend."

"This was the first time that I really understood the power of tax deferral. Did you realize that, based on my example, saving before-tax dollars would provide an average of $33,400 annually while saving after-tax dollars would provide an average of only $18,500. The ability to save part of a person's salary, tax-deferred, plus deferring the tax on the earnings from the savings, will provide almost twice as much as compared to paying taxes as he goes along.

"I'm only sorry that we didn't defer more when we were younger. It's water over the dam now, but it's a lesson that I will impression our kids," Joe emphasized.

> **People saving for retirement should maximize their tax-deferred savings.**

"But what if taxes increased?" Betty asked.

To answer Betty's question, Joe recalculated using various tax rates. He observed that the tax rate would have to increase over 40%, from the 31% rate used in the calculation, to a 45% marginal rate in order for the taxable case to be the preferred choice. Joe reasoned that it was unlikely that taxes on the middle and lower income groups would increase this much, though it may be more likely for the higher income group. Once again, he realized that different strategies may be needed depending on one's income level.

Joe decided to look into increasing his 401(k) contribution to the maximum.

Betty was concerned about her ability to save for retirement.

"Until your employer establishes a qualified plan such as an 401(k)," Joe explained, "your only hope is an **individual retirement account (IRA)**.

"Because of our **adjusted gross income (AGI)** level and since I already contribute to a qualified plan, any contribution that you make up to $2,000 will have to be with 'after tax dollars.' However, the income that you earn will grow tax-deferred. The advantage of this type of deferral based on my calculations is only about 2%.

"Somehow," Joe reiterated, "we need to work with your boss to install a qualified pension plan. With less than 100 employees, your company can set up a **Savings Incentive Match Plan for Employees (Simple 401(k) or IRA).** Let's get with your boss sometime and discuss this."

While the others were concerned about MUNIs, IRAs, and 401(k) plans, Mary Keane decided to investigate the advantages of **variable annuities**. She set up an appointment with Dan Palmer, their insurance agent.

At Dan Palmer's insurance agency

Mary learned, from Dan, that a variable annuity is in effect a mutual fund sold through an insurance company.

◆ Most variable annuities will give you a choice of investments similar to a mutual fund.
◆ In many instances the **investment advisors** are the same persons who handle investments for mutual funds.
◆ The advantage of an annuity is its tax deferral on capital gains and dividends without the contribution limit imposed on IRAs.

Dan advised her about the death benefit that guarantees the beneficiaries will receive either the amount invested or its current value, whichever is greater, free of probate.

Dan also described other aspects of the variable annuity, "Variable annuities come with annual contract charges by the insurance company from 0.75% to 2.25%. This charge is in addition to the cost of managing the investments, which is about the same as that of a mutual fund. A person needs to have a longer term investment horizon for a variable annuity," Dan continued. "The time needed for a variable annuity's tax advantage to outweigh the difference versus a mutual fund depends on the following factors:

1. "Taking the distribution as a lump sum versus. an annuity (periodic payments). The longer the number of annual payments, the quicker the break-even. Instead of taking the distribution all at once, spread it out in equal payments for years.

2. "The added expense of a variable annuity could range anywhere between 0.75% and 2.25%, depending on the insurance company. The lower the expense, the quicker the break-even.

3. "The annual rate of return (ROI). The greater the return, the quicker the break-even, the better off to invest in a variable annuity.

4. "Tax rates have to be taken into account, both during the accumulation period and during the distribution period.

5. "One other complication concerns taxes on capital gains. Capital gains are currently taxed at 28% versus. the highest individual rate of 39.6%. All distributions, including capital gains, from a variable annuity will be taxed as ordinary income ignoring the capital gains rate. If you are at the high end of the marginal tax bracket, a taxable investment with capital gains tax treatment at 28% may be a better deal. Any future reduction in the capital gains tax will mitigate this advantage."

Dan explained that, depending on the above factors, the time needed to break even can vary from one year to twenty-five years. A person has to work through the numbers to determine whether or not a deferred annuity makes sense for him or her.

"There is also a **contingent deferred sales charge (CDSC)** to be considered should an investor withdraw early from the contract," Dan said. "These charges normally relate to commissions paid to the agent that sold the investment. Sometimes, they are a static amount, such as 5% for five years, at which time the deferred charge goes to zero. Or it can decrease over time, 7% in year one , 6% in year two...until it reaches zero."

"Is that the range of time frames for the deferred charge?" Mary asked.

"Usually, for a variable annuity purchased directly from an insurance company," Dan answered. "But longer time periods, up to 15 years, can be found in some retirement plans with tax sheltered annuities (TSA)," he added.

"That can really get your attention, unless you were aware of it," Mary remarked.

"I agree," Dan said. "This charge should be spelled out ahead of time so investors understand the full scope of the product that they are purchasing. Conceptually, I agree with a deferred charge, particularly if it keeps a person from prematurely withdrawing and spending funds which should be saved for retirement. Before you go, Mary, you should also be aware of a **fixed annuity**. A fixed annuity is an insurance-based investment that earns a fixed interest rate for a period of time. The insurance company changes the rate after that period, then guarantees the new rate for a period of time."

"They are similar to Certificates of Deposit (CDs) offered by a bank," thought Mary.

"Insurance companies guarantee the principal of the fixed annuity," Dan explained. "The earnings on the investment grow tax-deferred until distribution, which is quite an advantage as compared to CDs. All in all, fixed annuities are considered very safe investments," Dan remarked. "However, a person should be cognizant of the financial strength of the insurance company itself. The insurance company is the primary guarantor of the dollars invested.

"*Insurance companies are reviewed by independent companies* and are given overall ratings. These can be confusing since each company uses a combination of letters or letters and numbers. To further confuse, rating companies do not use standard letter sequences to represent different levels of financial stability."

Dan went to his chartboard and listed the highest levels of several of the rating companies.

Level	A. M. Best	Standard and Poors	Duff and Phelps	Moody's Investors Service
1	A++, A+ Superior	AAA Superior	AAA Highest	Aaa Exceptional
2	A, A- Excellent	AA+, AA, AA- Excellent	AA+, AA, AA- Very High	Aa1, Aa2, Aa3 Excellent
3	B++, B+ Very Good	A+, A, A- Good	A+, A, A- High	A1, A2, A3 Good

"Notice how the "A" rating of one company is at a different level than the "A" rating of another company. This adds to the confusion," Dan said, as he pointed to the inconsistencies on the chart board. There are other lower categories. However, I recommend that retirees stick to insurance companies rated in the top three levels.

"While their ratings alone can't guarantee that an insurance company is immune to financial problems, these ratings are universally regarded as the most reliable tool available to access the creditworthiness of a firm," Dan continued.

"I thought the state guaranteed insurance policies," Mary countered.

"Many states, including Washington, have an agreement with the sellers of insurance in their states. These agreements, called **insurance guaranty funds,** basically assure the policyholder that, should an insurance company be declared bankrupt, the other insurers will be assessed to pay off any defaulted policies," Dan explained.

"Well, that's a guarantee isn't it?" Mary asked.

"It is and it isn't," Dan answered. "Unlike the Federal Deposit Insurance Company, there are no dollars set aside should an insurance company go bankrupt. In such a case, policyholders are forbidden to cancel their policy to prevent the defaulting company from becoming illiquid. Secondly, policyholders should be aware of the dollar limit that the insurance companies can be assessed. There is an annual cap, so it may take years to raise the full amount."

"Well, it's better than nothing," Mary commented and then asked. "Does the same concern about financial stability hold true for a variable annuity?"

"No," Dan answered, "because the investor, in effect, owns the underlying assets of the variable annuity. In this instance, the investor, not the insurance company, is taking the risk that the assets will be available when the payout begins. On the positive side, the investor is merely inconvenienced should the insurance company default on its contracts. In addition to the financial strength of a company, there are two other issues regarding fixed annuities," he explained. "The first is the interest rate itself. Generally, these rates approximate the rates of long-term treasury securities. But that does not guarantee they will hold up during periods of high inflation. Secondly, the annuity may prove to lack liquidity should you need a sizable sum."

"Why would an annuity lack liquidity?" Mary asked.

"Just picture the process," Dan answered. "A person either invests all at once or, over a period of time, purchases accumulation units. For this investment, the insurance company promises to make payment over the time period of the agreement. The payments can begin immediately or can be deferred until some time in the future. The investor receives only the amount promised at the time promised. Should the investor require a greater sum, generally it's unavailable."

"Can you have your cake and eat it too?" asked Mary.

"You can in a sense," Dan answered. "You do this by not, I repeat not, **annuitizing** your contract. That means you don't assign the funds over to the company. The act of annuitizing is accomplished by your signing an agreement that states the funds belong to the insurance company, and the company's only obligation is to pay you a specific amount over time. If you don't annuitize, but rather request specific withdrawals on a specific time schedule, you will retain the flexibility to withdraw larger amounts should your need them."

Mary thanked Dan for his counsel and promised to get back with him should she and Jim consider this type of investment.

That evening at the home of the Keanes

Earlier that day, Mary had suggested that they and the Meehans get together and review what they had learned. While the Meehans were interested in their need to increase tax-deferred savings, the Keanes were contemplating how to reduce their future income taxes. Betty was brought up to speed by Joe on the muni bond's tax implications and Mary shared with the group her meeting with Dan Palmer.

Jim had the final word. "I would like someone, perhaps a financial planner, to give me a comparison of our options. Based on our circumstances, he or she could determine whether we would be better off with MUNIs or annuities."

The rest of the evening was spent discussing all they had learned about planning for retirement.

"The impact of taxes really complicates investing, doesn't it?" Jim commented to Mary as they saw the Meehans to the door when they were leaving.

"I'll see you about 5:30 p.m. on Friday," Mary called to Joe as he got into his car.

Chapter 7

*"We do not quit playing because we grow old,
we grow old because we quit playing."*
Amy Ulrickson, MS

Take control of your personal environment

That following Friday evening Joe and Mary made the trip south to Centralia on I-5 to spend the weekend with Marie

Several of Marie's friends, all in their eighties, were just leaving as Joe and Mary pulled into their mother's driveway. As Marie reintroduced her children, she proudly announced that she and her three friends were planning a trip to Mexico. They were joining a group tour of other seniors leaving in about a month.

Marie was delighted the children chose this weekend to visit since, she would be spending the next several weeks choosing clothes, getting shots if necessary, etc., etc.

As they entered the house and in an attempt to discourage any argument against the trip, Marie confided, "You know I really need this trip. Dad would be so happy."

Mary, very reluctantly, agreed with Joe that the trip could be very beneficial, particularly if she went with a sponsored group. But she needed some time to digest this sudden announcement of Marie's. To gain some time, she quickly voiced another concern. "Mom, I notice that your friends still drive. Is that really a good idea?"

"Don't be silly. Of course we all still drive," Marie answered. "Usually I only drive around town. Even in town, one of our group got a ticket for driving too slow. Trust me, Mary, we recognize our limitations. More and more, we elderly seniors hear people complain about our driving. We are the first generation to live this long and drive cars. Our biggest concern is that the authorities will take away our mobility. To counter this concern, our group adopted the **driving rules** for elderly seniors:

- ◆ "Never drive after dark. Our eyesight isn't as good as it once was. We are more sensitive to headlights and glare.
- ◆ "Reduce driving on the freeway. Our tendency is to drive too slow and we could become a hazard.
- ◆ "Always signal when turning or changing lanes.
- ◆ "Always have at least one other person in the car.

◆ "Subscribe to a cellular phone service.

◆ "Join The American Automobile Association (AAA) or a similar auto service.

◆ "Have regular maintenance on all of our cars.

◆ "Have all drivers participate in a senior drivers education course.

◆ "Always wear our safety belts. Older drivers are more apt to suffer bone fractures and even die in crashes than younger people.

◆ "Never drive in inclement weather such as ice or snow.

◆ "Look at a map and know where we are going before we begin any journey to keep us from unnecessarily looking around while we are driving.

◆ "Be honest with each other regarding our driving ability.

◆ "Stop driving when others consider us to be a hazard and leave the driving to those who are more capable.

"Our entire group updated their driving skills by taking an eight-hour course offered by AAA and the American Association of Retired Persons (AARP). This driving course taught us how to drive defensively, and it taught us how the aging process and medications affect driving. We realize that we are getting older, but we believe seniors are good citizens and can be good drivers if they stay within limits," Marie replied to her daughter's concerns. "I also obtained a 10% discount on my insurance because I took the course."

"Mom, as always, you are one step ahead of us," Joe quipped. "What are some of the other rules that you and your group live by?"

"Every member of our small circle receives a phone call several times a day. This is not just to gossip. It's to make certain that the person is OK. We have all read the horror stories about people falling down and not being discovered for days.

"Most importantly, we keep physically and mentally active. We participate in aerobics at the senior center three times weekly and several of us are on the seniors dance team," Marie continued. "The dance team performs for hospital patients, school children and many other organizations. Some of the activities offered by our senior center would amaze you. For example, my friend Trudy is studying magic, of all things.

"Weather permitting, we always join the other seniors in the outings planned by the senior center. And of course, we attend all of the senior citizen seminars. All in all, we keep quite busy by trying to do meaningful things. We aren't content to just stay busy. Once a week, we visit the old folks home," Marie added smiling. "Just kidding, we don't really consider them old folks.

"My friends and I visit the nursing home residents each week. We play cards with them and even take some of them to the senior club activities. We don't want them to feel that they are forgotten. After all, we've known many of them for over 60 years. Remember how your grandmother visited her friend Grace, who had Parkinson's disease, every day for over 20 years? She visited just to let Grace's sister, who was her caregiver, have some time to herself. I often think that is what kept your grandmother so young in her outlook."

After they unpacked and while Marie was cooking dinner, Joe and Mary had a deep discussion.

"Joe, Mom is over eighty. Don't you think it time that she takes it a little easier?" asked Mary.

"How can I convince you that she is doing the best thing?" Joe replied. "Her hobbies seem to be both fun and challenging. They offer her the company of her peers and age group.

"People who volunteer tend to live longer and that's an irrefutable fact. It seems Mom has the good sense to enjoy life, but still retain her flexibility. She also has the freedom to reduce her activity if it comes to that. Besides, visiting a nursing home can lessen the fears of living in one someday."

"Yeah, I hear you Brother, but..."

At this point Joe interrupted. "There's always a but, isn't there? What does Jim intend to do when the two of you retire? I just can't picture him playing golf all day, every day. As for the business, your sons are more than capable of running it without him."

"My problem with Jim is to teach him that leisure is not being inactive. I want him to slow down gradually. He shouldn't work just as hard for ten months and then take two months off to golf. That's why we plan to spend at least two weeks a quarter at leisure. I also encouraged him to look into those *Elderhostel* classes."

"What is an Elderhostel class?" Joe asked.

"Elderhostel is for elder citizens who want new experiences," Mary explained. "It is a network of colleges and universities which offer low-cost, short-term, residential academic programs for older citizens," she continued. "Jim will always find a way to keep busy. He imagines himself as a budding van Gogh."

Joe responded with a puzzled look on his face.

"That's right! He bought an easel and signed up for some painting classes. I thought I had told you that!" Mary continued. "Someone he golfs with talked him into it."

"How about you and Betty?" she asked.

"Realistically, I see myself working at some type of part-time job," Joe replied. "Betty and I just don't have the money that you and Jim accumulated. I believe that I can use my accounting skills and work with small businesses. I also intend to volunteer, figuring my technical skills will be useful there as well. I don't intend to have a list of odd jobs to finish when I do retire. That would be the death of me. I intend to get out with people the same way I do now," Joe asserted.

Mary switched subjects. "Speaking of odd jobs, look around Mom's house. It's the same as when we grew up. It was wonderful to have all this room that gave all of us our private space. But is it the right place for mom? Now don't interrupt. Hear me out," she continued. "Notice how slowly Mom climbs the stairs, and the washing machine is still in the basement. I think the least we can do is to convince Mom to remodel so she can live all on one floor. Jim and I can easily handle the financial part, and you can convince Mom of the necessity as well as supervise the contractor."

"For once we both agree on something concerning Mom's welfare," Joe answered. "I work with my Kiwanis Club on building ramps for the elderly to help them get around their homes. I just never thought of Mom as being elderly and that she may need the same type of assistance. Let's discuss this with Mom at dinner and see how she reacts."

By dinner time, Joe had already sketched out how the living quarters could be rearranged to enable their mom to cope with her daily activities.

Mary liked his plan. "Widening the bathroom to enable future wheelchair access is a great idea. However, I would add grab bars even if Mom objects. I know that her friends keep in daily touch, but I also think we should look into items that Mom would need should something happen when she is alone."

"What kind of items are you talking about?" asked Joe.

"A cellular phone that she can keep near her, lamps that light with a touch so Mom doesn't have to fumble for a switch. Perhaps even an emergency alarm button that will connect to the fire station."

"Mary, you are absolutely right," Joe said. "Have you noticed that once you begin thinking about a topic, many useful ideas come to mind."

Joe continued. "As you were talking, I just thought of the **Red Cross** volunteer who spoke at a recent Kiwanis luncheon. She advised us to be prepared for a natural disaster. Here in the Northwest, an earthquake is a definite possibility, as is a volcanic eruption. Other parts of the country may be more affected by a flood or a tornado."

"What were some of the Red Cross's suggestions?" asked Mary.

"The volunteer described how she had two disaster kits, one she kept at home and the other in her car. Each kit included:

- "Water,
- "Non-perishable food,
- "Warm clothing,
- "Flashlights,

♦ "Extra medicine
♦ "Medical supplies,
♦ "Extra reading glasses and other items.

"The volunteer passed out a pamphlet listing all the items that one should have available. Having these supplies together in a bag of some type enables a person to just grab it and get to a safe place," Joe continued. "The volunteer described how water is the most critical item. In a disaster, the community drinking water almost always becomes contaminated. She explained that people need a gallon of water a day for drinking, cooking and sanitation. The first 72 hours are critical before organized aid can reach the disaster area," Joe explained. "The volunteer recommended strapping the hot water heater to studs in the wall. All gas heaters should be fitted with flexible gas supply lines. This setup will greatly minimize the danger from fire or explosion. This suggestion really impressed me because the water heater may be your only supply of fresh water during those critical hours."

Joe continued. "Some of the other suggestions included installing childproof locks to prevent dishes from spilling out of the china cabinet. Think of what could happen to your collection of Waterford glass and Belleek china."

"What a horrible thought," Mary said, with a shudder.

"The Red Cross volunteer also raised some other issues that pertain to Mom and also to ourselves. She mentioned such things as turning off the gas and electricity. I'm quite certain that Betty hasn't a clue as to how to do that."

"Betty isn't alone. I don't know how to do those things either," said Mary. "We all need to become more prepared for what can happen in a disaster. I'm going to call the Red Cross for copies of their material on disasters. I am also going to prepare some of those kits for the entire family, including you and Betty, and the kids, everybody."

At that point Marie called Joe and Mary to dinner. That dinner proved to be one the two siblings would remember for a long time. Surprising both her children, Marie readily agreed to their ideas about home improvement. She saw improving her home as an opportunity to let her children do something for her and figure that the improvements would extend the length of time that she could stay in her own home. The family had a very frank discussion on how their mom wanted to conduct her life in her twilight years. They agreed on topics in home care and alternative living arrangements.

"Mary, I would be delighted to have some help with the chores around the house and with the shopping," Marie said. "I promise that I will contact the volunteer chore program this week to arrange for those services. Thank you for your offer to pay for it. I don't need any monetary assistance right now. If I need some help, I promise I will come to you." Marie went on, "I want to stay in my own home for as long as I am able. When the time comes that I can no longer be self-sufficient, I will enter a retirement community that provides assisted living. But I want one in which I can furnish my own apartment. There is a retirement community, located just north of here, that would be ideal. I looked into it several years ago when both Dad and I had that siege of illness."

"Mom, you didn't tell us that you considered moving to a retirement community," Mary complained.

"You remember that time when both Dad and I were in and out of hospitals. After things calmed down, we took inventory of our lifestyle and decided to move a retirement community. Both of us wanted to be sure the other was settled in a good environment should something happen to either one of us. This particular community seemed to be ideal. It was like a small city where everybody knew each other and they had plenty of activities. For example, I could go to the opera with a group, and your father didn't have to attend. Think how easy that would have made both our lives. Your dad thought the living cost would be less than we spend now. For example, we would not need lawn care, and the cost to heat and maintain this place is enormous," Marie continued. "I also liked that retirement setup because it enabled a person to advance to the level of a skilled care facility without having to go to a different place. Besides, it's close enough for my friends to get up to see me on occasion."

"Why didn't you follow through?" Joe asked.

"That is a question that I have often asked myself," Marie replied. "I guess it was because we began to feel better and we put off making the decision."

Marie then changed the subject back to her present home. "Joe, your thoughts on remodeling are wonderful. I realize that I am not as young as I used to be, and these stairs are getting to be a problem."

Nevertheless, Marie set certain parameters. "Now, Joe and Mary, I don't want you to start anything until I get back from Mexico. I want to be involved in how everything goes together. I'm the one who has to live here."

It took some doing, but Joe and Mary convinced Marie otherwise. She finally agreed it was best to get the heavy remodeling work done while she was away. But they did agree to have a plan drawn up by a local architect, and receive her approval before they started anything.

Mary and Joe went to bed agreeing to help their mother maintain her sense of independence as long as she was able. They were delighted with the frank discussion that they had with Marie and wished they had done it years before.

As they were saying goodnight, at the doors of their respective bedrooms, Joe remarked to his sister, "Somewhere, I have a check-off list for retirees (Control of Personal Environment Checklist, Appendix 7a) who are considering relocating after they retire. I'll look it up. Do you remember? I sent you a copy. There may be something in it that would be useful to Mom."

Chapter 8

*"According to your latest figures, if you
retired today, you could live very
comfortably until about 2 p.m. tomorrow."*
Real Life Adventures

What are our financial needs?

At the Keanes' residence

Several mornings later, after she returned from a visit to Marie, Mary and Jim continued the discussion on their pending retirement.

"I'm serious about bringing in some professional to help us sort through our options," Jim emphasized. "It's beginning to get too complicated for me to keep track."

"I agree," Mary said. "I would like to begin gifting to our children so that they can enjoy some of our bounty while they are still young; and, furthermore, there is my mother to think about. I wish you had gone with me to listen when Anne Jahn spoke at the financial seminar that our company's retirement services department conducted," Mary continued. "Perhaps she can help us out. After all, she is a **Certified Financial Planner (CFP)**."

Anne Jahn, who has a Masters Degree in Business Administration (MBA), is a Certified Financial Planner (CFP) with a CPA license. She retired several years ago from a large corporation where she held a management position in the accounting department. Because she realized that she would have to live for a long time on her own investment decisions, she enrolled in the College for Financial Planning. After studying for several years and passing five national tests, she finally received her CFP certificate. Subsequently, an opportunity arose enabling her to take early retirement from her company. Anne decided to take early retirement and enter the newly emerging field of financial planning.

"How is your brother Joe going to feel if we get professional financial help?" asked Jim.

"He'll be okay. We will share our knowledge," Mary answered.

"All right. Let's have at it. Make an appointment with Anne," Jim replied somewhat reluctantly.

Several weeks later at Anne's office

Anne maintained her office with an attached conference room at the edge of a small shopping mall in the city of Lakewood, near the Keane Tool and Die Company. After the Keanes explained their retirement plans, Anne began Jim and Mary's financial planning education by covering the five major financial concerns of the retiree.

1. Living expenses
2. Medical costs
3. Mental incapacity
4. Estate planning
5. Financial advice

"Too often people's aversion to risk prevents them from investing at the level of return that they need for a secure retirement," she continued. "The greatest concern of all retirees should be, 'What's it going to cost us to live?' Understanding this factor, first, is more important than worrying about the return on their investments," Anne explained, "because the cost-of-living will determine the percentage (%) return they need.

"Not want, *need*," Anne said for emphasis.

Anne cited the following example. "I recently completed a plan for a widow whose current investments were returning less than 4%. She needed a return of better than 8% in order to live adequately until age ninety. Since there is no reason not to believe that she will still be alive at ninety, she had better plan to have finances to last her that long. In her case, she was investing far too conservatively and would run out of money while she was still in her early seventies."

"As a general rule," Anne explained, "it takes 75 to 80% of a person's gross working income to live at a comparable level during retirement. There isn't any magic drop in expenses when a person retires," she acknowledged. "Many retirees, who still owe on their mortgage, will experience only the elimination of their Social Security deductions and perhaps a reduction in their income tax. If this were the case, the percentage needed would be closer to 90% of their working income. For the first ten years, or so, your living expenses may actually increase. This occurs because you have more free time plus the freedom to spend that time where and how you want," Anne continued. "This energetic spurt is followed by a natural tendency to slow down as you age. Consequently, I always use at least two time frames when I project retirement living expenses."

Anne then explained that medical costs are also a major concern to retirees for these two reasons:

1. "They tend to increase two to three times faster than inflation.
2. "As we age, we require increased medical care.

"Regarding inflation," Anne continued "many planners use projections of 3.5 to 4%. I recommend using an average 5% inflation rate for any retirement projections. As my father used to say, it's like wallpaper; it covers a multitude of sins. While inflation has averaged only 3.1% for the past sixty-some years, it has averaged over 6.2% for the combined decades of the 70s and 80s," Anne explained. "Unfortunately, inflation isn't perfectly linear. It comes with peaks and valleys. A higher average helps to compensate for those peaks and valleys."

At this point Anne shared her philosophy on retirement planning. "I believe a person should plan conservatively to determine how practical it is for him or her to retire. Following retirement, if the actual return on investment exceeds what was planned, or if the actual inflation rate comes in lower than planned, then the retirees are just that much better off.

"I'm delighted to see that you both have a **durable power of attorney**," Anne said as she changed topics. "This document overcomes the third major concern of retirees which is: What happens if I become mentally incapacitated? We'll worry about the fourth concern, estate planning, after we calculate your retirement needs."

At this point Mary and Jim shared their goals and the financial statements that they developed in conjunction with Mary's brother, Joe.

"This is excellent," Anne said with pleasure. "Usually, getting people to develop this type of information is like pulling teeth. The purpose of this session," she explained, "is to enable me to fully understand your present finances and your goals."

Anne then took considerable time reviewing the statements with the Keanes.

While looking at their cash flow statement, she observed, "Most people detail their expenses, such as housing expenses, food etc., at a much more detailed level, but if you are comfortable with just a total amount and if it is reasonably close to your current spending level, then I have no quarrel with it.

"I notice, Mary, that your employer has a **defined benefit plan**," Anne commented. "The distribution from this plan can be taken either as a **monthly pension** or a **lump sum**. Let us, for the first go around, calculate your cash income as though you chose to receive the pension as a monthly annuity. Later, we will take you through an exercise on how to compare that option to a lump sum choice. Your monthly pension payments, if they are typical of most company pensions, may not keep up with inflation," Anne cautioned. "Your plan, unlike *military pensions* and other government retirement plans, does not have the protection of a **cost-of-living adjustment (COLA)** clause. So, for Mary's pension, we will plan for no increases in benefits. This is a conservative approach.

"I'll take the worksheets and other data that you have provided and develop a preliminary retirement projection. We will have retirement data to discuss at our next session," Anne said.

Anne then scheduled a follow-up session with Jim and Mary.

The Keanes' second session with their financial planner

Anne squeezed the Keanes in between two previously established appointments because they were so anxious to see the results of their retirement projection. Anne quickly described her retirement calculation.

"Before we look at the numbers themselves, you should understand the basis on which they are predicated," Anne began. She then passed out a listing of the assumptions that she used in preparing the Keane's retirement projections.

Jim and Mary Keane
Planning Assumptions

1. Inflation rate at 5%.
2. Return on investments at 8%. That's about the average long-term return on a portfolio consisting of 60% equity (stocks) and 40% bonds.
3. Begin drawing Social Security at your retirement age of 63.
4. Regarding Social Security, both of you qualify for the maximum amount. The amount that I calculated is the maximum less a deduction for early withdrawal. I only inflated Social Security at 4%. It is my opinion that future Social Security increases will most probably lag inflation.

Anne began her explanation, "Most people's initial retirement projections are based on their current expenditures. Then I ask the question: What would change if they were to retire today? The answer enables me, in conjunction with the client, to tweak the numbers until we arrive at an agreeable retirement expenditure in today's dollars," she said. "I calculated everything using today's dollars, often called current dollars. It's difficult enough for financial planners to relate to inflated dollars. For most people, the impact doesn't become real until the future value is converted into something they can relate to. Normally, I use a higher expense amount for the first ten years or so, following retirement. I have found that as people age, they tend to spend less in their later years. In your case, since you didn't detail your expenses, to be conservative I used the a level expense amount until age ninety. These, of course, are inflated 5% annually," Anne continued.

"My software program," Anne explained, "calculates and summarizes the expenses and income at the appropriate rates for inflation and return on investment. Then it calculates the present value of the net of that stream of income, less expenses, to arrive at the capital required to fund any deficit. In simple English, it converts all the future income and expense streams into today's dollars. That way, we can determine if you have sufficient resources, today, to last you through your retirement years," Anne explained.

"In your case, you have about $400,000 surplus which means you have the potential to live until age ninety using only 85% of your available retirement assets. I always calculate retirement projections to age ninety. Chances are, if you are married and alive at age sixty-five, one of you will be alive at ninety," Anne continued. "Remember, your retirement assets do not include such assets as your residence or vacation property. It only includes those items that we specified as being available to consume during your retirement.

> ## Chances are, if you are married and alive at age sixty-five, one of you will be alive at ninety.

"These results are based on your ability to average 8% return on your investments," Anne reminded Jim and Mary. "That ability is key to your retiring comfortably. You should consider investing in assets that have a reasonable chance of obtaining that level of a return. There are many investment opportunities that will provide you more safety of principal but will not enable you to obtain your needed return.

Retirement Projection		
Mary & Jim Keane		**January 19xx**
Retirement Inflation Rate		5%
Assumed Investment return rate		8%
Retirement age		63
Gross annual living expenses	$	144,000
Cumulative inflated retirement expenses	$	8,294,512
Less (-) the total income from Social Security and Mary's pension.	$	(1,692,988)
Equals (=) the retirement income deficit	$	6,601,524
Present value of the retirement income deficit	$	(2,233,764)
Retirement assets available	$	2,638,376
Retirement assets surplus	$	404,612

"Finally, understand that you use these numbers in a relative sense. Whatever happens in the future will in all likelihood be different than anything we may project today," Anne acknowledged.

"I realize that's a real mouthful to digest all at once, so let's go over the numbers carefully. Feel free to give me a call after you leave should you have any questions, because I really want you to understand the implications of this projection. I will have your plan completed by the next time we get together. Now let's take the time to walk through all these numbers to make sure that you understand them.

"The key numbers are:
- ◆ "How much you need each year,
- ◆ "The inflation rate,
- ◆ "The investment return rate,
- ◆ "And how long you will need the retirement income."

"How did you come up with that $8 million retirement expense number," Jim asked.

"The $8,294,512 is what you will spend over the course of your two lifetimes until age 90," Anne explained. "This is the accumulation of all the $12,000s per month, inflated annually by 5%.

"You will receive $1,692,988 from Social Security and Mary's pension," Anne continued, "based on a **cost-of-living adjustment (COLA)** for Social Security at 1% below the inflation rate. Remember, we have not inflated Mary's pension and you are taking an early withdrawal of Social Security."

"The deficit amount of $2,233,764 is the **Present Value (PV)** of the difference between the retirement needs and the income," Anne explained.

"How did you compute the retirement deficit amount?" Mary asked.

"That's a present value (PV) calculation," Anne replied. "We needed a method to compare the cash that is spent over the length of time of your retirement to the assets you have on hand today to finance that outflow. Present value translates the dollars you will spend, and receive, in the future to their worth in today's dollars. Very simply, it means that a dollar you receive two years from now is not worth as much as a dollar you have on hand now. For example, if you could earn 10% on your money, then one dollar you receive two years from now would be worth only 83 cents today. Why? Because you can earn interest on the money you have now. Does that explanation help?" Anne asked.

"Okay, I'm comfortable with that explanation," Mary replied.

Anne went on, "We then compare the present value of your retirement cash outflow to the worth of your current assets at the time of your retirement to determine if they are sufficient. You have a surplus of over $400,000," Anne concluded, glancing at her watch. "I'm sorry to have to end the session so abruptly; but unfortunately, as you are aware, I have another engagement and have to run," Anne said. "Next time, we will cover some additional retirement issues."

Mary and Jim left Anne's office with a good feeling regarding their ability to retire comfortably. They were getting excited about the whole planning process. They resolved to explain as best they could to Joe and Betty how Anne calculated the projection. Jim was delighted with the process and the results.

"I'm glad I took your advice. I think Anne will do a good job for us," Jim said to his wife. He showed his gratitude by taking Mary out to dinner.

Later that week at the Meehans

During dinner one evening, Jim and Mary described Ann's process that to Joe and Betty. Though Joe was sorry that he did not attend the session, he was intrigued with the outcome. After the Keanes left, Joe and Betty discussed their next step in retirement planning. "*Projecting-our-retirement* is the piece that we were missing," Joe proclaimed. "I'm confident that I can do for us what Anne did for Jim and Mary."

"To be honest, I didn't understand all that stuff about present value that Mary was talking about. Do you understand it?" Betty asked.

"Fortunately, I have a computer spreadsheet with built in formulas that compute present values. When I run some examples, I will illustrate how it works," Joe answered.

Later that same week at the Meehans

After spending some time thinking about the approach, Joe described to Betty how he intended to project their retirement income. "We have to take these factors into consideration," Joe explained, as he wrote them down.

"OK, I can understand why you need to inflate the expenses and the income, but the present value still throws me," Betty said.

"It's a difficult concept to understand," Joe replied. "So let's take it slow and walk through the entire process.

"When we set our goals, we decided on certain things that we wanted to accomplish.
♦ "Retire at fifty-seven.
♦ "Pay off our mortgage before retirement.
♦ "Set up an emergency fund of $10,000.
♦ "Increase our retirement savings.

"To adjust our current living expenses to reflect these goals, we adjust the numbers as though these changes have already taken place by the time of our retirement," Joe said. "Then he described the process that he intended to follow to compute their retirement projection."

"First of all, we need to calculate the amount of pension that I will receive at age fifty-seven. My company gives me an annual report of how much I will receive at age six-five, but I have to deduct about 5% annually for each year that I am under that age.

```
┌─────────────────────────────────────┐
│     Retirement Factors and Approach │
│                                     │
│  1.  Develop pension income by year.│
│                                     │
│  2.  Increase Social Security       │
│      annually by 4%.                │
│                                     │
│  3.  Extend retirement assets by a  │
│      pre-retirement rate of return  │
│      until year of retirement. This │
│      includes all monthly           │
│      contributions to 401(k) and    │
│      SEP plans.                     │
│                                     │
│  4.  Adjust current expenses to     │
│      represent the amounts          │
│      anticipated at the year of     │
│      retirement.                    │
│                                     │
│  5.  Inflate the current expenses   │
│      by 5% annually until age       │
│      ninety.                        │
│                                     │
│  6.  Subtract the inflated expenses │
│      from the income of the         │
│      investments beginning with     │
│      year one of retirement.        │
│                                     │
│  7.  Add any surplus or subtract    │
│      any deficit from the asset     │
│      balance and use present value  │
│      to recompile the annual        │
│      income.                        │
│                                     │
└─────────────────────────────────────┘
```

"Fortunately, we received those **personal earnings and benefit estimate statements** from the Social Security Administration. We will use the age 62 early retirement amount. Annually, we will increase this amount by 4% (1% less than the cost-of-living estimate). We also have to take into consideration the fact that I will retire five years before we will begin to receive Social Security.

"Let's use 8%, the estimate that Anne used in Jim and Mary's projection, for both our pre-retirement and the post-retirement return on our investments. However, before we can apply this percent, we need to determine how much our retirement savings will grow before the date of our retirement. We begin with our current retirement account of $96,000 and add our future savings, plus that portion that my company will match. Every year we increase our savings by the pre-retirement rate of return.

"That takes care of the calculations to arrive at the retirement income portion of our plan," Joe explained.

"For our living expenses," he continued, "we will begin with our final cash flow plan, the one that we developed several weeks ago.

"First we need to adjust several of the expenses to reflect our outflow during retirement. We will follow Anne's approach and compute two time frames, first a 15-year period and second a ten-year period," Joe said. "These are the categories that we need to adjust and why." (Box on following page)

"It took a lot of work, but I can see the value of examining the different types of expenses," Betty said admiringly.

"This should give us a good start," Joe went on. "Now we adjust these numbers annually to reflect inflation. We will use the 5% that Anne used in preparing Jim and Mary's plan.

Revised Downward:

Housing — because there will be no mortgage payments.

Food — fewer lunches out since we will no longer be working.

Clothing —more casual, less expensive clothing.

Utilities —With more travel, less time will be spent at home.

Taxes —no Social Security deductions, plus a lower income tax bracket.

Work-related expenses —will be zeroed out.

Savings and Contingencies —will be fully funded by the time of retirement.

Revised Upward:

Transportation —because of more extensive travel plans.

Recreation—associated with more travel.

Medical—to recognize anticipated cost increases

"Finally, we get to your question on present value," Joe acknowledged. "Present value translates everything back to the current worth of today's dollar. This calculation is done to enable us to compare what we have saved to the assets we will need for our retirement. Both of these calculations reflect today's dollars."

"How do you do that?" asked Betty.

"The computer formula uses a present value factor based on the interest rate provided to convert future dollars into present dollars. For example, if we could earn 8% on our money, then receiving $108,000 dollars a year from now has the same net value or current worth as having a $100,000 right now," explained Joe. "On the worksheet for each year, I subtract the expenses in inflated dollars from the income in inflated dollars to determine if we have a net increase or decrease. I then use the present value formula to convert each specific year back to this year's net worth. I then add or subtract the total from our retirement assets valued at the time of our retirement to determine if we have enough money to retire. Let me give you a simple example," Joe said.

"Assume that we begin with $150,000, earn $60,000 in the first year and spend $52,000. The $8,000 difference between what we earn and what we spend translates into $7,407 in today's dollars. This amount is then added to our beginning balance," Joe said as he pointed to the illustration. During the early years of our retirement, the net difference between income and expense will be a surplus, and the present value amount will increase the asset balance. As the years go on, the inflated expenses will, more than likely, exceed the inflated income," he continued. "At that time, the asset balance will begin to decrease."

	Retirement Asset Balance in Current $	Annual Income Inflated @ 8%	Annual Expense Inflated @ 5%	Net	Present Value in Current Dollars
Begining Balance	$ 150,000				
Year one		$ 60,000	$ 52,000	$ 8,000	$ 7,407
Balance @ end of year one	$ 157,407				
Year two		$ 64,800	$ 54,600	$ 10,200	$ 8,745
Balance @ end of year two	$ 166,152				

"I follow you so far," Betty said.

"We are trying to find out how much we need when we retire to keep the asset balance from reaching zero or going into negative territory," Joe explained. "To find the answer, I first have to set up the columns and formulas on my spreadsheet," Joe said. "I'll get to it some evening this week."

Later the following week

After working on the projection through the weekend, Joe sat down with Betty to discuss the output from his labor.

"The expenses look like they are right in line with what we discussed the other day," Betty said.

"That's not our problem," Joe lamented. "I calculate that we will need to save an additional $600,000 in order to retire at this rate. That's an impossible target."

"Don't tell me that. I don't want to hear it," Betty sighed. "Where do we go from here?"

"I'll just have to keep working the numbers until we determine when, and at what level of income and expense, we can afford to retire," Joe answered.

About a week later

After a number of iterations, Joe and Betty sat down to discuss the revised numbers.

"These are the revised assumptions that I made. First we will accept the retirement expense projection as being reasonable," Joe said. "This means a more drastic change to our current spending." He then explained the changes that would have to take place.

Retirement Projection Joe & Betty Meehan	Final Working Plan	First 15 Years Retirement	Second 10 Years Retirement
Expenses:			
Cash Expenses	$ 400	$ 400	400
Housing	$ 750	$ 150	150
Food	$ 400	$ 360	360
Clothing	$ 300	$ 240	90
Transportation	$ 400	$ 600	400
Medical	$ 350	$ 525	1045
Total Insurance	$ 175	$ 175	175
Recreation	$ 700	$ 1,050	490
Utilities	$ 175	$ 157	157
Joe Work Related	$ 130	$ 50	50
Betty Work Related	$ 110	$ 1,436	1436
Contributions	$ 50	$ -	0
Taxes	$ 1,915	$ 200	0
Other Expenses	$ 200		
Total Expenses	**$ 6,055**	**$ 5,343**	**$ 4,753**

1. "Wait until age sixty-four to retire.
2. "Earn 9% return on our investments.
3. "Reduce our transportation and travel expenses beginning immediately to have sufficient retirement assets.

"Waiting until later to retire will increase the pension that I will receive from work. Also, Social Security kicks in sooner," Joe explained.

"How do you feel after you had your heart set on retiring early?" Betty asked.

"I thank God that we found out early enough to change our savings and spending habits. Because without making these changes, we would not be financially able to retire at all. Retiring at fifty-seven is a nice thought, but it simply isn't practical," Joe replied.

> **Without making these changes, we would not be financially able to retire at all.**

"I don't mind traveling less, and the amount of transportation and recreation planned is more than adequate," Betty said. "But is the average return on investment of 9% achievable?"

"That is always an open question," Joe replied. "I did one other calculation to test the sensitivity of the impact of the return. I reduced the return by 2% to 7% and reduced the **inflation** by only 1/2% to 4.5%. This improves our surplus dramatically. I was really surprised at how much impact inflation plays on a person's ability to retire. I now feel comfortable with the final results, and, yes, I believe that we can achieve them.

Both Joe and Betty began to feel better about their ability to retire securely even though it would happen later than they had hoped. They couldn't wait to share the results with Mary and Jim.

Chapter 9

*"Selecting the appropriate retirement package may be the most
important financial decision that most people make in their lifetime."*

Select the appropriate retirement package

The following week at Anne's financial planning office

Jim called Anne, their financial planner, and asked if they could bring Betty and Joe to their next appointment. Since the intent of this session was to obtain an understanding of the types of options that their company pensions offered, the Keanes reasoned that this would be invaluable knowledge. Mary was surprised that Betty was reluctant to attend. She talked her into going by explaining that knowledge of pensions was as important to the wife as to the husband.

"Betty, I understand your reluctance to take time off from work. However, this is a very important subject, and you should be knowledgeable about it," Mary emphasized. "In my opinion, a wife needs be fully aware of her husband's pension plan."

Joe was delighted that Betty finally agreed to attend. He had been trying to get his wife more involved in their long-term finances.

"Anne Jahn, I would like you to meet Mary's brother Joe and his wife Betty," Jim said as he introduced them.

Joe liked Anne immediately. He was most impressed that Anne hadn't pressured Mary and Jim into investing in a product. She respected their desires to become educated first. In Joe's mind, putting education first is the true mark of quality in an advisor.

Anne spent the initial half-hour being brought up to speed on the Meehan's goals and progress in their planning effort. She asked numerous questions about their companies' pension plans. Anne was pleased that all of the participants had an in-depth knowledge of tax deferral, "that should simplify our discussion. I also want to thank you for supplying an advance copy of each of your company's plans. I was able to review them before you came. As you are aware, many employers have turned the job of investing over to their employees. The decisions on investing and the responsibility for insuring that a pension will be available are now in many instances the responsibility of the individual employee," Anne emphasized.

"Both Jim and Joe have a **defined contribution plan**. This type of plan is called a **401(k) plan**, and it was named after a particular section in the tax code. As you are aware, 401(k) plans enable you to contribute pre-tax dollars. Bear in mind that a 401(k) plan requires you to be your own money manager. Your company has turned the investment decision-making over to you. If there aren't sufficient funds for you to enjoy retirement, it is your fault and not your company's.

"Betty, your company has recently established a **Simplified Employee Pension (SEP)**. The **SAR-SEP** has been replaced with a SIMPLE Plan. Though all companies can establish a **Simplified Employee Pension Plan (SEP)** only companies with 100 or fewer employees can establish a **SIMPLE-Plan**. A SIMPLE-Plan can take the form of an IRA or a 401(k). If it's an individual retirement plan, which means you are fully vested with a higher contribution level than the $2,000 of a normal **IRA**, you can contribute up to a maximum dollar limit and the employer must also make a contribution. The original $6,000 deferral election limit is indexed in $500 increments, based on the rate of inflation.

"Mary, in addition to having a 401(k) plan, your company also has a **defined benefit plan**, which means that your employer invests for you and will provide you with a pension when you retire. Your pension will be based on the average of your last 3 years' salary and your number of years of service. You are fortunate that the plan has an early retirement option which, incidentally, begins at age 55. This means you can opt out earlier than 65 and still get a partial pension once you are fully **vested**.

"Vesting simply means that you have a right to all or a portion of the pension funds, even if you terminate your employment," Anne explained. "However, your pension will be about 4% less for each year that you are under age 65. The plan enables you to take the pension as an annuity, meaning you will receive a **monthly pension**, or you can take a **lump sum** distribution. I will show you later in the session how to determine which is more suitable for you."

Anne then led the group in a discussion on investing in their various plans, the risks involved, and the options available when they wish to retire. With a 401(k) and a SAR-SEP, your employer makes available a number of investment options. Also, you can change the percentage of your salary deferral every quarter, if you desire, up to the maximum allowed. How wisely you invest during your wealth accumulation years will be the key determinant to how well you will live during retirement."

> **How wisely you invest during your wealth accumulation years will be the key determinant to how well you will live during retirement.**

"Won't the fact that we are investing with tax-deferred dollars provide us with enough dollars to retire?" Betty asked.

Anne expounded on Betty's question. "Unfortunately, statistics tell us that most people have invested all their funds in the **fixed option** of their 401(k). The fixed option is usually invested in a

guaranteed investment contract (GIC). A GIC is nothing more than a **certificate of deposit (CD)** whose rates and principal are guaranteed by an insurance company."

"We have all seen what happens to CDs when interest rates drop. The same thing happens to GICs. Furthermore, they are only guaranteed by the insurance company itself and not by the **Federal Deposit Insurance Corporation (FDIC)**, as is the case with bank CDs up to $100,000," Anne continued.

"While many employers have covered losses to employees when the insurance company had problems, there is no guarantee that all employers will. I am concerned that GICs are too conservative an investment for 100% of your salary deferral. The **Department of Labor (DOL)** has released statistics which show that 75% of all workers with a 401(k) or similar plan have none of their contributions invested in stock. This oversight is a mistake that people will regret when they go to retire," Anne declared. "Their retirement funds simply will not grow to a sufficient size to enable them to retire securely.

"Many people also make a second mistake. They invest too much in their company's stock, out of a sense of loyalty. Often a company will match a portion of your investment and invest this amount into its own stock. In many instances, this is sufficient exposure to a single company stock for most people. People ought to invest their money in a more varied manner.

"Moderation pays!" Anne declared. "During their wealth accumulation years workers, should put 60 to 70% of their contributions into stock. While a portion of this investment can be placed in their company stock, the vast majority should go to a stock fund. In many company plans, the stock fund will be an index fund which mimics the market, such as the S&P 500. When a person invests in such an index fund, it is as though he has invested a small portion of their pension in each of the top 500 companies in industry. Such investing provides both an opportunity for growth and wide diversification for minimizing risk. The remainder should be invested into the fixed option, normally a GIC or a bond fund."

> **Decide on an allocation between stocks and bonds and stick with it regardless of the volatility in the market.**

"Let me see if I can summarize what you just covered to make sure that I understand it completely," Joe interrupted. "I should split my monthly contributions to my 401(k) plan between stocks and bonds with the greatest emphasis on stocks. Furthermore, I should continue to do this regardless of the volatility in the stock market."

"Well done. I wish I could condense my presentation as well as you did. Thank you, Joe," Anne said. "In your case, Mary, your defined benefit plan has its own series of risks."

Anne continued. "Many companies and many governmental units, such as state and municipality pension funds, are underfunded. Thus, sufficient funds are not available to pay their debt to the employee's retirement should the company become bankrupt. The employees of

Eastern Airlines found themselves in this predicament several years ago. Inadequate funding can also occur because interest rates drop and the companies have not earned the returns that they had assumed in their projections. This phenomenon is cyclical and is of little consequence for most companies. However, there are exceptions. For example, a large automotive company is estimated to be underfunded by over twenty-two billion dollars. This company has reached a settlement with the Pension Benefit Guarantee Board to pay ten billion in cash and stock into the company's pension fund to bring the deficit down to a more manageable size.

"On a personal note, I don't know how any company can fully make up that large a deficit," Anne commented. "This deficit could severely impact the stability of that company.

"Furthermore," she said, "a recent article in the Wall Street Journal estimated that state and municipal pension funds are underfunded by $1.4 trillion. So you can see that governmental employees are in the same boat in many instances."

"I'm only an employee. What can I do?" asked Mary.

"There is a bright side," Anne answered. "Qualified pensions are covered by the **Pension Benefit Guarantee Board**; and if worst came to worst, they would pay a good portion, but possibly not all, of your pension. Congress should become involved, because the Pension Benefit Guarantee Board is almost bankrupt. Writing to your Representative and Senators expressing your concern will be of some help. Concerning your company, Mary, I don't think you have any worries because of their current financial strength. But it is something to keep in mind for the future."

Anne then turned the discussion to Betty's situation. "Betty, you are in a most enviable position. Because the IRA established under your SAR-SEP is exclusively yours, you can even withdraw the money next week if you desire. However, I don't recommend any such action.

"First of all, since you are under $59\frac{1}{2}$, you will pay a 10% penalty on any withdrawals. Secondly, when you prematurely withdraw before retirement, you lose the growth that tax deferral provides. You give up the compounding of the earnings. This will cost you dearly when you need the money for retirement," Anne explained.

Even though Joe and Betty were not ready for immediate retirement, they stayed to hear the next topic. This discussion centered around the decisions which need to be made when a person retires.

"In my opinion," Anne said, "selecting the appropriate retirement package may be the most important financial decision that most people make in their lifetimes. While most companies try to help, they are limited in their assistance because of their fear of liability. A company might get sued if an incorrect investment decision is made based on their advice.

"Some companies offer two choices for receiving retirement benefits from qualified plans.

1. "**Annuity**, and
2. "**Lump Sum.**

"Mary, your company's plan offers you such a choice. However, most companies only offer the annuity option.

"Let's discuss the annuity option first. An annuity is a sum of money payable at regular intervals, such as a $1,000 a month for life.

"The forms of annuities are normally the following:

> **Selecting the appropriate retirement package may be the most important financial decision that most people make in their lifetimes.**

◆ **Single life annuity**—This is the highest pension amount available. It is based on the life of the pensioner only. The payments end with the death of the pensioner.

◆ **Joint annuity**—The **Employees Retirement Income Security Act of 1974 (ERISA)**, unless you and your spouse request some other form in writing, requires that you receive a joint annuity. With a joint annuity the pensioner and the spouse receive a monthly benefit for as long as both of them live. If the pensioner dies before the spouse, the spouse will continue to receive a benefit for the remainder of his or her life. Because there is the potential of paying this benefit for a longer period of time, the monthly benefit is lower than a single life annuity. The reduction will depend upon the percentage of the benefit that the surviving spouse receives. These are often expressed as:

> **100 % joint annuity**—The spouse will continue to receive the same monthly benefit as was paid when the pensioner was alive.

> **50% joint annuity**—This choice reduces the payment to the surviving spouse to one-half that amount that was received by the pensioner. However, the amount paid to the pensioner is slightly higher than the 100% option."

"There are all types of variations in company plans. Some plans offer a *sum certain* which guarantees a specific amount regardless of how long the recipients live. Other plans offer a *term certain* such as a guarantee for at least 10 years. Each variation pays out a different amount."

"With so many options, how can anyone make a realistic choice?" Mary asked.

"The approach I've developed is quite simple in concept, since it assists you in quantifying the cumulative amount that you will receive for each year under all of the options," Anne answered. She then passed out an illustrative worksheet. "The worksheet helps you understand how much you would receive under different circumstances. Let me explain. My approach highlights the point at which the payments cross over. For example, option 1 may pay the highest cumulative amount until year 8. Then option 2 becomes the best choice. So if you believe that you will survive longer than 8 years, you should choose option 2."

"Only you and your spouse can make the final determination as to which option is best for you," Anne advised. "The numbers on the worksheet are for a hypothetical couple. Let's assume the husband is the pensioner. The figures in the row for year one are the annual amounts that his qualified plan would pay under each of these options. Year two is simply two times (X) year one or the total amount that the plan would pay out in two years. Year three is three times (X) the annual amount and so on."

Pension Calculation Woprksheet*

Year	Single Life	Joint 100%	Joint 50% Pensioner	Joint 50% Spouse
1	$ 24,816	$ 21,060	$ 21,864	$ 10,932
2	$ 49,632	$ 42,120	$ 43,728	$ 21,864
3	$ 74,448	$ 63,180	$ 65,592	$ 32,796
4	$ 99,264	$ 84,240	$ 87,456	$ 43,728
5	$ 124,080	$ 105,300	$ 109,320	$ 54,660
6	$ 148,896	$ 126,360	$ 131,184	$ 65,592
7	$ 173,712	$ 147,420	$ 153,048	$ 76,524
8	$ 198,528	$ 168,480	$ 174,912	$ 87,456
9	$ 223,344	$ 189,540	$ 196,776	$ 98,388

*limited to 9 years for illustrative purposes only

Anne continued with the explanation. "If the couple chose the single life annuity and the worker lived nine years, they would have received $223,344 in total. However if the worker only lived three years and the spouse many years longer, collectively they would have received only $74,448. Bear in mind, this option stops paying at the worker's death."

"That's pretty scary," Betty stated.

"Yes it is," Anne agreed. "The option is provided for any retirees who are single."

Returning to the worksheet, Anne pointed out, "The 100% joint option would have paid $189,540, assuming the spouse lived nine years (or six years longer than the retiree). The 50% option would have paid three years for the retiree ($65,592) and six years additional for the surviving spouse ($65,592)—$131,184 total for both," Anne said as she pointed out the two amounts from the third year row of the pensioner and the six year row of the spouse. As you can see," she continued, "the worksheet allows a couple to play 'what if' games until they get comfortable with the option they select."

At this point Joe jumped in. "Why doesn't everyone just select the single life annuity and purchase life insurance with the difference between the options to cover the spouse?"

"This, too, is an option," replied Anne.

"It's a strategy to maximize your pension that is often exploited by insurance salespersons. Before anyone chooses this option, I recommend that he or she use a sharp pencil. A life insurance payout is beneficial in that the proceeds are received free of income tax. This provision gives the beneficiary a lump-sum payment and greater control. However, these proceeds generally come later in life, when the surviving spouse is often ill equipped to make such financial decisions.

One must also consider that the additional pension amount received is taxable income which, after being taxed, may not leave a sufficient surplus to purchase the appropriate amount of life insurance. Finally, the illustrative interest rates used in the demonstration by the insurance company may be too high. Should interest rates fall, the purchaser will end up paying a higher premium to obtain the same death benefit."

Anne continued. "Furthermore, the insurance policy payout may come at a time of low interest rates. The beneficiary, then, may be unable to invest the proceeds safely at those low rates to produce the necessary income. In addition, if the pension is indexed for inflation, then the couple foregoes this opportunity to obtain an annual increase by not choosing the pension option.

"This explanation maybe a long winded answer to your question, Joe, but I wanted you to understand the decisions involved," Anne said. "For most people this option just doesn't pencil out, and they are better off just choosing a lower paying, but steadier, pension option.

"Mary, you have the additional choice of a **lump sum** payment of your pension. Under this option you would receive your pension in one payment. The amount is calculated based on your accrued benefit at the time of retirement. The company actuaries use a current interest rate and a statistical number of retirement years based on your age at retirement. You are faced with the problem of how to equate the total lump sum amount with the monthly inflow of dollars that you would receive under an annuity over many years?

"Often the company gives you a choice to accept a total amount such as $180,000 lump sum or accept $20,000-a-year for life. To help solve this dilemma, I again rely on our old friend, the present value calculation," Anne said. "Present value discounts future cash flows which allows us to equate the current worth of receiving $20,000 for the next 'x' number of years to the $180,000 in terms of today's dollar. Now comes the key question, 'What is the rate of return that must be earned on the lump sum in order to be equal to receiving $20,000 a year for the next 'x' number of years? In the above example, the couple would have to earn about 10% compounded annually for thirty years on their $180,000 in order to equal receiving $20,000 a year for the same thirty years."

"Is this reasonable?" Anne asked. "If you believe it is, then choose the lump sum."

Betty asked, "why don't we just compare the $180,000 to the pension calculation worksheet? If I understand it correctly, using the joint 100% option, we would receive $180,000 in less than nine years."

"An excellent observation" Anne said. "But you overlooked your ability to earn interest on the portion of the $180,000 that you haven't spent. At the end of nine years the lump sum would be more valuable that just the receipt of the annuity, which is why I use a present value calculation. It brings the interest into the equation. Today, with the aid of personal computers, the ability to use present value calculations is available to almost everyone. Unfortunately, qualified plans are not the only choices that people have to make when they retire. They also have to decide what to do with the funds saved in their 401(k) plan."

"Companies are only required to maintain these plans for you until age 65. Again, you have a choice. You can either take the money and pay a tax immediately or you can do a **direct-transfer-rollover** to an IRA and continue to defer the tax. If you don't do a rollover to an IRA, the distribution constitutes ordinary income which may push you into a higher tax bracket. Should you need some of the funds, you can roll over a portion and take the remainder as a taxable distribution.

"Your taxes can be reduced if you qualify, which all of you do, for a **tax-forwarding-average**, be aware the 5 year averaging no longer applies after 1999. To take advantage of this, you must choose a 100% taxable distribution which means nothing can be rolled over. Tax forward averaging significantly reduces the immediate income tax that you pay. But in most instances, it does not provide the advantages of tax deferral. I would consider this option only if you need all the money sometime in the near future.

> **It's *really important* to directly transfer a rollover from a qualified pension distribution to an IRA.**

"The direct transfer rollover is the best approach for most people. You simply tell the holder of your qualified plan to transfer the distribution directly to the custodian of an IRA that you have already established. All companies are now familiar with this technique. Should you fail to do a direct transfer rollover, the company is required by law to withhold 20% of your distribution, even if you roll over the remainder. Ironically, the Internal Revenue Service (IRS) considers this distribution to be taxable. Now, you not only have less money until your next tax return is filed, but a portion of it is considered income and is taxed in its own right. Believe me, I have never understood the logic for that ruling.

"Joe, the work that you did in demonstrating the advantages of tax deferral, (Chapter 5), illustrates very clearly why this is the best approach for most people," Anne confirmed. That remark concluded the topic on retirement plans. The discussion turned to when the parties could get together again. Anne had an opening available in a couple of weeks, which was quickly accepted by both the Meehans and the Keanes.

On the way home, the two couples admitted to being very tired but better informed, although still slightly confused.

"I hadn't realized how tiring financial planning could be," Jim said, "and I hardly participated in the discussion. I'm looking forward to going to work to get some rest."

"Amen to that," said the others.

Chapter 10

"Social Security is one of our most precious institutions. At its core are the twin American values of work and family. It sustains us when we face the major events of life: retirement, disability, death and illness. It is the most efficient way to deliver that sustenance. The main problem is that we Americans have little idea what we are buying when we pay our Social Security taxes."

Andy Landis, author of *Social Security, The Inside Story*

Social Security, Medicare, and Medigap insurance

The following Sunday at the Meehans

Mary and Betty sipped their almond lattés that Betty made with her new espresso coffee maker. Betty, along with some of her work colleagues, had become addicted to the flavored coffee drinks. She was proud of her homemade brew even though it wasn't up to par with the coffeehouse product. The men refused to try the new fad and stayed with their 'hi-test' version. Jim was anxious hear his in-laws' thoughts on the financial planner he and Mary selected. Joe said he was particularly pleased and looked forward to the next session. As they sat around, Mary brought up a subject that was on her mind.

"If I were to retire next year," Mary asked, "should I take Social Security right away or should I wait until I'm sixty-five? The only thing that I know about Social Security is that Mom is receiving it."

Betty spoke up. "I recently attended a seminar about Social Security and Medicare. Let me share with you what I learned.

"As a general rule, early retirement will pay about the same amount of benefits as delaying until you are sixty-five. The seminar leader told us that early retirement pays out over a longer period of time. Since it pays out longer, naturally the amount received monthly will be lower. In fact, it's $\frac{5}{9}$ of 1% less per month. This amounts to a cumulative 20% deduction at age sixty-two.

"Our seminar leader, who used to work for Social Security, explained that Social Security also pays a greater amount for each year you delay receiving benefits past age sixty-five until you reach age seventy," Betty continued.

"Does everything have to be so complex," Mary moaned. "I just want to know if I should take it sooner rather than later?"

At this point, Joe intervened, "It seems to me the 'present value techniques' that we used in determining the best retirement option will be helpful here. Let me take a crack at it and get back with you. That is, if Betty will share her knowledge with me," he said with a smile as he looked at his wife.

Later that week at the Meehan's

Joe spent considerable time both working at his computer and reading the material that Betty received at the seminar. Other extensive research included long sessions at the library to further his education on Social Security. He reviewed his completed worksheet with Betty before the next get-together with their in-laws.

That following Sunday at the Keane's

Joe and Betty were primed to show how social security pays out. Joe led the discussion.

"Betty and I set up a case study. We assumed that a person would receive the maximum amount allowable and draw Social Security until age eighty-two."

"Why so young?" Jim questioned, "I expect to live until my nineties."

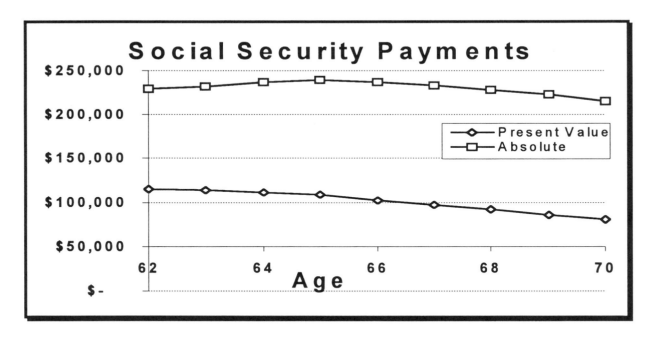

"And you may well live until your nineties," Joe agreed, "but we had to cut it off somewhere. Besides, when using a present value method, it doesn't make any difference. We determined that in total (absolute) dollars, the age that pays the most is sixty-five. However, when we use present value, which, as you remember, helps us to account for the length of time that the money is available to us, age sixty-two is the winner. This graph illustrates both of these approaches. Notice how the circles begin to diminish after age sixty-two," Joe pointed out.

"Mary, you and Jim are fortunate to be the ages that you are," Betty said.

"There is now a new term—**normal retirement age**. This means that people born after 1938, such as Joe and I, will have to wait for a period of a few months up to two years longer before they receive full benefits. This change compensates for increased life expectancies."

"Is the percentage paid for delaying taking Social Security after age sixty-five the same rate for each year?" Jim asked.

"No, it increases depending upon your date of birth. For example, if you were born in 1940, you will receive a 7% increase for each year that you delay. People born in 1943 or later will receive 8%," Betty replied.

"I picked up a **Request for Earnings and Benefit Estimate Statement** for each of us. It's simple to fill out, and in a couple of weeks the Social Security Administration will send each of us a record of our Social Security earnings and an estimate of our Social Security benefits for ages sixty-two and sixty-five. It's easier to let them calculate your retirement benefits for you. The seminar leader said that we should request this information every three years. Mistakes in reported earnings do happen. He told us about one very large company which had an entire year's earnings for over 10,000 employees overlooked. Think of the problem that would have caused their retirees if that error had not been corrected. If a large corporation can be missed, so can an individual," Betty continued. "Beginning in 1995, people sixty years of age and older, who are not currently receiving Social Security, will receive the Personal Earnings and Benefit Statement automatically. By the year 2000, about 123 million people will be on the mailing list.

"One other point, Mary. You have to file three months before you are entitled to draw Social Security in order to receive your first check on time."

"Don't rush me, I'm only thinking about it," Mary quipped.

"What are the other dos and don'ts about Social Security that we should know? For example, can I earn Social Security if Jim doesn't retire?" Mary asked.

"That is one of the most popular questions," Betty answered. "Yes, you can receive Social Security before Jim retires. However, you have to have been employed and have established a Social Security benefit under your own name in order to file at age sixty-two or later." she continued. "If the benefit you receive based on your earnings is less than 50% of your spouse's benefit, your benefit will be increased to the 50% level when your spouse retires."

"Would I be entitled to receive a Social Security benefit if I had not worked and established my own account?" asked Mary.

"If you have not worked, then your must wait until your working spouse retires," Betty answered. "At that time, you will receive a spouse's benefit equal to 50% of the worker's benefit. To be eligible, on your own work, you need ten years of work in an employment that paid into the Social Security System. The system uses the term 'work credits,' of which four can be earned a year. Forty work credits are required to be fully covered. The amount that you have earned in a quarter is used to determine a work credit."

Joe intervened. "You should understand that this is not half of the worker's benefit. It is an additional benefit which is calculated based on the amount to which the worker is entitled."

"If I were *widowed* or even *divorced* what would I get?" asked Mary.

"You, of course, have your own earnings record, which we covered already," Betty replied. "In the event of a divorce, if a marriage has lasted ten years prior to the divorce, and if the person is sixty-two or older and currently unmarried, he or she is entitled to a spouse's benefit even if the former spouse has not retired and is still working. This benefit is different from the spouse's benefit of a still-married couple.

"An unmarried widow is entitled to benefits as early as age 60, although this would only be 71.5% of the full coverage. If the widow is disabled, she can collect Social Security as early as age fifty. The widow's or widower's benefits are limited to the amount their spouse would have received had they been still alive," Betty explained. "The checks will continue to come if they wait until they are past age 60 to remarry. This also goes for you, Jim, since it covers a widower as well as a widow. Mary, even your mother is entitled to receive benefits based on your earnings record provided she receives one-half of her support from you or Joe."

"Social Security is a really wonderful benefit, isn't it," Mary commented.

"I recently read, in a Social Security pamphlet, that there are over three million children of deceased or disabled workers who receive benefits. Almost two million of these children are orphans under age eighteen. When you consider that the surviving parent also receives benefits, Social Security goes a long way to put a safety net under young families," Joe remarked. "When you think of it, Social Security puts a safety net under a lot of us," he continued. "Think about what it would cost if, as individuals, we had to provide for retirement, disability, family dependents, survivors, divorced spouses, and all that Medicare covers."

At this point Jim jumped into the conversation. "Do I get any credit for my time in the **military service?**"

"According to another pamphlet I read, people in the military have been paying into Social Security since 1957," Joe answered, "and inactive duty, such as the reserves, has been covered since 1988. In answer to your question, Jim, it depends, since additional earnings credits are given for the period during which you served.

1978 and Later

A service person is credited with $100 in additional earnings up to a maximum of $1,200 for each $300 active basic pay.

1957 through 1977

A service person is credited with $300 per quarter for each calendar quarter in which active pay was received.

1940 through 1956

No Social Security was deducted during this time. However, a service person may be credited with $160 a month. To receive this, he or she has to be still active, honorably discharged or a survivor of a dead veteran. A veteran can't double up by receiving both these additional earning credits and a military pension for the same years."

"However," Joe continued, "a person can get both Social Security and a military pension. The benefit may be reduced if a government pension is paid for a job in which Social Security taxes weren't paid."

"Betty, what about income taxes on Social Security?" Jim asked.

"I'm going to defer to Joe. He knows a whole lot more about taxes than I do," Betty answered.

"Based on my research," Joe said, "taxes enter the picture several ways. First of all, each of us contributes a percentage of our wages to Social Security, and this amount is matched by our employer. These contributions build the pot from which our benefits are paid. Self-employed people must contribute double the amount of an employed person to cover both portions."

"Tell them about Social Security income being taxed," Betty said.

"A portion of our Social Security benefits must be included in taxable income," Joe answered, "when our gross income plus 50% of the Social Security benefits received exceeds a certain amount. Married couples with income over $44,000 and single filers with income over $34,000 are taxed on 85% of their Social Security benefits over this amount. This provision is a very complicated calculation, as this worksheet shows," Joe said as he passed out a Social Security Benefits Worksheet from the IRS 1040 instructions which is sent annually to all taxpayers.

"Here's another catch. Tax-exempt interest is included in income when calculating the amount of benefits which will be taxed. Those MUNIs that you own, Jim, aren't totally tax free after all. It's a small wonder that CPAs welcome changes in the tax law."

"Everything is taxed anymore, isn't it?" mused Jim. "How does Social Security handle inflation?"

"Social Security is meant to be inflation-proof because it provides automatic increases," Joe answered. "Annually, the change in the **consumer price index (CPI)** from the 3rd quarter of one year to the 3rd quarter of the next year is used to increase the benefits at the beginning of the following year. You also may be interested in knowing that you can earn some income before Social Security benefits are discounted. The earnings allowed and the discount differ by age brackets. The dollar limitation is indexed annually. Under age sixty-five, the amount is currently about $8,000 and the discount is two dollars for every one dollar earned over that amount. Between sixty-five and seventy you can earn over $11,000 with a three dollar for one dollar discount. At age seventy, none of your earned income is considered."

"I remember some Hollywood performer collecting Social Security at age seventy-two to publicize the no-limit benefit," Mary remarked. "The newspaper article stated the amount would be donated to charity."

Joe went on, "There is also a portion of your contribution, plus that of your employer, that goes to pay for **Medicare**. Medicare comes under the Social Security Law. This contribution is currently 1.45% of your wages which adds to the payroll costs. Self-employed persons pay 2.90%."

"Speaking about Medicare, is that something that concerns Mary and me?" asked Jim.

"Medicare is health insurance for people sixty-five and older," Joe replied. "As I explained, you and your employer pay for it during your working years. To be eligible to collect on Medicare, you need to sign up for Medicare at sixty-five, even if you don't retire. Betty, please remind me to give Jim a copy of the booklet on Medicare."

Joe continued, "The easiest way to explain Medicare is to emphasize what it doesn't cover."

"**Medicare, Part A** covers just hospital bills, skilled nursing facilities and hospice. Part A does not cover doctor bills. Part A pays for all hospital-covered services for the first 60 days—except an amount called the insurance deductible. This deductible is adjusted annually and is currently around $700. This amount must be paid for each separate hospital stay," Joe stressed. "From sixty to ninety days," he continued, "the patient pays a portion of the daily charge. The patient pays coinsurance, currently around $180; Part A pays the difference. There are, of course, conditions. For example, your admittance to a hospital must be prescribed by a doctor. You must also spend three days in a hospital before going to a skilled nursing facility in order to be eligible. Medicare doesn't pay for long-term nursing home stay, but you have 100 days in a skilled nursing care facility if you need daily treatment by a nurse or rehabilitation therapist. The first twenty days are at no cost, but following that you pay a portion."

"**Medicare, Part B** is partially paid for by a monthly premium which will increase as medical costs increase. The government pays the rest."

"To prevent people waiting until they get ill before applying," Joe explained, "there is a window of opportunity at age sixty-five. If you miss this opportunity, then you have to wait for specified annual periods to enroll. The **initial Medicare enrollment period** covers the three months before the month of your sixty-fifth birthday and the three months following. Of course, coverage begins sooner if you enroll sooner."

"What about a person who wants to continue working after age sixty-five for an employer who pays for his health plan?" Jim asked.

"This contingency is covered by a **Medicare special enrollment** during a seven-month period beginning with the month that employees are no longer covered by their employer. However, if you fail to enroll during this period, there is a 10% penalty for every twelve month delay plus a waiting period before Medicare becomes effective. Now listen to this. Enrollment occurs during the first quarter of each year, but coverage doesn't begin until July of that year. If a person's special enrollment period ends in April and he fails to enroll, fifteen months will go by before he can enroll and begin receiving Medicare coverage."

"That could get a person's attention," Jim remarked.

"In addition, there is a deductible and co-pay feature associated with Part B as well as Part A," Joe said as he finished his explanation.

"What about buying an insurance policy to pay for medical costs? Does that make any sense to someone age sixty-five?" Mary asked.

"In my opinion," Joe said, "it makes all the sense in the world. Between the co-pay and deductible schedule, it will cost you over $5,000 should you need to stay in a hospital or skilled nursing facility for ninety days. This type of insurance is called **Medigap**. Its purpose is to fill in the gap left by Medicare. Congress passed a law in 1992 standardizing Medigap insurance policies," Joe explained.

"Now all Medigap policies must supply basic coverage. Basic coverage pays the patient's portion of the basic hospital and doctor's bills covered by Medicare. Basic coverage includes:

♦ "Cost of 365 days hospitalization over a person's lifetime.
♦ "Daily charges for hospital stays.
♦ "The 20% co-pay for doctor bills.

"There are ten standardized policies," Joe explained. "Each succeeding one covers the basics and adds additional features. The key to success is determining which policy is best and most economical for you. For example, some policies include coverage for a portion of drug costs. If you are on expensive medication, then you should opt for this coverage," declared Joe. "It pays to do an in-depth review before you choose a policy. Some are more lenient with hospital or nursing facility stays while others want you home as soon as possible to save costs. Keep in mind, if you make a poor first choice and your health deteriorates, it could cost you dearly to enhance your policy in the future," Joe stressed.

He continued, "You only are assured of coverage, regardless of health conditions, during the six months following your application for Medicare Part B. For example, in the State of Washington, no one can be denied Medigap coverage because of a pre-existing medical condition during this six-month period. However, there may be a delay in receiving coverage for that preexisting condition, e.g., a six month waiting period.

"It may be cheaper in the long run to purchase a more expensive policy which will cover medical needs in the future and whose premiums will remain relatively stable over the long-term. Policies whose premiums are based on people's 'attained ages' (their current age) usually increase in cost every year. A policy purchaser should ask the insurance company to estimate future premiums," Joe said.

"It also would be worthwhile to deal with an insurance company which gets billed directly from the doctor to reduce some of the complexity. After all, who needs complexity?

"As my final point," Joe said, "it pays to shop around. I have read where some policies covering the same exact features cost up to twice as much as a less expensive policy. You also may want to take advantage of group rates. For example, The American Association of Retired Persons (AARP) offers such policies."

"Isn't all this very confusing to the older American?" asked Mary.

"You bet it is," Betty answered. "It gets even more confusing when some doctors don't play by the rules. That's right! Some doctors try to get around Medicare rules by having patients sign blanket agreements to pay for services or procedures not covered by Medicare."

"It may be appropriate in unusual circumstances to agree to a specific service or procedure not covered by Medicare. However, no one should sign a 'blanket agreement' allowing a doctor to perform these services at his or her option," Joe said.

Joe continued. "How much Medicare will pay is confusing. The limit that Medicare will pay is called the **approved** or **accepted charge**. Participating physicians have agreed to accept this approved charge as the amount they will charge. If the medical provider doesn't accept assignment, they can only charge 15% more than the Medicare approved charge. Remember that Medicare only pays 80% of the approved charge, leaving any additional charges to be paid by the patient."

"Fortunately," Betty interjected, "nearly all states have set up Medicare counseling programs. These services assist enrollees on everything from eligibility to overcharges by healthcare providers. They even assist in appealing Medicare decisions. The State of Washington initiated a program of trained volunteers called the Senior Health Insurance Benefits Advisors (SHIBA 1-800-562-6900) to educate and assist senior citizens. This program is being implemented in many states around the country. As an additional service, AARP has volunteers who assist enrollees under their **Medicare/Medicaid Assistance Program (MMAP)**. People can get information about counseling services in their state by contacting their local area agency on aging."

While the coffee cups were being gathered up by the women, the subject turned to a more general topic on social programs.

"In your opinion, Joe or Betty, will Social Security be around when you guys decide to retire?" asked Jim.

"Wow, that's a toughie," said Joe. "The critics of the system forecast gloom and doom even to the point of generational warfare. These folks are concerned that the system will run out of funds by about 2010. Many critics call for a means-test and want to cut off payments to those whose incomes are above a certain level. One critic calls Social Security 'the welfare program for the well off.' That's the dark side."

At this point Betty jumped in. "On the other hand, the supporters of the system point out that the system is running a $60 billion surplus. They estimate the surplus will increase to $300 billion annually to a total surplus of $3.0 trillion by the year 2020. The supporters see a stockpiling by and for the baby boomers."

"Others see the crash of the system not taking place until 2029." Joe said.

"Betty and I, based on our research, fall into the middle of the road, somewhere between the pessimists and the optimists. In our view the government will continue to tinker with the system, without making radical changes," Joe said. "For example, they may raise the ceiling on the maximum taxable payroll earnings and eliminate early retirement."

Betty intervened, "Already they are in the process of delaying full benefit retirement until age sixty-seven."

"If worst comes to worst, they may just reduce the benefits," Joe continued. "In the future, we will be older before we start to collect our Social Security. Most probably, we will be taxed on the full amount. I wish that this tax would be added back to the Social Security trust, rather than just go to some general fund. On the whole, Joe and I see Social Security being around through the 21st century. Hopefully, by then all retirees will have enough savings to be self-sufficient and won't need the government's safety net," Betty said.

"Unfortunately, that just a wishful thought," Jim replied.

"What about all the newspaper articles stating there is no real money reserve, just paper debt from the government? Aren't young reporters claiming that the only payment will come from taxing the post boomer generation?" a concerned Mary asked.

"Think of the Social Security trusts as being similar to a mutual fund investing in government bonds," Joe replied. "There are no dollars in reserve supporting a mutual fund investment, just the assurance of the government. Yet, investors consider government bonds as the safest investments. Remember, the government, like large corporations, doesn't pay off its debt. It rolls it over by replacing the old debt with new debt. The only way to reduce government debt is to get the deficit under control to reduce the interest payments."

"Do you agree with a means test?" Jim asked.

"I tend to agree with those who oppose a test based on your income," Joe answered. "Even today, people who are single and are high income earners will not get back the dollars they and their employers pay into Social Security. This means these folks are subsidizing the lower wage earners. You should understand that the system is skewed toward the lower wage earners. I would opt for increasing the income tax, rather than reducing the benefits." Joe answered.

Then Mary asked, "Is **Medicare** in as good a shape?"

"Unfortunately, no," Betty answered.

"Medicare may well be broke within five years," Joe said.

"On the bright side, however," Joe continued, "the Administration and Congress seem to recognize the magnitude of the problem. Currently, the thought pattern is to herd enrollees into bigger groups and to push people to join **health maintenance organizations (HMOs).**"

"As we are all aware, the best measure of stopping runaway medical costs is for all of us to take better care of ourselves," Betty emphasized.

Joe was the first one to suggest leaving, "I have a long day at work tomorrow. It's the start of monthend closing, so let's call it a night."

"Please don't forget to file your 'Request for Personal Earnings and Benefit Estimate Statement,'" Betty reminded her in-laws as the couples parted.

Chapter 11

"It's your home and your community, learn how to secure them."

How to create peace of mind in retirement

During one of their visits to spend time with their Mom, Mary and Joe accompanied her to a seminar at her senior center

The topic of the seminar was *how to create peace of mind in retirement*. Joe was looking forward to the session to learn more about how he could improve security for Marie. He was uncomfortable about her living alone, but did not want to share this concern with his sister. He was well aware of Mary's fear for her mother's safety and did not want to intensify that fear.

After they were seated, an announcer introduced the first speaker. This topic was selected in response to a number of requests from the membership on making our environment safer. The lecturer, Officer Chris Franklin, was from the Centralia Police Department. The seminar was focused on empowering retirees to provide for their own security. His opening statement surprised most of the audience.

"The older we get, the safer we are.

"This is, of course, in relative terms, since the more violent crimes are the ones that happen least to senior citizens," Officer Franklin explained.

"Why is this important to you?

"To enjoy peace of mind in retirement, you need to be in control of your life," the officer continued. "News reporting today exaggerates the impact of crime and violence, which adds to the fears of senior citizens. Unwarranted fears of crime and violence rob you of that peace of mind. I hope I can alleviate some of those fears by helping you understand the difference between news reporting and reality."

Officer Franklin continued. "The more violent crimes, such as rape, robbery and aggravated assault, are most often committed against teens and young adults, but elder-abuse is on the rise. Increased elder abuse often results from what we term the 'sandwich generation,' where elder parents reside with their children who also have children of their own. If anyone tends to be abusive in the home, the elderly parents usually become victims of the abuse."

"What can we do about it?" asked a person in the audience.

"You have to get involved," Officer Franklin answered. "Far too often, the victims and their friends or family don't take any action. They either hope the abuse will stop or they are afraid of destroying the 'good name' of the individuals involved. Abuse won't go away by itself. It will only fester, get progressively worse, and pass on the traits to the next generation. People who abuse other people need professional help. If they won't obtain this help themselves, then they have to be reported to the authorities. We can't help if we are kept in the dark. Call your local police department. It might surprise you how helpful we can be in these situations."

The officer continued, "Crimes which most often impact the senior citizen are:

♦ "Theft without contact.
♦ "Simple theft with contact, such as purse snatching.
♦ "Aggravated assault.
♦ "**Con-games** and **bunko-schemes.**

"Theft without contact, burglary when the resident is not at home, is the most prevalent crime against the elderly. Bear in mind that burglars do not like to be observed," said Officer Franklin. "Programs such as **Block Watch** where neighbor helps neighbor, are very effective in preventing burglary. To assist you in implementing this program, I'm passing around a sign-up sheet for those interested in receiving more information. If you are undecided at this time, just call your police department, and we will be glad to get you and your neighbors started."

"We already have Block Watch on our street," said the person sitting next to Marie.

At this point, Mary asked a question. "How effective and how safe is it to have senior citizens involved in Block Watch?"

"Seniors can be most effective and very safe," Officer Franklin answered. "Understand however, that implementing Block Watch does not mean you will confront criminals. That's our job. Block Watch reminds the burglar that neighborhood observers report the presence of suspicious people."

"Prompt reporting is our most valuable aid," Officer Franklin continued. "Seniors usually are home much of the time and are knowledgeable about the comings and goings in their neighborhoods. That makes them ideal candidates for Block Watch."

The police officer continued. "People can also minimize burglaries by improving their home security environment. Ask yourself if your shrubbery shields your home from view," he said. "If so, it gives a potential thief a place to hide. Prune back your bushes or replace them. Do you have proper lighting?" Officer Franklin asked. "Consider getting some of those outside passive lights that become active with motion. Thieves often will not wait around when a spotlight comes on suddenly. We have found that this type of lighting is far more effective than leaving outside lights on."

"How do we keep burglars out of our homes?" asked a man in the audience.

"To prevent forced entry, lock your doors and windows," Officer Franklin answered. "About one-third of all burglars enter through unlocked doors and windows. I recommend that you lock them even if you are in your yard. It only takes a second for someone to sneak into your house."

"Burglars can get past locks," the man persisted.

"Secure all entries with dead bolts that have at least a one-inch throw," Officer Franklin suggested. "Dead bolts are very effective, and for sliding patio doors, use a Charley Holder. This rod folds down to secure the door from being opened and prevents the door from being lifted. For those of you who can afford it, private protection with an alarm system is also very effective as a deterrent. To prevent invasion of your residence, you must harden the target by making it difficult for unauthorized entry. Make your house looked lived-in at all times," he continued. "Get one or more timers to turn lights on and off at night. Always keep your garage door closed to prevent someone from knowing whether you are home or gone. Tell a neighbor when you will be out of the house, ask him to keep an eye on it for you and offer to do the same for him when he is out. In many communities, the local police will also keep an eye on a house when the owner is away for an extended period of time.

"Simple theft, with contact, is the next crime most often committed against older people," Officer Franklin stated.

"What does that mean?" asked another attendee.

"Pocketbook snatching and pick-pocketing are examples," the officer explained. "Often, carrying a pocketbook is just force of habit. If you don't need a pocketbook, leave it at home. The same goes for a wallet. Even though I'm a police officer, I often just carry my driver's license and leave my wallet at home to reduce the chance that I can have it ripped off.

"**Elder abuse** in the form of aggravated assault is becoming more commonplace," Officer Franklin reemphasized. "As I said earlier, this crime often occurs when the elderly are in residence with their children and grandchildren—as sad as it may seem. Often, this abuse goes unreported because it makes the elder person being abused seem a failure in rearing his or her children. These crimes need to be reported. If you suspect this is happening to a friend, neighbor, or relative, please report it. A visit by a uniformed patrol person can often prevent a reoccurrence."

The officer then changed to the next most prevalent crime against seniors. "Bunko-schemes or con-games are also on the rise among the elderly. There are so many different types it would be difficult to discuss all of them in the time I have left," Officer Franklin said apologetically. "I'll just give you a list of don'ts. If you follow these, you should avoid most of the heartache of being duped.

1. "Don't ever give your credit card number over the phone unless you initiated the contact.

2. "Don't ever give money to anyone in order to receive a gift sometime in the future.

3. "Con artists making phone solicitations often demand an immediate decision. Whether it's a once-in-a-lifetime investment or a cemetery plot, tell them to send their proposal to you in writing.

4. "No legitimate company or bank is going to get their customers involved in helping to 'catch a an employee in the act.' Banks and companies use professional detectives and investigators. Report this type of approach to the police immediately because you are most probably dealing with a con artist.

5. "Don't contract for home improvements, driveway repairs, etc., with someone who knocks *uninvited* on your door. They often tell you of a great opportunity because they are working the neighborhood and have some material left over. Often the work will be shoddy and unnecessary. If you need work done, find a reputable local company or try the Yellow Pages®. It may cost more, but the work will be necessary and finished correctly. When in doubt, call the police or the Better Business Bureau. It is better to apologize to an honest vendor than to be ripped off by a dishonest one.

6. "Don't let a contractor or other supplier con you into extra work after you accept his bid. There are times when a contractor, partially through a job so that you can't call it off, will begin to sell you on additional work. Learn to say no!

7. "Check any investment opportunity that you don't originate with a trusted advisor, before signing anything or sending any money."

"How can we tell if a person is honest?" asked someone in the audience.

"Unfortunately, there is no sure way to know," answered the policeman. "Many scam artists get away with it because they look and talk like that nice boy next door. You have to use common sense. If someone promises you a high return that is risk-free, don't believe him. Check it out with a professional advisor. Don't be afraid to ask questions. After all, it's your money.

"One more point to be aware of. Scam artists often prey on elderly people by using fear tactics. Take your time before entering into an agreement with someone you don't know, no matter how urgent he seems to make it. Time works against all con artists. Like a burglar they want to get out fast. So use time to your advantage. Delay making a decision. Tell the person to come back after you have taken his or her offer into consideration."

"Before you are unfortunate enough to be robbed, the following advice can help you," Officer Franklin stated.

♦ "Put an identification number on appliances and other items that can be carried away and pawned. Etches can be borrowed from your local police department. Your Social Security number etched into your camcorder, computer, television will greatly assist in recovery. Often a thief will simply not bother to take it.

♦ "Take a video of your home and its possessions and keep it in a safe deposit box. This will help you remember what was taken if a robbery occurred. It is also provides proof when you report your loss to your insurance company.

"These are some thoughts on preventing burglary and other crimes against older citizens," Officer Franklin said. "In the back of the room, I have placed a number of booklets and pamphlets on the topics I've discussed. Please pick some up when you leave. Your state's attorney general also provides literature on crime prevention for seniors, and I recommend that you call for that information. The number is in the phone book. Thank you for listening. The more involved you are, the easier my job is."

The announcer invited the officer to stay for lunch and asked if there were any more questions.

Mary, still concerned about her mother's pending trip to Mexico, spoke up. "A number of people here are planning to travel to a *foreign country*. What advice do you offer them?"

"It pays to be extra careful in any unfamiliar area," the officer answered. "Before you depart, learn as much as you can about the areas that you plan to visit. It helps to have a small English translation dictionary. Stay away from high-risk areas, like portions of the Middle East, Latin America, etc. Call the State Department (1-202-647-5225) which provides recorded traveler's warnings."

"How about advice on being mugged or robbed?" Mary asked.

"Most people travel with a group and should stay with members of that group. Unless you are familiar with the area, never travel alone," Officer Franklin advised. "We all have heard stories of the flower vendor in Spain, for example, who turned out to be a pickpocket, or of the child in Italy who crawled under a table in a restaurant to steal a purse. They all are probably true. It's up to you to protect your possessions when you travel. If you put something down, keep it secure between your legs. Other advice that I can offer would be to:

♦ "Go to your local bank and obtain sufficient foreign currency to tide you over for the first few days of your trip. Get just enough to provide time to become familiar with the differences in currency values.

♦ "Take traveler's checks and only keep that amount of currency that you anticipate spending that day in your pocket or purse. It's best to count out your money in private each morning before you leave the hotel.

♦ "Use one of those money belts, the kind that wraps securely around your waist and fits underneath your clothes. Use it for your passport, credit card, traveler's checks and most of your currency.

♦ "Take only one credit card. I recommend either a Master Card or VISA because these are almost universally accepted. Always check to be certain that *your* credit card has been returned.

♦ "Utilize travelers aid at airports and train stations if you are unsure of where to stay.

♦ "Exchange currency at banks rather than stores to minimize your flashing cash in public.

♦ "Take one of those fanny packs and wear it in front to free both of your hands and to eliminate the need for a purse.

♦ "If you find yourself in an unfamiliar area, walk with determination until you get into a more public place.

♦ "Ask for directions from cab drivers, police or retail establishments.

"Traveling in many foreign countries is as safe as traveling in the United States. Simply use the same amount of caution that you would use in visiting a strange city in the U.S. Enjoy yourselves—I wish I were going with you. Thank you for listening."

Later that evening at Marie's house

Joe, Mary and Marie discussed what they learned from the day's seminar.

"I made a lot of notes on his suggestions regarding traveling in a foreign country. On Monday, I'll type up my notes and send you a copy for your Mexico trip," Mary said, speaking to her mother.

Joe was more concerned about the safety of Marie's home than her planned trip. "There's not a lot of valuable things to steal, but etching makes a lot of sense. I'll get a hold of one of those markers somehow and do that the next time I'm down."

"Don't forget to do your own possessions and send it over to Mary and Jim to do theirs," Marie reminded him. "I've got a lot of friends whose children do things for them, but never get around to doing them for their own families."

"Tomorrow, I'll look at the outside of your house and see if any shrubbery needs trimming," Joe said. "Also, we need to 'harden the target' as the officer said, and add some of those sensing lights. If you intend to remain here, I intend to make you as safe as I can, and I promise to look at my own house as well."

"We've installed one of those home protection systems," Mary said. "I got nervous after a neighbor's house was broken into and insisted on more protection. I sleep better now. Jim and I would love to pay for the same type of protection for you, Mom, if you will let us."

"Let's discuss it when we finalize the plans to renovate the house," Marie said. "Now get to bed. It seems that you two have a lot of work to do tomorrow before you go home."

Chapter 12

"No matter how hard investors try, they still haven't found a reliable way to see the future."
Morningstar

Tame the investment risk

At their financial planner's office

The Keanes and the Meehan's met with their financial planner, Anne Jahn, for the second time. This time they intended to improve their knowledge of investing. Joe was curious about Anne's ability to keep up with all the changes in investment strategies.

"Anne, before we get started, would you tell us how you keep up-to-date on all the changes that take place?" Joe asked.

"I would be happy to," Anne answered. "As a CFP, I need to take 30 hours of continuing professional education every year. To maintain my CPA license, I need 40 hours, plus 13 hours for insurance. In addition, I'm a prolific reader, and believe me, I receive gobs of material to read."

"That's a lot of studying," Betty remarked.

"Fortunately, some of the seminars can count toward more than one requirement," Anne replied.

Anne led the conversation about investing by helping the Keanes and Meehans understand **risk**.

"Before we concern ourselves with investing," Anne said, "let's talk about the risk involved for the retiree. In my opinion, the understanding of risk is by far the most important element of investing. Retirees face greater risk than do younger investors because many retirees live on pensions and Social Security. Therefore, they do not receive the annual salary adjustments that often cover the increasing expenses due to inflation. Also, due to their age, there is

> **The understanding of risk is by far the most important element of investing.**

insufficient time to recover from a bad investment, and today's investments are very complex. Finally, most retirees are concerned only with the fear of losing their principal. They are afraid of losing all their money. It can be a scary time when a retiree realizes that a paycheck no longer is coming in, and he has a tendency to preserve what he has saved."

Anne continued. "As a result, retirees often invest too conservatively. Their passion to protect their principal blinds them from the other risks that they face.

"Before we go on, let's try to understand what I mean by risk. I define risk as *the possibility of not having sufficient funds to live decently in retirement.* More than anything else, most retirees fear the possibility of outliving their money.

"As a financial planner, I try to help people understand the down side of investment risks. There are, of course, many other types of risk which we will hit on briefly, but the following list includes the *seven basic risks* which should concern the retiree investor.

> **Inflation is the most serious of the basic risks.**

1. "Inflation.
2. "Stock market decline.
3. "Financial survival—I call this the bankruptcy risk.
4. "Interest rate changes.
5. "Liquidity and marketability.
6. "Tax law changes.
7. "For the international investor, the change in the value of the dollar.

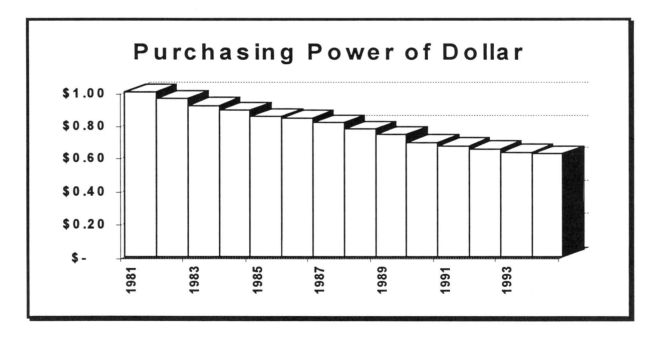

"If the retiree investor understands these risks and uses the tools available to minimize their impact, then he or she will be a stress-free investor. A stress-free investor is one who doesn't panic every time a mutual fund or stock price goes down. He or she is a person who can sleep at night," Anne said.

"What is the most serious risk of the seven risks that you mentioned?" Betty asked.

"**Inflation,** in my mind, is the most serious risk," Anne answered. "It will impact most retirees negatively, because of the conservative way they saved for retirement. Inflation is harmful because it is insidious," Anne continued. "That is, inflation has a gradual and cumulative effect. It compounds! The 2.7% increase in the **consumer price index (CPI)** last year is added to the X% of the year before and so on and so on. Inflation is deadly to retirees who live on fixed incomes. Let's look at some exhibits that I use in my seminars." Anne began describing the first chart on the Purchasing Power of the Dollar, illustrates the impact of inflation on a couple who retired in 1982.

"I selected this period because most experts agree that during this time period, inflation was considered to be 'under control.' If this couple had been receiving a fixed income of $1000 a month, their relative quality of life income is now at a $620 per month level, a 38% loss in purchasing power," Anne emphasized. "Their major fear of having insufficient funds to live decently has been realized and in each succeeding year it will get only get worse. It's a self-fulfilling prophecy."

> **T-Bill**
>
> **Short-term U.S. government debt sold initially at auction.**

"Anne, don't most fixed income investments cover inflation?" Jim asked.

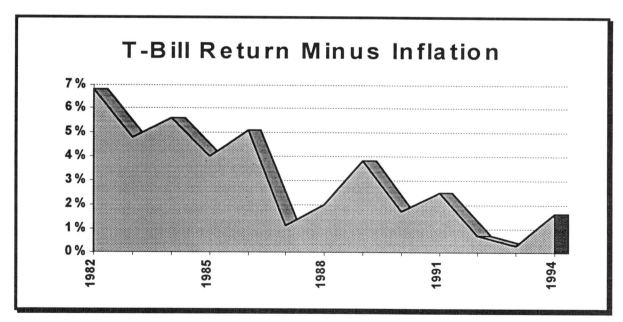

"Unfortunately, as we age, many of us take too conservative an approach to our investments. Far too often, in our attempt to protect our principal, we sub-optimize the income we can earn on the investment. Let me demonstrate this with a chart which looks at the **treasury bill (T-Bill)** return over the same time frame as exhibit one. I use the T-Bill as a surrogate for all fixed income type investments."

Anne continued. "Even though this exhibit illustrates that the return on most fixed income investments has exceeded inflation during the last decade, the same cannot be said for the prior decade. In the 1970s inflation exceeded the T-Bill return in seven out of ten years. If we included the impact of income taxes, the results would be far worse."

"The second item of note, the average return of T-Bills and most fixed-income investments, such as CDs, yielded only 3.2% after inflation for the period illustrated. With such a low return, a person would need a $350,000 investment to withdraw $1000 per month to supplement Social Security and other income without invading their principal."

"Let us take a look at how well an investment with some growth ability did over the same-time frame. The stocks and bonds minus inflation chart illustrates the average return, *after inflation*, for an investment of 50% stocks and 50% bonds."

During this time period, a mix of stocks and bonds had an average return of 10.5% after inflation. That return assumes that a person's investment did as well as the average of the market. With a 10.5% return, an investment of only $110,000 would have provided $1000 monthly, without invading principal," Anne explained. "Now, that's quite a difference from needing $350,000.

No matter his or her age, every investor needs some growth investments to offset the ravages of inflation.

From these exhibits, you can begin to see the advantage of appreciation or growth," Anne pointed out. "However, even though the return is significantly greater, due to **market volatility**, there were several years that the net after inflation was negative."

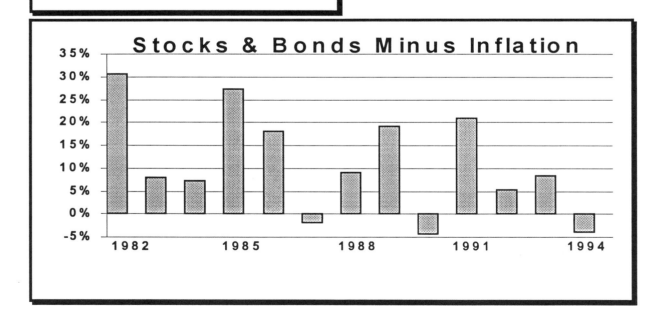

Anne continued the discussion about risks. "The actions of the **Federal Reserve System Board of Governors (FED)** impact inflation and market volatility. The FED, a committee of seven governors appointed by the President, independently manages the nation's monetary growth and credit to meet the needs of the economy. Controlling inflation has been high on the FED's agenda since the double-digit rates of the mid-1970s and early 1980s. The cause of inflation during this period can be traced to prior FED policies to stimulate demand for goods and services to minimize the negative aspects of the business cycle. Business cycles include four phases: a trough, a recovery, an expansion and a peak. These economic activity fluctuations are irregular, have differing durations and magnitudes, and cannot be predicted with any degree of certainty. Though the forces of supply and demand fashion the business cycle, the FED uses its control over the banking system to influence the cycle. The stock market is *said* to anticipate the business cycle. The attempts of the stock market to predict both the business cycle and the actions of the FED frequently results in market volatility.

"Market volatility refers to the change in the stock market as a whole. This is often called **systematic risk** and is expressed as the **Greek letter beta (β)**.

"Because most stocks move in tandem, through the length of a business cycle, in a down market your investment will decline in value just by your being in the market at that time. However," Anne continued, "some stocks are more sensitive to market swings than others. Beta expresses that market sensitivity. If the beta of a stock or stock mutual fund equals one ($\beta = 1$), then that stock moves either up or down exactly the same as the overall market. A beta of less than 1 ($\beta < 1$) tends to be less volatile than the general market while a beta greater than one ($\beta > 1$) is more responsive to market swings. For example, a stock with a beta of 1.20 is expected to increase 20% greater than the market on the upside and decrease 20% more on the downside," she explained. "A negative beta is considered to be uncorrelated to market swings and tends to move more independently. Often when assembling a portfolio, seasoned investors try for an average beta of less than one (< 1). The use of the beta statistic often helps to minimize the drastic swings of the general market and therefore makes for less volatile investing," Anne concluded.

"How does a person find out what the beta is for stocks or mutual funds?" Mary asked, reflecting her interest in statistics.

"You can ask your broker about specific company stocks. For mutual funds, publications such as '*Morningstar*' indicate the beta for those mutual funds that they track," Anne answered. She continued her explanation of some of the statistical measures used in gauging the volatility of an investment. "The measure that I consider more appropriate than the beta statistic is the **standard deviation**. While the beta statistic measures how well a stock, bond or mutual fund correlates to the movement of the market, the standard deviation compares a stock, bond or mutual fund's volatility to its own average return. Standard deviation is a measure of the consistency of an investment's return. Think of the standard deviation as the average difference from the compound return for the investment during a specific period of time. It may be easier to understand if I demonstrate how to use it. Though the calculation is relatively simple, I'll leave the calculations up to the mathematicians."

"A good idea, or we will be here all night," Mary agreed.

Leaning over to Jim, Betty asked, "Do you understand any of this?"

"For once, I do," Jim answered. "We use statistics in our business for quality control. This enables us to make certain our product meets the customer requirements. The smaller the standard deviation, the closer the product is to the customer's specifications. Just keep in mind, a small standard deviation is better than a large one."

Anne continued by illustrating on a chartboard how to use a standard deviation.

	Mean (avg. monthly total return)	Standard Deviation	
Investment A	10%	5%	5% to 15%
Investment B	15%	20%	-5% to 35%

"The standard deviation describes, in one number, the distance or spread of the actual returns from the investment's average return," Anne continued. "The wider the spread, the greater the volatility. This factor is illustrated by looking at the range for the two investments. You add and subtract the standard deviation from the average return to obtain the range. Although investment B has a greater average return, its higher standard deviation makes it a much more volatile investment. Therefore, investment B is considered the more risky investment."

"Anne, thank you for that explanation, but I didn't understand a word of it," said Betty.

"Thank you, Betty, for bringing me up short," Anne replied. "Statistical concepts are very difficult to understand. Let me try to explain by telling a story."

Anne described a young investor who attended one of her seminars and a follow-up complementary consultation. Anne advised him to begin investing in a mutual fund that purchases stock in medium-sized companies to achieve both growth and income. The young investor subsequently attended a seminar by a stock broker and was advised to invest in a different fund. The young investor returned to Anne and asked what he should do.

"What did the stock broker say when you told him about my recommendation?" asked Anne.

"He said that the fund you recommend is more risky," the young investor replied.

"We took the time to compare the two funds," Anne said as she wrote on the chartboard. "Using the *Morningstar* report, we collected the following data."

	Fund A (Anne)	Fund B (Broker)
Mean (Average Rtn.)	21.0%	11.5%
Standard Deviation	12.50	8.0
Range (one Std. Deviation)	8.5% to 33.5%	3.5% to 20.0%
Frequency Distribution*		
-15%	2	1
-10%		
- 5%	1	1
0	2	3
5%	8	12
10%	10	9
15%	3	2
20%	1	
25%	1	

* **A frequency distribution describes the number of times an incident has occurred.**

Anne explained the data, "The fund recommended by the broker had returns which were more consistent with the mean or average return of that fund. This smaller spread, in many circles, translates to less risk. However, the level of the average return also must be taken into account. The return of fund A was almost twice the return of fund B for the seven year period that we reviewed their results. An investor would have tripled their value by investing in A as compared to only doubling their value by investing in fund B."

"What is a frequency distribution?" Betty asked.

"A frequency distribution shows the number of times that an amount has fallen within given intervals. Notice how both funds had one occurrence where they lost 5%, where only fund A had returns greater than 20%. This is how it would look if we were to graph the data.

"The risk to an investor in fund B was to forego the opportunity to make a greater return."

Betty whispered to Jim, "That doesn't agree with what you just said about the smaller the deviation the better."

"It depends on the product," Jim answered. "In our business, one type of metal may have more variations than another, but it will always be stronger. So, when in doubt, we use the stronger metal because even its poorest performance is better than the best performance of the lower quality metal. I think that's what Anne just said about mutual funds."

"I believe it's extremely important to understand the implications of the word 'risk.' A person should always ask, '*Please explain what you mean when you say that one fund is more risky than another?*'" Anne emphasized.

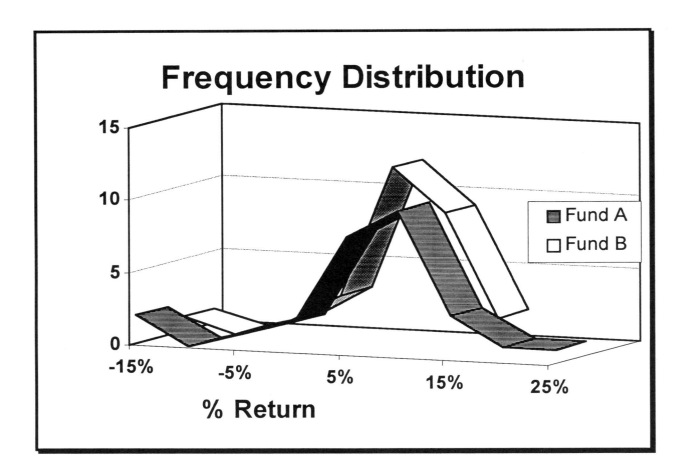

Anne summarized her short discussion on the use of statistics to measure market risk, "A wise investor takes into consideration both of the beta and the standard deviation. There are others, of course, but full explanations would do more to confuse you than to educate you, and I want to make one final point. To fully realize the benefit of a statistical approach, the statistic should be calculated on an investor's entire portfolio and not just on individual investments within the portfolio. We will discuss this further when we cover investments. Finally, it is most important to recognize that even though statistics help us to explain the past, no one has come up with a foolproof method to predict the future of the market."

Always ask!

Please explain what you mean when you say that one fund is more risky than another?

"Shouldn't we just get out of the market when it goes down?" asked Jim.

"Jim, you are talking about **market timing**. Frankly, it is very difficult to time the market. Companies sell timing services which try to predict when a person should be in and when a person should be out of the market. Timers have several opportunities to be wrong on the same decision:

> ## "No one has come up with a foolproof method to predict the future of the market."
> *Morningstar*

1. "The market can go up, instead of down, after you pull out.
2. "The market can go up while you are out and before you can get back in.
3. "The market can go down after the market timers put you back in."

"A market timer must be correct about 70% of the time to break even, which is very difficult. Most of the gain during an upswing in the market comes in short spurts. If you missed that spurt, you missed the gain. For example, during the 1980s if you were out of the market for only the 40 best trading days, out of some 2500 trading days, your annualized return would have been down by almost 14%. That's an average of 14% per year for the entire decade. Therefore, I recommend that if retirees consider timing the market, it should only be with a minimal portion of their portfolio. Keep in mind the fact that you don't lose money when the market goes down. You only lose money when you sell in a down market. We will discuss this later when we cover the investment philosophy for the retiree," Anne continued.

"How concerned should an investor be about a company going bankrupt?" Jim asked.

"That's a risk called **financial survival.** The company in which you invested may go bankrupt," Anne answered. "Long-time employees and retirees of a company most often have significant holdings in that company. Company loyalty is an admirable trait. However, having a disproportionate share of your portfolio in a single company significantly increases your risk."

"How about the company owner? Doesn't he need to hold the majority of a company's stock?" Jim asked.

"Often these owners are not holding the stock as an investment. Instead, they are holding the stock in order to control the company. That's an entirely different reason for owning stock," Anne answered.

Anne continued. "Investors can minimize their financial risk—that is, the chance of a bankrupt company wiping out their entire portfolio—by diversifying their investments so that they do not hold significant amounts in a single company's stock."

"**Diversification** involves spreading investments among many stocks. However, spreading your investment over different stocks, or even stocks in different industries, will not assure that you are protected from market volatility," Anne advised. "If the stocks in which you invest correlate with each other on market swings, then you have just averaged the same risk. Correlated stocks move the same way at the same time. An example may be the lumber market and the home building industry. One would expect these two industries to have a good correlation over time."

"How many specific companies stock should a retiree own?" asked Mary.

"Many experts tell us that an investor needs at least 30 individual stocks, which are not correlated, to obtain sufficient diversification." Anne explained further, "To be *perfectly diversified* the investments need to move in opposite directions. When stock one declines at the same time stock two increases, a person has perfect diversification."

"Isn't that unrealistic?" Mary questioned.

"For all practical purposes it is," Anne answered. "However, even though *perfect diversification* is unrealistic, every investor should build his or her portfolio with diversification in mind."

> **Common Stock:**
>
> **Evidence of partial ownership of a corporation which may pay a dividend or appreciate in value.**

"Doesn't investing in mutual funds provide diversification?" Betty asked.

"When a person purchases a mutual fund, he immediately diversifies his investment into the number of specific stocks that the fund owns. I recommend that a person invest in more than one mutual fund. Having more than one type of mutual fund in your portfolio will greatly improve your diversification. As long as the prices do not move in parallel, diversification will always reduce risk."

> **Bonds:**
>
> **Promissory notes issued by either corporations or the government, which carry a fixed rate of return.**

"Doesn't the fact that a person owns bonds help him avoid the market volatility of stocks?" Joe asked.

"It does, in a sense," Anne answered. "However, bonds bring their own form of volatility when interest rates change. **Interest rate changes** are a considerable risk to anyone who invests in fixed rate instruments, with bonds being the most notable example. However, an increase in interest rates will also negatively impact utility stocks, bank stocks and insurance company stocks."

Anne continued. "When interest rates change, they affect the income or the value of your investment. Interest rate changes impact the income paid by such investments as bank accounts and money market funds. A drop in interest rates during the time you hold CDs can reduce your ability to invest at the same rate when the CD matures. Many authors call the inability to invest at a comparable rate **reinvestment risk**."

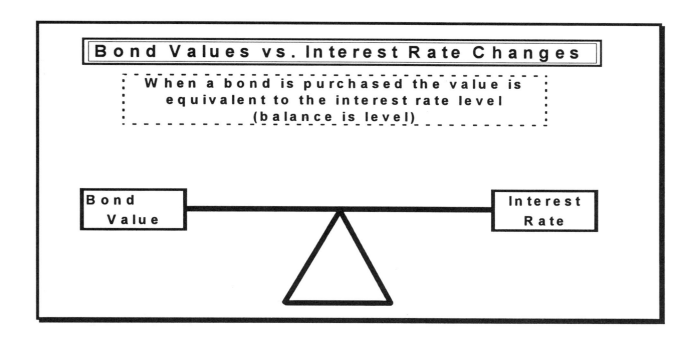

"A number of my friends have experienced this risk," Betty said. "When they went to reinvest their CD proceeds, they had to settle for a lower rate."

"The impact of interest rate changes on bonds is a little more complex. If you hold, or a mutual fund holds, a bond until maturity, there will be no impact from an interest rate change. That's simply common sense. When the government or a corporation promises to pay you 6% on a bond with a face value of $1000, they will pay you $6 a year and $1,000 at the maturity of the bond. That is what they agreed to do when you purchased the bond. This promise works exactly the same whether the bond has been purchased separately or is included in a mutual fund," Anne continued.

"However, suppose you have to sell that bond to another investor, perhaps because you need the money. Then an interest rate change will play a very big part in how much that investor will pay you for your bond. No one can predict when changes in interest rates will occur. Let us suppose that the interest rate for bonds with five years to maturity increased to 8%," Anne said. "This means that currently an investor can collect $80 annually for a $1,000 bond. It's not very likely that the investor will pay you $1,000 for the 6% interest bond that you want to sell. It's more likely the investor will pay only $919."

"Think of it as a balance. When you purchase a bond, the balance is level because the bond value and price are equivalent to the current interest rate. As interest rates decrease, the value of the bond increases and when interest rates increase, the value of the bond decreases. That's where volatility comes into play in the bond market," Anne explained. "When you sell a bond at a time that interest rates are different than when you purchased that bond, the bond will be worth more or less."

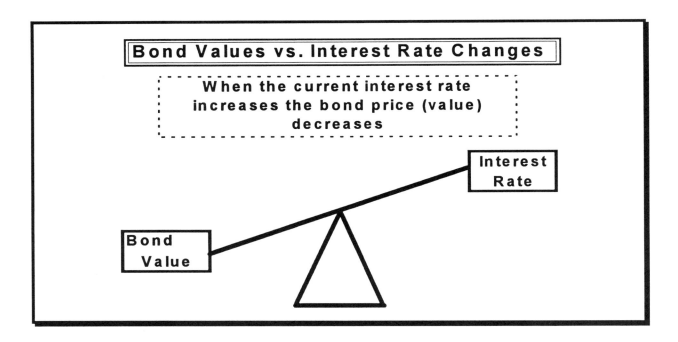

"That explanation answers the question of why bond prices change. Now tell us about marketability and liquidity" Mary requested.

"Marketability and liquidity represent the risk of being unable to sell when you need the money. These risks most often occur with something like real estate, residences or small-businesses, which may not be easily marketable at the time you wish to sell. You may have to reduce the asking price to find a buyer—hence the risk. The efficiency of the stock market and the liquidity features of mutual funds have made marketability and liquidity risks a non-issue for most investors. But that doesn't mean that they are non-existent," Anne said. "Let's take MUNIs, for example. There are 1.2 million issuers of MUNI bonds as compared to the 30 thousand issuers of corporate bonds. Many of these MUNIs are rarely traded because there is no central exchange for trading them. Even sophisticated dealers working for mutual funds may not know the true market price until they find someone willing to purchase that specific MUNI bond," Anne explained. "The same holds true for small company stocks sold **over the counter (OTC).** That doesn't mean that you shouldn't invest in MUNIs or small company stocks. I just caution you of the risks of not being able to bail out some or all of your money when you need it.

"**Limited partnerships** are even less marketable," Anne continued. "I don't recommend this type of investment for retirement purposes. I believe it is too risky."

Anne continued describing the basic risks, "**Tax law changes** are an ever-present risk. Congress annually tinkers with the tax law and at least once a decade makes major changes. Rumors of potential changes abound. For example, in recent years, there was a scare that investments in variable annuities would lose their tax deferral status. The administration changed its mind when it felt the fury of the insurance industry. According to a 1992 magazine article, an Assistant Secretary of the Treasury advocated a one-time tax on pension plans."

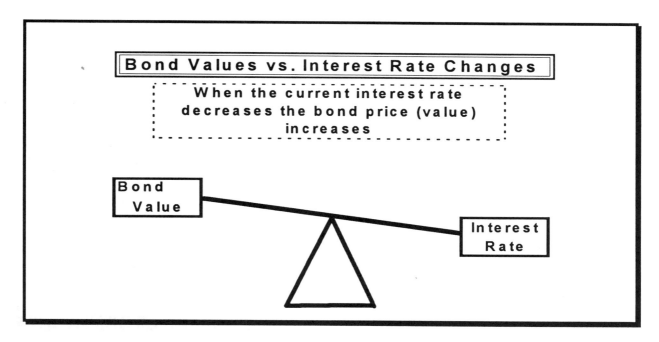

"Is nothing sacred?" Jim asked.

"Regarding taxes, there are several certainties." Anne pointed out:

1. "Laws will be changed to meet the current perceived needs, regardless of future consequences.
2. "Tax laws rarely give a favor without asking for one in return.

"A person implementing a plan today cannot predict the whims of future tax laws. I suggest that retired people don't do anything too exotic. In addition, they need to keep their plans current," Anne said.

"Our last basic risk, the **change in the value of the U.S. dollar**, is one of the additional risks facing the international investor. The value of currencies floats in the world market because of trade deficits, interest rates and many other factors. A weak dollar enables the U.S. to sell more products overseas. When the U.S. dollar strengthens—that is as it appreciates in value when compared to a foreign currency—the international investor loses money when the foreign currency is translated back to U.S. dollars."

> **Municipal Bonds (MUNIs)**
>
> Debt obligations of states and their political subdivisions. Interest income is generally tax-free.

Anne continued, "Some international mutual funds have hedging strategies in an effort to manage currency exchange risk. A **hedge**, often called a derivative, involves the purchase of an option to offset the loss if the market moves in the opposite direction.

Even experts or professionals cannot predict future exchange rates accurately. If a mutual fund hedges its exposure to a foreign currency and that currency rises, the fund will forego its opportunity to participate in the currency's appreciation. While trying to protect itself from the downside, the fund may hurt itself on the upside."

Anne continued, "We discussed the basic risks that a retiree faces in investing, and there is one thing that all investors must bear in mind. No one can eliminate risk. All we can do is minimize it. Investors have to think in terms of their overall portfolios. It's the combination of investments, within a portfolio, that will have the greatest impact on minimizing risk.

"We have also covered some of the techniques available to investors to reduce or minimize a specific risk. Let me reiterate:

♦ "For inflation protection, have a portion of your portfolio invested with assets that tend to appreciate. I recommend that all investors, regardless of their age, have at a minimum 30 to 40 % of their portfolios in stocks with the intention to outperform inflation. Use cash and cash equivalents for short-term parking of funds only. These instruments barely keep ahead of inflation in the long run.

> **It's the combination of investments, within a portfolio, that will have the greatest impact on minimizing risk.**

♦ "Diversify your investments to protect against financial risk and to minimize market volatility.

♦ "Interest rate changes affect long-term bonds to a far greater degree than they do short-term and intermediate bonds. If you invest in individual bonds, then you should stagger the maturity dates as a hedge against interest rate changes.

♦ "Be mindful of marketability and liquidity risks. Keep sufficient funds invested in liquid assets, such as the stock market, to tide you over until you can sell the less-liquid assets.

♦ "Be aware that tax laws change. Be cautious of investing in new schemes touted as tax-savers before they are fully tested in court.

♦ "Invest some of your portfolio overseas in a mutual fund. I recommend 10% to 20%. There is a risk concerning revaluation of U.S. currency, but it can also work to your advantage.

"Since 1972, the average return of an international investment outperformed its domestic counterpart," Anne stated. "But the diversification advantage is more important.

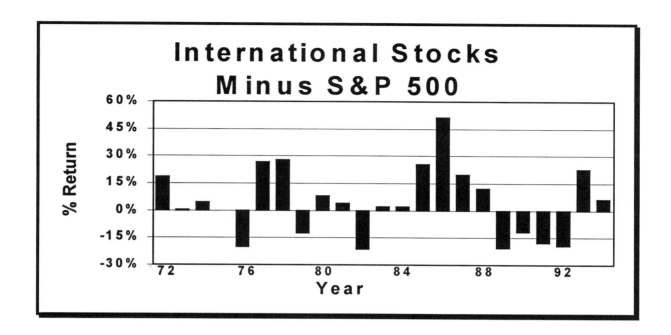

"Foreign investments have performed counter cyclical to U.S. investments. This chart illustrates how foreign stock investments have outperformed or under-performed U.S. investments since 1972. Notice the cyclical pattern and bear in mind we are comparing differences. In 1978, for example, non-U.S. stocks had a positive return of greater than 34% while U.S. stocks had a positive return of 6.5%.

"Finally, never, ever, invest in anything that you don't understand or that sounds too good to be true.

"There is a saying in Chicago, *'for a guaranteed method to make a small fortune in the commodity market, start with a large fortune,'*" Anne said with a smile. "This saying reminds us that even knowledgeable professionals get burnt on risky investments."

Anne continued, "There is one more useful technique that can minimize loss in investing. Retirees should never invest for short-term gains. They should invest for the long-term. First of all, you enjoy the **magic of compounding** because your earnings produce additional earnings. Most financial planners advise people to invest for five years or longer.

> **Retirement is not the time to begin investing in exotic products or gimmicks to increase your return. Avoid speculative investments at all costs.**

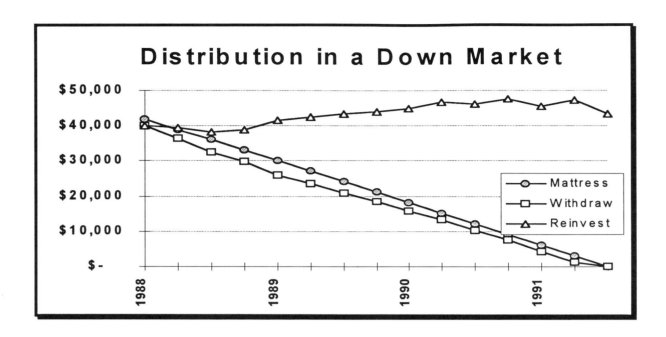

Anne explained further, "This advice is based on the long history of the market, which demonstrates that the longer that funds are invested, the less likely it is that you will lose any of your principal. Unfortunately, most retirees cannot afford to leave all of their investments five years or longer without touching them," Anne pointed out. "I learned this lesson while giving seminars for senior citizens. Based on that experience, I developed a investment philosophy for a retiree. Let me describe the circumstances. A elderly couple complained about the return on a small investment that their broker recommended. They intended to use the principal and income from this investment to supplement their pension. However, in less than three years, their principal was gone.

"Using simple division, the principal alone should have lasted over 3.5 years, based on their rate of withdrawal if they had merely put it in their mattress and taken out what they needed," Anne explained. "Over the time they were taking a withdrawal, the investment would have made a 10% compounded return if, and I repeat if, they had been able to reinvest the dividends and capital gains. Take a look at the reinvest line on the chart.

"What happened?" Anne asked to emphasize her point as she illustrated on the chartboard using a graph.

"During the first two years the investment lost money only to make a considerable recovery in year three. Unfortunately, the couple's withdrawals during years one and two did not leave sufficient principal to fully take part in the recovery. In that instance the couple would have been better off to keep the money in their safe deposit box or mattress and take out the amount that they needed each month," Anne remarked. "Like a good wine, an investment needs time to mature and earn a reasonable return."

Anne went further. "I studied the market returns for the last twenty years and determined that an investment for only one year in either stocks, bonds or some combination of stocks or bonds would have lost money 20% of the time. That means they would have lost money one year out of every five. However, if an investor were capable of investing for two years he would have lost money only once over this same time frame.

Retirement income needed	**$ 48,000**
Less: Social Security	**$(12,000)**
Pensions	**$(24,000)**
Other income	**$ -**
Net Income	**$ 12,000**
Times two years	**X 2**
Equals Living expense fund	**$ 24,000**

"My strategy consists of a retired person, or couple, protecting the net living expenses he or she needs for the next two years." Anne continued explaining as she wrote on the chartboard. "The net amount represents the total amount needed less income from other sources, such as Social Security. Assume that $48,000 is needed and $36,000 is coming from secure sources. Then the retiree would need to protect the principal for the $12,000 unsecured need times two (2) or $24,000 to cover a two-year period.

"Since he or she is going to live on these funds, the funds should be invested for safety in a CD or MMF. I call the returns for these investments savings rates. Keep in mind, the purpose is preserving the principal and not earnings or growth. With two years living expenses set safely aside, the retiree can invest the remainder of his assets like anyone else. In the above example, if the $24,000 represents 10% of the retiree's portfolio, the remaining 90% can be invested at market rates which over time will significantly outclass the savings rates. The current volatility in the market would not affect his or her ability to live for the next two years. This strategy enables retirees to sleep at night. At the end of year one, you need to make a decision. Ask yourself the question: should I transfer some of my investment to my principal protection account or should I let it ride for another year? I use the following as a rule of thumb," Anne said in answer to her question. "If the retirement assets appreciated—that is, gained in value—then transfer an additional year's worth of net living expense to the principal protection account. Don't forget to allow for inflation. Remember, if the market had a bad year, you have the option to delay for another year before you need to make a transfer. This annual look hopefully will prevent the need to sell in a down market," Anne explained.

"There is sure a lot to consider," Mary commented to Jim, as Anne suggested taking a short break.

"You are going to have to explain a lot of this to me when we get home," Betty said to Joe after taking a deep breath.

> **If you can avoid selling into the teeth of a down cycle, you most probably will avoid a loss in the market.**

"I understand most of what she is telling us and I'll cover it with you later," Joe replied. "In the meantime, do the same that I am doing—taking a lot of notes."

The couples enjoyed the break while consuming some of the refreshments that Anne's secretary provided.

Chapter 13

*"Buy stock when it's low and sell it
when it high, if it doesn't increase
then don't buy it."*
Will Rogers

Should retirees manage their own investment portfolios?

Still at Anne's office

Following the short break, Anne continued her dialogue with the Keanes and Meehans. "I hope you have a better understanding of the need to manage the many types of risk. Now we will spend a little time discussing retirees who invest themselves, that is, retirees who actively trade in stocks and bonds. Investing the bulk of their securities in specific company stocks and bonds, in my opinion, is not the wisest choice for the majority of retirees.

"Remember what I said when we discussed risk. There is insufficient time for most retirees to recover from a bad investment, particularly with the complexity of today's investments."

Anne continued, "Retirees, in particular, should be in control of their own investments. They can do this by being specific in describing their needs and risk tolerance to their financial planner, stockbroker or investment advisor. They should instruct their advisor to telephone only if the suggestion fits within agreed upon parameters. Avoid unsolicited phone calls, aptly named cold calls, from stockbrokers. Most people don't realize that brokerage houses inventory securities and need to sell this inventory. Often a cold call describing a hot tip is nothing more than a plea to buy from inventory. This doesn't mean that you shouldn't talk with your stockbroker. But as an investor, you need to be in charge. A good broker will understand this and provide only those opportunities that fit your specifications."

"Also, it would be nice not to be interrupted by so many calls from my broker," Jim said with a smirk.

Changing gears slightly, Anne explained her opinion that people invest in a specific company stock for one of the following reasons:

1. "Company loyalty—Retirees hold a strong loyalty to the company that made their retirement possible.

2. "Family Interest—Often retirees will invest in a company which employs one of their children.

3. "Big score—People invest in specific stocks and to a lesser degree bonds to hit the big one. Frequently, a friend or relative lets the retiree in on the big secret. This one can't miss! All of us want to be among the first to invest in the next Microsoft, Nike or Starbucks.

4. "Bragging rights in the neighborhood—Investing is often the topic of conversation at the golf club or other social occasions. Even describing losses enables one to enter the discussion. You don't have to bet the farm in order to participate in the conversation."

Anne continued. "I want you to understand. *I am not opposed to retirees investing in specific company stocks and bonds.* I just believe they should do it in moderation. My rule of thumb suggests that retirees should invest only about 10% of their portfolio in specific stocks, 20% at the very most. Those who invest above the 10% range should have the financial capacity to handle the risk and the mental ability to handle the complexity. Even the 10% target should be lower if your portfolio includes investments which *time the market.* The remainder of a retiree's portfolio, eighty plus percent, should be handled by professional money managers. We will discuss the various types of money managers in a later session.

"Why am I concerned about investing in specific stocks for the retiree?" Anne asked for emphasis.

"Picture, if you will, a small boat on a large ocean." she said in answer to his question. "The swells of the ocean make the boat a lot more volatile than the ocean itself. The stock market is similar to the ocean, while a specific stock is similar to a small boat. The stock is not only moved by the waves and currents, but it also gets moved by the piloting of those aboard. Retirees should just try to ride the waves.

"Even though individuals own over 50% of the outstanding stock, most of this stock is bought and held," Anne emphasized. "Today, Wall Street is managed by professionals employed by pension funds, insurance companies and mutual funds. They do most of the daily trading. In the less complex market of yesteryear, the investor tried to beat the market," she continued. "Today, with the untold thousands of professionals who set the expectations, it would be poor advice to suggest that a retiree take them on. I believe a retiree should strive to attain his or her goals with the least amount of risk and complexity.

"Two different measures determine how well a specific stock fares," Anne continued. "Let's call the first measure *expectations* and the second *results.* The stock market acts on expectations and reacts on results. In other words, the market anticipates what will take place and invests accordingly. The market consensus of many observers of specific stocks forms an expectation of how well that stock will do in the near term. These expectations are based on many factors, such as how well the overall economy is doing, in addition to how well a particular company is doing in that economy.

"Consider this excerpt from the Wall Street Journal. *When the actual results became known, that a company's profits **only grew** 3.6% and sales **only grew** 2.2%, the stock got hammered.*

'Weak earnings and sales growth for the quarter. The results sent the stock down $5, or 7.4%, and shook the stocks of the entire sector.'

"Why?" Anne asked. "Not because it didn't make money," she answered, "but because **it** *didn't live up to the expectations* of the market analysts. An investor needs to be knowledgeable about the expectations, not just the results. Few retirees have the connections to be privy, on a timely basis, to this knowledge."

"I've got lots of friends who make money in the market," Jim countered.

"Many retirees do quite well investing in the stock market," Anne agreed. "Why! Because they take the time necessary to understand and follow the market. People need to be responsible for their own financial decisions. I'm most concerned about those retirees who don't or won't get personally involved."

"If I wanted to handle my own investments, what advice would you give me?" asked Jim.

Anne's recommendations to Jim.

1. **Understand the risk/return relationship.**

2. **Develop an investment strategy.**

3. **Pay attention to asset allocation first.**

4. **Be well diversified.**

5. **Invest for the long-term.**

6. **Use dollar cost averaging to enter the market.**

"First of all I would advise you to understand the **risk/return relationship**."

"There will always be risk *to your principal* when you invest, except for risk-free Government bonds. Investors, in other than government bonds, should be compensated for the additional risk taken," Anne declared. "As the risk increases, so should the return that you expect. If you choose to accept a lower risk, accepting less chance to increase the appreciation on your investment, then you must be prepared to settle for lower return over the long-term."

"My second piece of advice, would be to develop an **investment strategy** and stick with it. Quite often, those who become trade junkies lose the most because they are out of the market in the upturns. Most of the gains in the market are made in short spurts. Retirees have to understand that they need to be in the market during these short spurts. Think back to our discussion regarding marketing timing when we described the seven basic investment risks."

Anne continued with her third piece of advice. "Pay attention to **asset allocation** first. In other words, balance your financial risk." Anne explained. "There is one very well documented study[2] on 91 large pension plans' data for nine years. The study looked at how these pension funds made money, and the results were a surprise to most investment professionals. The study concluded that almost 94% of the profits resulted from asset allocation. Security selection accounted for 4.5%, and when the security was bought or sold, it accounted for only 1.9%. This finding supports the analogy about the ocean current and tides that I alluded to earlier. The market itself determines most of the return.

Investment Strategy

1. **Determine the overall percentage for each of the major categories in your portfolio.**

2. **Allocate within each major category.**

3. **Select individual securities.**

4. **Determine the time-frame over which to be fully invested.**

5. **Develop a strategy for making adjustments to the major categories.**

6. **Review your entire portfolio at least annually.**

"Consider the following steps when you develop an **investment strategy**," Anne said as she wrote on her chartboard.

"First of all, decide the overall percentage to invest in the major categories of stocks, bonds and other assets. Real estate is an example of another asset. Next, apportion the stock percentage into large company stocks, small company stocks and international stocks. The bond percentage can be broken down into short-term, long-term, MUNIs and high-yield. Only after you take these steps should you decide on the specific investments. The fourth step involves 'dollar cost averaging' which I'll discuss in a few moments. Finally, decide what triggers readjusting your portfolio, perhaps a change of 5%. For instance, if you determined that 10% should be in international bonds and, upon review, you find that they have appreciated to 15%, sell 5% of those bonds and reinvest in a category that has less than the desired allocation percentage. As you can see, there is a subtle market timing in this approach. You are selling high and investing low, thereby locking in your profit."

"This is a lot to swallow at one sitting," Jim commented.

"Perhaps you could you draw us a picture to describe the process," Joe said.

---

[2] Gary P. Brinson, L. Randolph Hood, and Gilbert L. Beebower, *Determinants of Portfolio Perfamance*, Financial Analysts Journal, July-August 1986, pp. 39-44.

Step 1	
Cash	5%
Bonds	25%
Stocks	70%
Other	0

"I'd be happy to," Anne replied. She then drew the following on the chartboard, and walked through each step.

"First, in Step 1, determine the portfolio's overall percentages. A number of factors go into making this decision, including the investor's need for income and tolerance for risk. Next, in Step 2, determine how to allocate the overall percentage within each category. For example, cash can be invested in CDs, money market funds or savings accounts, while bonds can be invested in such types as corporate or US Government, municipal, high yield, international government. This selection is also based on the same set of factors that drove the overall allocation percentage. In addition, we are adding a degree of diversification.

Step 2

Cash	Bonds		Stocks	
Money mkt. fund 5%	Corporate	15%	Large co.	35%
	MUNI	5%	Small co.	20%
	Intl. govt.	5%	Intl. stock	10%
			Specialty stk.	5%

"Step 3 adds the dimension of market research. Here again, it is critical to understand the rationale behind the original allocation. For example, if the investor needs income, then stocks which pay regular dividends should be considered.

Step 3

Cash	Bonds	Stocks
Specific money market fund	Specific bond issues	Specific stock issues

"Step 4 involves the movement of the investor's money into the market. If the investor is already in the market and merely reallocating, then the movement should be immediate. On the other hand, if the investor is currently out of the market, or investing for the first time, then he should enter the market over a period of time. This approach is called dollar cost averaging which we will get to in a minute.

"Steps 5 and 6 involve the maintenance of the portfolio. Over time, changes will occur. These planned steps bring the portfolio back into overall alignment."

"Thank you," Joe said. "Things really clear up when you can visualize them."

"If everyone is comfortable with what we have covered so far, I'll move on to my fourth suggestion, diversification."

Since there were no dissenters, Anne continued. "Research has suggested that a portfolio should consist of ten to twenty individual stocks for minimum diversification and at least thirty stocks to be well diversified. This, in effect, says that for minimum diversification, you need an investment of about $30,000 to $50,000 if you are investing in specific stocks.

"The investor needs to choose stocks which don't correlate with each other. As I said earlier, a downturn in the housing market will undoubtedly hurt the lumber industry. These two industries correlate with each other.

"Many advisors recommend that 10 to 20% of your portfolio be invested internationally," Anne went on. "This recommendation recognizes the dramatic change in valuation which has taken place across the world, and the shift will only intensify in the future. Countries from Latin America to China and Russia are moving more and more of their industries to private enterprise. These industries may well be the investment growth areas of the future.

"What is your risk when you lack diversification?" Anne asked for emphasis. "The entire Japanese stock market, the Nikkei index of 225 stocks, fell 57% in less than two years. If you had been overextended in that market at that time, it could have been a disaster.

"Number five on my list of suggestions is to invest for the long-term."

Anne continued. "Even at age sixty, a person could be looking at decades of investing. History has shown us that the longer investors keep their investment in the market, the less chance they will lose principal."

Anne pointed to the history of investments displayed on an overhead projector screen. "I chose this period to avoid the years impacted by the depression, which I consider to be an unusual event that, I'm certain, we all hope will never be repeated. Notice how the chance of losing principal decreases as the investment term increases. This chart represents how well the S&P500 stocks did in those years. The loss percentage decreases even faster when bonds are substituted for a portion of the stock. Don't forget to consider the risk/return tradeoff. Too heavy a substitution of bonds for stocks in a portfolio could reduce its long-term appreciation potential. Not only does a long-term investment offer protection, it offers opportunity as well," Anne emphasized.

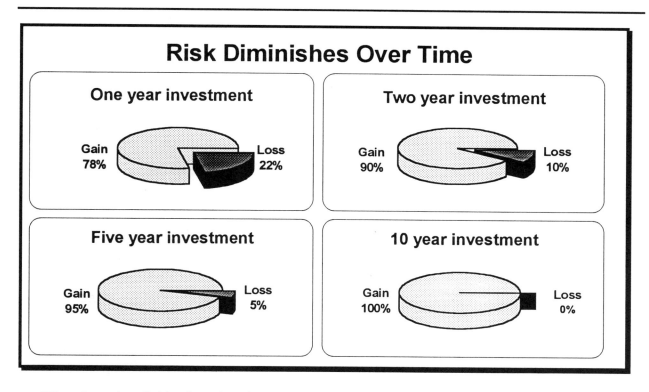

"By reinvesting dividends and capital gains, you enjoy earnings on your earnings. Even 2% makes a difference. With each 2% increment in earnings your portfolio will grow about 10% faster in five years and about 18% faster in 10 years. Often, mutual funds will demonstrate how a small amount invested in their fund, long ago, grew to a phenomenal amount today. The next time you see one of these advertisements, pay particular attention to how much the reinvestment of the dividends and capital gains had to do with the growth. Many call this process the **magic of compounding**.

"My sixth suggestion is to use **dollar cost averaging** when investing," Anne said. "Dollar cost averaging is based on the underlying presumption that, regardless of where the market is currently, the long-term trend of the market will be up. Dollar cost averaging involves the continuous investment of the same dollar amount at fixed intervals. When the market is down, the investment purchases additional shares. When the market is up, the shares purchased at a lower cost are now worth more. The average share price will always be worth more than the average share cost while you are in the accumulation phase."

"Does it follow that a person using dollar cost averaging will never lose money in the market?" Joe asked.

"I wish it did," Anne answered with a smile. "Just because the average share cost is less than the average share price doesn't always mean that you have made money. If the market drops sufficiently, then the earlier purchases will diminish in value. If these shares are sold before the market recovers, then of course a person will lose money."

"When is a good time to use dollar cost averaging?" Joe asked following up on the topic.

"When a person is accumulating his or her retirement assets," Anne answered. "Monthly investing in a 401(k) is dollar cost averaging. I also recommend a person dollar cost average when he has a significant amount of money to invest. This could be from a lump sum retirement distribution or, perhaps, from an inheritance."

"Why not just invest the money immediately?" asked Jim.

"I have a concern when I hear about a person receiving a large inheritance one day and being fully invested the next day," Anne answered Jim's question. "No one knows how the market will fare in the short-term. Therefore, I just feel more comfortable when clients to money at a measured pace over a year or a year and a half. I also suggest that if the market takes a sharp decrease during that time, it may provide a buying opportunity. In that instance, I suggest that a person double or triple his or her normal monthly amount."

Anne went to the chartboard and reiterated the six recommendations that she made to Jim on how to handle his own investments.

She concluded this discussion with some thoughts on investing in specific issues of stocks and bonds.

"Before you buy a stock," Anne said, "develop a strategy for when you should sell that stock. I once purchased stock because my daughter was employed by the company. When she left, I sold the stock. Buy stocks in companies that you know something about," she advised. "You may know that a company has implemented a process to ensure that its products are produced to specific quality standards, giving that company a competitive advantage. In time, this advantage will translate into profits and sustained growth that is not matched by its competition. Investors who are value-minded look for these competitive advantages. Try a hands-on approach," Anne continued. "Look at what you are buying. I recently shopped in two stores. One was a toy store which was crowded with shoppers, and the other was a retail clothing store which was nearly empty. If I were choosing a stock, which one do you think I would buy? Incidentally, the retail clothing store recently filed for bankruptcy.

"If you purchase bonds," Anne continued, "buy investment-grade bonds only and purchase them with the intent to keep them until maturity. Bonds are graded by such companies as Moody's and Standard & Poors. I believe retirees should select only those bonds rated A or above.

"Regarding MUNI bonds, many advisors will tell you to only purchase **general obligation bonds (G.O.)** because they have the full faith and credit of the taxing authority behind them," Anne explained. "I used to advise retirees only to purchase G.O. bonds. I relented after a manager of a MUNI bond fund for an insurance company described his bias for **revenue bonds**. In his view, G.O. bonds will always have a political risk. It's possible that a state could reach such extreme negative financial straits that it may become politically expedient to stop paying interest on its bonds. To avoid paying interest, the state would have to declare bankruptcy. Bear in mind this hasn't happened yet. However, interest paid on revenue bonds by a publicly owned utility is just another cost of doing business. According to the fund manager, even during the depression revenue bonds paid interest."

"That hasn't always been the case, has it?" Joe asked.

"Of course, there is always one exception to any rule. The one fly in this ointment is WPPS, pronounced 'Woops,'" Anne answered. "These were bonds offered by the Washington State Public Power Supply to obtain revenue to build a number of nuclear plants. The plants were never completed, and most investors lost heavily. However, many smart investors understood the risk involved, and they took out insurance. Every one of these risk adverse investors was fully paid."

"What do you mean, they took out insurance?" Jim asked.

"Municipal bond guarantee insurance has been around since about 1971," Anne replied. "The lower the rating of the bond issue by Standard & Poors or Moody's the higher the interest the municipality must offer to sell the bonds. When they issue bonds, municipalities can take out coverage to guarantee the payment of interest and principal. This type of insurance shifts the rating from the bond issue to the financial strength of the insurance company and often lowers the interest rate the municipality must pay to bondholders."

Anne continued on with her final points:

♦ "Always keep market abnormalities in mind. Even if you do everything right, as far as investing conservatively, it is still possible for you to lose money.

♦ "As a retiree, never ever borrow money to invest. Never buy stock on margin and never ever speculate. Understand what the risks are *before you put your money down*."

With that advice Anne suggested another short break before discussing professional money managers. After the others readily agreed, she excused herself to look over the phone messages which her assistant piled up on her desk.

During the break, Mary and Jim discussed their feelings regarding how they have managed their investments.

"I think she is right on the money," Jim said. "I have been blindly following our broker's advice, and quite frankly I really can't tell you how well we have done in comparison to the market. I'm open to a better suggestion, because I don't want to spend my retirement receiving phone calls every week to buy and sell stocks and bonds."

Chapter 14

*"A paradox, if the advice reaches enough people and they act
on it, knowledge of the advice destroys its usefulness."*
"A Random Walk down Wall Street," Burton G. Malkiel

Should retirees let others manage their investments?

At Anne's office

As the couples enjoyed the cold soft-drinks Anne offered, they talked among themselves about how well this session on investments was going.

"That was really interesting," Betty commented. "I don't pretend that I understand everything Anne was saying, but I know more now than when I started."

Anne, caught up on her phone messages, returned and continued the discussion on investments. "Most retirees will be better served to let professionals manage their money.

"In years past, investors tried to beat the market. Today the majority of the daily transactions on the New York Stock Exchange are directed by institutional investors. These are the investment advisors for the insurance companies, pension funds and mutual funds.

"Even though the small investor owns the majority of stock outstanding," Anne explained, "most of their holdings are rarely traded. This group includes owners who hold on to their stock to ensure control of their company. Therefore, at least in the short run, the institutional investor has a greater impact on the price of a stock than does the performance potential of a company. Consequently, since most retirees lack the timely information available to the institutional investor, most retirees are better off letting these professionals invest their money.

"If a retiree can't do as well as a professional investment advisor, then the retiree is better off joining them," Anne remarked. "Let's first discuss the most popular money manager, the **mutual fund**."

"What is a mutual fund and how does it work?" asked Betty.

"Mutual funds are investment companies which pool their investors' money and invest on their behalf in a portfolio of stocks and/or bonds in accordance with the investment objectives of the fund," Anne answered. "Individuals invest in a mutual fund by purchasing the shares of the fund. Each fund share represents ownership of a fractional share of each of the fund's underlying assets. Dividends and capital gains are paid out in proportion to the number of fund shares owned. As the underlying assets increase or decrease in value, the net asset value of the fund share increases or decreases proportionately. The net asset value multiplied by the number of fund shares owned determines the fair market value of your investment. Investors delegate the buy/sell decisions to the fund."

"How do you know which fund to invest in?" Betty asked.

"Think of a mutual fund as being a large specialty store, one which buys quality products in bulk. When you are in the market for a specific item, you go to the specialty store that sells that item. It's the same with mutual funds. Investors select mutual funds whose objectives are similar to their own. If investors desire income, they select funds with objectives to maximize current income. To help you get a better understanding, let me begin by describing how a mutual fund is organized and then we will discuss how it works," Anne said, as she passed out an illustration of a mutual fund's organization.

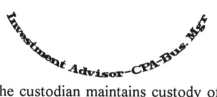

"Mutual funds have many of the same characteristics as a corporation. The fund is managed by a **board of trustees**, who are elected by the investors in the fund (**shareholders**). The investments of most mutual funds are transacted by an **investment advisor**. Often this advisor is a separate corporation which may be an independent contractor of the mutual fund. Families of mutual funds generally use the same investment advisor. The investment advisor does the research and manages the investments portfolio. This corporation also places orders for security transactions in accordance with the policies of the fund. The **custodian** is the fund's transfer and dividend paying agent. In this role, the custodian maintains custody of the fund's securities, cash and records of each shareholder's account. Generally, the custodian is a separate bank or trust company. Of course, like other corporations, the annual report must be audited by a **CPA** firm. The duties and responsibilities of the fund's management is spelled out in the **prospectus**, a legal document which describes what you should know before investing in a mutual fund. Here is a copy of my write-up on what I consider the relevant information that one can find in a prospectus (Appendix 14a)."

Always the pragmatic one, Jim Keane asked, "How much is it going to cost me?"

"Well, that all depends on your definition of cost," Anne answered with a smile. "In my definition, I include a cost for lost opportunity, which means I am interested in obtaining an above-average return for an appropriate level of risk. Therefore, I am interested in selecting those funds that have a greater potential for earning more than average return.

"You should understand that 80% of the professionals do not, over time, outperform or even equal the average performance of the market.

"So, Jim, in answer to your specific question, the following are the costs an investor may encounter when investing in a mutual fund.

"**Opportunity cost**—The cost associated with investing in funds which under-perform funds with similar risk characteristics. In effect, the cost of accepting a lower return."

"How can you measure opportunity cost?" Joe asked.

"Generally, the cost of lost opportunity is measured by comparing your actual return to the return of an index or the return of a specific mutual fund," Anne answered. "For example, if you had invested 100% in bonds over a five-year time period through year end 1994, you can compare your actual return to the average return of a portfolio composed of 50% stocks and 50% bonds for the same time period. The difference between these similar risk returns is the lost opportunity cost of holding 100% bonds."

"Thank you," Joe said, as he wrote down the example.

Anne continued describing the various costs associated with mutual funds. "I am going to generalize about the remaining costs. Keep in mind that funds have the latitude to use their own nomenclature when describing costs. Never assume—always read the prospectus.

"**Commission expense**—In the trade, these expenses are referred to as **loads**. A load is a commission the investor pays to receive investment advice. Loads compensate financial planners for their help in choosing the right investment for a client and not just for providing access to a fund. A percentage of this load normally goes to the brokerage firm in addition to the salesperson.

"For example, I earn most of my income by advising people how to invest. This is a service that I perform," Anne said.

"There are several different types of loads or commissions associated with mutual funds," Anne explained. She then discussed the various load types.

♦ "**Front-end loads (Class A shares)**—This type of commission is deducted immediately from your investment, and the level of the charge is reduced as you pass each breakpoint. The fund prospectus explains this action. This one-time charge is most appropriate for long-term investors.

♦ "**Back-end loads (Class B shares)**—These funds are sold without an initial sales charge. However, deferred charges are incurred when shares of the fund are redeemed before a certain time. Usually, the deferred charge decreases by one percent for each year the investment is retained. If you are a long-term investor and cannot obtain a sales charge break, you may be better off with a backend load. However, most class B shares will have a slightly higher expense ratio and therefore have lower returns than class A shares. Many funds will automatically convert class B shares to a class A shares classification after a designated number of years.

♦ **"Level loads (Class C shares)**—These mutual funds are also sold without an initial sales charge. However, they may bear, for a short time, a deferred sales charge, and they will have overall higher annual expenses for the life of the investment. A portion of this higher expense ratio is often shared with the original salesperson. If the investor intends to remain in the fund only for a short time, a class C share maybe the most beneficial. This type of charge is similar to a wrap fee which we will discuss shortly.

♦ **"No-loads**—True no-load funds are without an initial sales charge of any type. It is like shopping in a discount store. If you understand the cost, quality and know what you want, it's the place to go.

"Just a couple more thoughts about loads," Anne continued. "As with most investment transactions, the larger the amount invested, the smaller the load. Here is a rate structure followed by many load mutual fund families for their stock funds. Bond funds usually have lower initial loads." Anne then passed out a copy of typical front-end sales charges.

Sales Charges (Loads)	
Break-point	**Sales Charge %**
Less than $50,000	5.75%
$50,000 but less than $100,000	4.50%
$100,000 but less than $250,000	3.50%
$250,000 but less than $500,000	2.50%
$500,000 but less than $1,000,000	2.00%

"As you can see when investing larger amounts of money, the load factor as a percentage becomes less of a concern," Anne commented. "I often tell my clients to invest as though they are amortizing the load over five years. On an investment of $250,000, in the same fund family, the load reduces the return by less than a half percent (.05%) a year over those five years. Often the differences in other expenses between mutual funds far exceed this amount.

"Other annual expenses of mutual funds are included in the expense ratio include the management fee, other fees, and 12b-1 distribution costs," Anne said, as she continued.

"**Management fee**—This fee is the investment advisory fee paid to the fund for portfolio supervision. These fees usually range from .50% to 1.00% of the average fund balance.

"**Other expense fees**—These fees are paid to the fund to compensate for the cost of record-keeping and auditing as well as for legal, shareholder services, transfer agent services and custodian expenses.

"**12b-1 distribution expense**—A majority of the funds charge separately for advertising, marketing and distribution services. Often the financial planner or original salesperson receives a portion of this charge to encourage him or her to continue servicing the account.

"There is one additional cost of investing, called brokerage costs, that is neither well-known nor well-understood," Anne said.

"**Brokerage costs**—This term refers to the cost the investor incurs to buy and sell securities. Often it is called a **hidden or invisible cost**. For stocks that don't trade on an exchange, the brokerage cost is built into the bid/ask spread. If the investing organization does not have a 'first-class' trading capability, trades maybe executed at unfavorable prices. The more efficient the mutual fund, the lower the brokerage cost.

"Even with all of the above costs, the fact is, mutual funds are the more cost effective vehicles for most investors. Let us take a look at what those costs buy for us," Anne said as she listed the advantages of investing in mutual funds on her chartboard.

Mutual Fund Advantages:

Instant diversification—The mutual fund investor immediately owns a portion of all the stocks or bonds purchased by the fund. In some instances a $250 purchase will enable the mutual fund investor to own a stake in 100 to 800 different companies.

Professional money managers—The employees of the investment advisor, who often are **Certified Financial Analysts**, have one job and one job only and that is to pursue the investment objective of the mutual fund as described in the prospectus. They work at this full time.

A high level of regulation and evaluation—Because of its size, the mutual fund industry is the most highly regulated segment of the securities industry. Each fund has to prepare annual reports as well as an annually updated prospectus. The content of these are prescribed by the **Securities and Exchange Commission (SEC)**. Independent evaluators such as *Morningstar* and *Valueline* continually report their opinions on the more popular funds.

Values are published daily—Unlike the value of individual bonds, mutual fund net asset values (NAV) and offer prices are published daily in financial papers, like the *Wall Street Journal*, and in most daily newspapers.

Liquidity—Redeeming a portion of your investment, in most instances, involves only a phone call, often to an 800 number. The check or, if you wish, an electronic deposit to your bank account usually arrives within a week.

"Retirees can select to automatically receive the distribution of dividends when paid by the fund or they can receive a specific amount on a monthly basis. These arrangements can be set up or canceled at any time," Anne explained. "The investor often overlooks what I call the *efficiency of investing.*

"**Investment efficiency**—We have already discussed 'brokerage cost.' Mutual funds have a decided advantage because of the sheer volume of trading and the fact they only trade in per-selected stocks and bonds. Stockbrokers, on the other hand, are driven by the desires or needs of their clients, which often translate into sales of less than 100 shares called **odd lot**, as well as **over-the-counter-transactions (OTC)** for small company stocks. These types of trans-actions will drive up the cost. Markets are made for over-the-counter-transactions through the **National Association of Securities Dealers Automated Quotation System (NASDAQ)**. In past years, this market sold the stock at the higher 'asked' prices and paid the seller the lower 'bid' price. The SEC is forcing brokers to let their customers buy enter 'limit' orders which enables the investor to specify the price that is acceptable. However, there are no real teeth, as yet, in the SEC's position since a broker does not have to accept a limit order.

"**Investor efficiency**—Mutual funds allow the investor to purchase and sell units of any size, which efficiently utilizes the investor's money. Compare this advantage to a monthly dividend from a bond that languishes in a low return broker's cash account because it is insufficient to purchase an additional bond."

"Nothing is simple anymore, is it?" Jim mused. "What are some of our other investment man-agement choices?"

"There are several other categories such as annuities, wrap fee accounts and money managers," Anne answered.

"A **variable annuity** is almost a second cousin to a mutual fund. In fact, they are mutual funds sold through insurance companies. In some instances, the **investment advisor** is the same corporation that handles transactions for a mutual fund."

Anne then expounded on the major differences between mutual funds and variable annuities.

♦ "The commission expenses are covered by back-end loads, called **contingent-deferred-sales-charges (CDSC)**, similar to loads for class B share mutual funds. The investor does not pay the commission unless he withdraws from the annuity within a certain time period. Commonly, these charges begin at 7% and decrease by 1% annually. Most insurance companies will allow the purchaser to withdraw 10% of the value annually without paying a deferred charge.

♦ "Earnings from variable annuities are tax-deferred until distribution. In this respect, they are similar to a non-deductible IRA.

♦ "Most variable annuities offer some death benefit guarantee.

◆ "Many variable annuities have only a handful of stock, bond and money market investment accounts to foster diversification. Look for those funds with ample selections, including solid stock funds. Through what is known as a **1035 exchange**, an investor can often move 100% of his or her account to another annuity tax-free.

◆ "Some variable annuities have outperformed others over time, so it pays to shop around to find proven track records."

"Variable annuities sound like a good deal," Jim said.

"They well may be the right investment for some people," Anne responded. "Among the considerations are:

1. "Understanding the relationship between the tax-deferred benefit and the additional cost of insurance. Depending on your tax bracket, the additional insurance cost will exceed the tax deferral benefits for an investment period of anywhere between 3 to 10 years. Often these calculations are based on a lower tax bracket during the distribution phase. In any event, investment dollars need to be locked up for a period of time to take advantage of the tax deferral benefit. Keep in mind, the highly taxed investor foregoes the advantage of the lower rate capital gains tax. All distributions from variable annuities are taxed at the ordinary income rate.

2. "Because of the tax deferral, variable annuities have early withdrawal restrictions. Similar to an IRA, there is a 10% penalty for a withdrawal before age $59\frac{1}{2}$. An annuity comes with the additional advantage of unlimited contributions as compared to the $2,000 of an IRA. You can also defer distributions to age 85 as compared to the $70\frac{1}{2}$ limit for IRAs.

3. "Ability to diversify may be limited. The majority of variable annuities does not contain the wide range of options offered by a mutual fund family. Some are limited to bond investments and money market funds only. An investor should question the logic of investing in a money market fund which carries an extra .50% to 1.00% for insurance coverage. Money market funds are generally considered to be one of the least risky investments. Why park your funds there for safety's sake if they are already guaranteed?" Anne asked to emphasize the point.

4. "There is no 'step-up' in basis at the time of the annuitant's death. This means the beneficiaries will be liable for income taxes. Gains from mutual funds, on the other hand, do qualify for the 'step-up' in basis.

5. "While you are purchasing accumulation units during the investment phase, your only risk exposure is the volatility of the underlying assets, because the funds of variable annuities are maintained in separate accounts and are not available to the creditors of the insurance company. At distribution time, a decision must be made whether to annuitize or not. When you annuitize, you agree to have the insurance company pay you in equal payments for a

specified period of time. However, should you choose to annuitize, the money goes into the insurance company's general pool and loses the creditor protection.

"I often counsel people not to annuitize because I believe they should keep control of their money," Anne added.

"How about fixed annuities? Are they a good idea?" Mary asked.

"**Fixed annuities** look a lot like bank CDs," Anne answered. "However, like variable, annuities they also allow earnings to build tax-deferred. Early withdrawal penalties under the tax law can be avoided if the distribution is over the life of the annuitant(s). The initial earnings rate is guaranteed by the insurance company for a specific period, usually one to three years. Then the rate floats according to the current return potential of the insurance company's investments."

Anne continued describing fixed annuities. "Periodic payments begin at a stated or contingent date, at retirement for example, and continue over a fixed period or for the lives of the annuitants. Investors face several risks. They have to be concerned about creditworthiness of the insurance company itself and about the investments themselves. If an insurance company invests in **collateralized mortgage obligations (CMOs)** for example, it faces the threat of a change in interest rates. Should rates fall, homeowners are apt to refinance their mortgages, leaving insurance company the option of only investing in lower-interest-bearing instruments. Should interest rates rise, the insurance company is stuck with a rate below the current market. Though a high rating by a ratings firm like Moody's or Standard and Poor's is not absolute assurance of the future financial vitality of an insurance company, it's the only assurance available."

"Everything has its price," Mary said. "What else is available?" she asked.

"Finally, let's discuss **wrap-fee accounts**," Anne answered. "In this instance money managers charge a percentage based on the size of the portfolio for managing all the investments.

"Proponents of wrap-fee investing argue that a properly structured wrap-fee account program offers a vehicle for long-term, disciplined professional asset management at a reasonable price. There is a certain ego inflating message when one talks about *my money manager* which appeals to some people," Anne continued. "I direct some investors to a portfolio manager because that investor wants to talk to only one person and to have that person handle *all* their investments. Financial planners and brokers who utilize money managers usually meet with the investor on a quarterly basis and discuss his or her individual portfolio."

"Earlier, you seemed to advocate Mutual Funds. Isn't a money manager a better choice?" Jim asked.

"Jim, there is one thing you should understand," Anne replied. "Most portfolio managers, in effect, operate a mutual fund. Think about it for a minute. They don't meet with a client and then select the appropriate investments. Generally, each money manager has a particular investment style. Money managers *pre-select* the stocks and bonds that meet their investment criteria, and then put their client's money into that series of stocks and bonds. Only by pre-selecting investment opportunities can they work efficiently. As a further complication, there is a growing trend for money managers to utilize no-load funds. These money managers often call themselves **fee only planners**. For an annual amount, usually 1% of the portfolio value, they invest their client's money into pre-selected no-load mutual funds. The cost over time to the investor is very similar to the Class C load funds. To adequately address the risk tolerance of the client, and in some instances, to obtain sufficient diversification, a client may have to choose two or more portfolio managers because each manager's investment style varies. In my view," Anne continued, "the difference between the portfolio manager and the mutual fund manager is slight. Often people choose money managers because of a closer working relationship than that afforded by mutual funds."

"Can people have their cake and eat it too? That is, can they invest in mutual funds and still have a close working relationship with their investment advisor?" Betty asked.

"I like to think that most financial planners fill that role," Anne replied with a smile. "An investment advisor who acts with reasonable impartiality and meets periodically with the client to take into account his or her overall portfolio structure, regardless of where the investments are placed, fulfills that role. In other words, consider any investment advisor who puts the client's interest first. Mutual funds pay trail commissions to encourage just that type of behavior. In the past, one difference had been the wrap-fee, an annual percentage applied to the ending balance of the portfolio," Anne said, continuing her discussion of money managers. "Today, however, through the use of class C funds, some mutual funds are copying the same type of fee structure."

"With a mutual fund manager, you buy into an already established position and assume the cost basis in existence at the time of purchase. If the underlying asset had increased in value before your investment, then you purchased an unrecognized capital gain. When the fund subsequently sells that investment, unless you are in an IRA, you are liable for the capital gains tax. With the portfolio manager, your investment begins fresh. This adds more initial flexibility to your investments, particularly when it pertains to capital gains recognition."

"Earlier, you advised that at least 80% of our portfolio should be handled by some type of professional money manager. How do we choose one?" Mary asked.

"Your best bet, in my opinion, is to use some type of independent rating service. After all, there are over 5000 mutual funds and an estimated 17,000 money managers. For mutual funds, I use *Morningstar Mutual Funds*," Anne continued. "Morningstar is an independent company which provides information, data and analysis on over 1200 funds. Since I favor funds with some whiskers—that is, mutual funds that have survived several different market cycles—I start my filtering process by selecting funds that have at least a *5 year track record*.

"*Morningstar* facilitates this search with their star ratings," Anne went on. "It uses a risk-adjusted rating of one to five stars, with five being the highest rating. The star rating views a fund in isolation and is a representation of how well a fund has balanced risk and return in the past.

"My initial selection criterion is simple," Anne said. "If a fund has less than a 10-year track record, I select only those funds with an average historical star rating of 4.0 or better. If a fund has been around longer than 10 years, I include those funds with an average historical star rating 3.5 or greater. This process reduces the 1200 original population to about 250 funds, of which about 60% are load funds. Next, I develop statistics for the selected 250 funds. I then look for funds that have achieved better than average returns for their category. I also use the standard deviation, Beta (β), and the style boxes provided by *Morningstar*. The fund selected must be a member of a fund family which has a number of funds that meet my criteria. Of course, I also choose funds that charge a load since this is how I earn my living."

"It appears that you do extensive research to earn your commissions," Joe remarked.

"Thank you," Anne said. "Investors have a right to understand their advisor's selection criteria. Before we leave mutual funds, let's touch briefly on the impact of the load and of other expenses. There are many people who shop around to get the cheapest price—often to their chagrin. I can't tell you the number of times in my life that I purchased on price instead of on quality only to regret my decision," Anne said as she continued. "Since about 80% of the funds in the long run return less than the average of the market, a lot of people are sub-optimizing their investment opportunities—which relates to the lost opportunity cost that we discussed earlier. Most comparisons of load versus no-load funds make the simplistic assumption that each fund makes exactly the same return," Anne continued. "They are simply telling us that if all returns are equal mathematically, the larger amount will always win out. In reality, with so many choices, an investor is supremely better off in a well-performing load fund than in a poor-performing no-load fund. In addition, if you were to choose only no-load funds, you would miss the opportunity of investing with some excellent managers such as John Templeton, the legendary chairman of Templeton funds.

"Remember—this choice is either/or, the products are different. It's not like going into a discount store and buying the same product at a lower price. A load fund can only be purchased by paying the load. Keep in mind that all markets are not equally efficient. Information is not readily available in some markets and some managers are better at selection than others. As I said earlier, to keep my clients targeting on a longer-term-focus, I tell my them to conceptualize amortizing the load over five years even though it's usually paid in year one. The amortized load is usually less than 1% a year. I have a perception that investors in no-load funds are more apt to jump ship in a shaky market. All too often, they sell after the market is already down—thereby taking a potential temporary loss and making it a permanent one. This type of response impacts the entire fund since either the fund must sell into the teeth of a decline or must maintain an overabundance of cash in order to pay out. Often, the cost of the load, already incurred, will be sufficient incentive for many investors to benefit by staying the course.

"In a good fund family you can usually transfer some, or all, of your plan's assets to another fund in that same family, whenever you like, at no cost," Anne continued. "It just takes a phone call, which explains why I only recommend a fund family with at least several funds that meet my criteria. Pay attention to the expense ratio of the fund. The range of fund expenses from the lowest to the highest rarely exceeds 1%. The advantage of a superior manager to an inferior manager often is many times greater. You pay your money and you take your chances."

"Are there services that rate the other types of professional investors?" Mary asked.

"*Morningstar* also rates variable annuities," Anne answered. "Money managers, on the other hand, are more numerous, and less information about their performance is available to the average retiree. To compensate for my lack of knowledge about good or bad money managers," Anne continued, "I utilize a firm which specializes in selecting and monitoring money managers. Even this firm contracts with an independent company to perform the evaluation. The evaluators look for better-than-average returns as well as the consistency that the money managers display in following their stated investment objectives. I wouldn't have the a clue on how to choose among the many money managers without a source such as Pershing's PEAK 1 program[3]," she concluded.

At this juncture, Jim Keane leaned over and told Mary that he agreed with Anne's conclusion. "From now on. a significant portion of our investments will be handled by the professionals," he said.

"We have just enough time to cover one more topic," Anne said. "Let's discuss how retirees should invest."

After looking at their watches, the Meehans and Keanes begged off.

"I'm bushed," Jim said. "Let's set up another session for sometime next week." All those in attendance quickly agreed to Jim's suggestion and thanked Anne for a most informative session.

"This session was really interesting, but my brain couldn't absorb anymore," Jim said, on the way home.

---

[3] Pershing, Division of Donaldson, Lufkin & Jenrette Securities Corporation.

Chapter 15

*"In this line of work, you never have to retire. You keep right
on until your through. Which is fortunate. I've had lunch with
people who've retired. All they talk about is their illnesses.
They're so boring."*
Julia Child, 81-year-old chef

Anyone who can read can cook

During a visit with their Mom, Mary and Joe again accompanied her to a seminar at her senior center

Mary was particularly interested in attending this seminar about food preparation. She and Jim had experienced a change in their eating habits since their children left. Mary realized they had fallen into the habit of eating fast-foods for convenience. She attributed her lower energy level to this change in their diet and resolved to correct the situation.

"I think you will really enjoy today's topic," Marie said.

Joe and Mary were surprised to see that the auditorium was set up as a large dining room. The arrangement of the cooking facilities particularly fascinated them. A large slanted mirror, installed over the range and work area, allowed the audience to observe the food being prepared and cooked.

"This is the best part of belonging to the Senior Center," Marie explained. "We learn all about cooking and then enjoy what we have learned."

Nancy Tarpey, the speaker, was a local author who recently published a book entitled *Eating Healthy When You Are Alone*.

"Thank you for inviting me," Nancy said. Then she asked, "Why are nutrition and good eating habits important to senior citizens?"

"To keep us healthy," came an answer from the audience.

"That is absolutely correct," Nancy answered as she began her presentation. "New research is discovering that deficiency of vitamins and nutrients may be the cause of many of the conditions that we have been attributing to old age, including cataracts and slow-healing wounds. It's vital that seniors eat healthy meals.

"Today, I'm going to prepare a meal with absolutely no fat content to illustrate how we can obtain fat-free nutrition without sacrificing taste. Also, I want to demonstrate how easy it is to cook, even though I realize that most of you have cooked all your lives. However, I notice a number of men in the audience who may not have the same experience. I believe that *anyone who can read, can cook*," Nancy stated.

"Unfortunately, it's almost impossible to prepare food economically for one person or even for two people," Nancy continued. "That is why many supermarkets have opened bakeries and salad bars, and that's why they offer fried chicken or even Chinese meals. Pizza parlors and fast-food enterprises entice many seniors because of the convenience. All of these conveniences are much more expensive than the same portion prepared at home. Furthermore, they are high in fat, salt and calories, which senior citizens don't need. What is the one ingredient that many seniors have in abundance?" asked the speaker.

"TIME!" Nancy answered with enthusiasm. "Use that time profitably by doing your own cooking," Nancy advised. "It saves you money, and it improves your outlook on life. You are in a better frame of mind after preparing a good meal. You are better off physically because you are getting a more wholesome diet. *So long, depression!"* Nancy announced.

"How do you start?" she asked. "Having a freezer is essential and having a microwave is nice. Never cook for one person. Always cook for four or more and then freeze what you don't eat. A wholesome meal is only a microwave away."

"Do we need all those fancy gadgets like food processors?" someone in the audience asked.

"Fancy gadgets such as food processors and microwaves help, but are not essential," Nancy replied. "Anything the food processor can chop, you can chop with a knife. If you have these appliances, by all means use them. However, I often ignore them when I'm doing small jobs because I don't like to clean them after I'm finished."

"I haven't bought your book *yet*," said another person, to the laughter of the attendees, "so please tell us how to buy food for one or two people."

"I live alone and I happen to like fish," Nancy replied. "Once a month I go to a fish store and have them filet a whole salmon. I take the fish home and cut the filets into meal size pieces. I keep one piece for that evening's meal because I love fresh salmon, and I freeze the rest. I do the same thing with bread. Monthly, I go to a good bakery, buy a month's quantity and take it home and freeze it. The kaiser roll for my sandwich comes out of the freezer and I pop it into the microwave. Earlier, I explained that you should cook in quantity and freeze the leftovers. Let me take it a step further. Freeze the leftovers in quantities that fit your meal requirements. If you are like me and live alone, freeze the leftovers into meals sized for one person. If there are two of you, then, of course, make larger batches. Mark the batch clearly with a description of the contents and the date."

"How long can leftovers remain in the freezer?" asked another participant.

"As a general rule of thumb, I try to use everything within three months," Nancy answered, as she continued to chop vegetables for the ensuing luncheon.

"Suppose you can't cook?" a male in the audience asked.

"If you can read, you can cook," Nancy replied with a smile. Get a good cookbook. Remember, it doesn't have to be fancy," Nancy said. "My most used cookbook is a $1.29 version of Fanny Farmer. It doesn't contain any fancy pictures of how my meal should look. However, the essential instructions and exact measurements are clear. I just follow instructions. This presentation is not just directed at the women in the audience. Men, too, can cook. If you are married, take the night off once a week, Mom, and let Dad do his thing. Both of you will benefit."

"How can I get my husband interested in cooking?" asked another, as she nudged her spouse with her elbow.

"Take him with you to a cooking class," Nancy answered. "Cooking is fun and it is fun to learn in a group. I first got hooked on cooking by attending a class at my local community college. While attending, I met a lot of people whom I now call friends. A cooking class can be a fun experience, and the benefit can last for a lifetime. If you have to live alone, then learn to be on your own. Knowing how to cook is essential," Nancy commented.

"We have just talked about how to eat. Now let's talk about what to eat," Nancy continued. "Due to any number of reasons, varying from dietary constraints because of heart conditions to dental problems, many of us find it more difficult to digest certain foods as we age. With this in mind, we have to learn to eat the right stuff and not just the good-tasting or the easy-to-prepare stuff. The Food and Drug Administration has recently developed a standard labeling approach to enable the consumer to understand the nutritional value of the product. I recommend paying particular attention to the number of grams of fat. We should only eat between 65 and 80 grams of fat daily. A few helpings of potato chips could consume our daily fat ration rather quickly. Learn to use the labels when preparing your meals. As we age, we tend to eat less. Therefore, it is essential that we eat nutritious foods," Nancy said, as she led into her description on how to eat nutritiously.

1. "Strike a balance between the four food groups and include each in the planning for a daily meal—meat—poultry and fish—milk products, fruits and vegetables, fiber—bread, pasta, cereal—plus a liberal amount of water.

2. "Find out your nutritional deficiencies and satisfy those with your diet. For those of you who have the potential of osteoporosis, which is the leaching of calcium from the bones, calcium intake is critical. One way to obtain calcium is to consume several glasses of skim milk or several cartons of low-fat yogurt. Other sources of calcium include green vegetables. If you don't get calcium from your food intake, you may need to take a calcium supplement.

3. "Avoid sugar. Keep in mind that some processed foods contain up to 70% sugar. Each year, many Americans eat more sugar than their body weight—which is a major cause of obesity. Rather than relying on sugar, consider carbohydrates, such as bread and cereal for example, as another source for energy. Carbohydrates provide necessary fiber, which is vital in proper elimination and in the prevention of colon cancer.

4. "Consider vitamins, whether you take them in food or in pill form. Either source provides equal benefits and they convert food into energy. People who smoke should take 100 to 150 milligrams of vitamin C daily. Vitamin B6 and vitamin E help with blood circulation and they help the blood to carry oxygen. Such vitamins are often called the runner's cocktail because so many joggers and runners take these vitamins daily.

5. "Reduce your caloric intake by substituting vegetables. For example, use raw vegetables such as carrots, broccoli and celery as a snack and dip them in a 'nonfat' salad dressing. A banana a day will normally satisfy your potassium needs. Some portion of our food should be in raw form since cooking leaches out most of the vital nutrients. When you prepare cooked vegetables, use the microwave or steam them to help preserve these nutrients."

Nancy continued. "Take some time today to review your eating habits. In talking with senior groups, I find that, far too often, eating has become just that—a habit. I want to help make it an exciting experience for both large and small appetites. Cooking brings satisfaction, and satisfaction brings happiness. Look at how much fun I'm having.

"I just have to add the pesto sauce to the soup, and it will be ready to serve. Sit back, take a break for a few minutes, and enjoy the soup. By the way, the bread is from your local bakery," Nancy said.

With the assistance of some volunteers, Nancy served the soup and bread.

As the participants enjoyed their soup, Nancy continued preparing the main course.

"While I continue with the food preparation, I want you to notice my use of a sanitizer," Nancy said. "A sanitizer is just a cap of bleach in a gallon of water. I use it to wash my utensils and clean my cutting board every time I move on to a new dish. With the present concern about salmonella and e-coli, we should all get into the practice of handling food properly. I recommend that we:

♦   "Defrost meat and poultry in the refrigerator and refrigerate all reusable cooked food immediately following the meal.

♦   "Wash and repackage meat and poultry, then wash your hands after handling either.

♦ "Wash any plate or utensil that is used to prepare or carry fresh meat or poultry before reusing this dish. This idea is something we need to keep in mind when barbecuing. How often do we see an outdoor cook reuse the same unwashed plate?

♦ "Properly cook food, particularly meat and poultry. Avoid rare or medium rare burgers, particularly if young grandchildren will be eating.

"I can't emphasize proper handling too much. It is vital to good health. Just a few other odds and ends about eating," Nancy continued as she began to cook the main course.

♦ "Consider eating five or even six times a day rather than the normal three. Digestion works best when we are active. Smaller meals served more frequently help the digestive and assimilation process. These smaller meals should consist of the same balance of wholesome nutrition and not just of 'junk food.'

♦ "Eat sufficient fiber. Your colon will thank you. Fiber can be found in fruits, vegetables and grain.

♦ "Watch your weight. Your blood pressure will appreciate it. Consider using nonfat or skim milk and nonfat salad dressings.

♦ "Fish protects blood vessels. Eat it several times a week. Some research indicates that it helps inhibit kidney disease.

♦ "Frozen food has as much nutritional value as so-called 'fresh food.' Why pay more?

♦ "Vegetables are cholesterol-free and your heart thanks you.

♦ "Starchy foods, such as potatoes, are a less fattening way to get protein.

♦ "Avoid dehydration. Drink sufficient quantities of water.

"Science is beginning to come to grips with the fact that common-sense eating habits not only aid your body, but also help you maintain your learning ability," Nancy remarked, as she began to serve the main course. "Now, won't you all come and join me in the meal that I prepared using the suggestions that I have been explaining."

As Joe and Mary were leaving their Mother's house following the seminar

Mary commented to her mother, "I notice you already follow many of the suggestions offered today."

"This hasn't been the first cooking class that I have taken," Marie answered, smiling.

As they turned onto I-5 heading back home toward Tacoma, Mary began to mentally revise hers and Jim's eating habits.

Chapter 16

"Far too often, a retiree's portfolio is neither properly diversified nor sufficiently growth-oriented."

How should a retiree invest?

On the way to Anne's office for another session

Mary commented on the amount of time that she was taking off from work.

"If you think you have a problem," Betty countered, "I have to take time off without pay, because I haven't earned any vacation as yet. But the meetings have been worth the cost and effort since both Joe and I need to understand investing."

"I feel very fortunate that the boys can run the business without me," Jim added to the conversation.

Anne's assistant greeted them, escorted them into the conference room and poured the first round of coffee. Shortly thereafter, Anne joined them.

Mary, speaking for herself and Jim, began, "Anne, we all want to thank you for your time and patience as we have gotten better educated on investing. As you know, Jim and I are going to retire within a year. What specific investments should we be considering?"

"Well, Mary, we discussed many aspects of investing for the retiree, and all of them should play a role in your investment decisions. Before I answer your specific question, let us review some of those recommendations," Anne said as she began to write on the chartboard.

"The two years living expenses should be covered either from an on-going source or from

> **Anne's Recommendations:**
>
> ◆ **Establish how much income you are going to need.**
>
> ◆ **Set aside two years of net income to live on.**
>
> ◆ **Invest the remainder of your retirement assets intelligently for the longer term.**

savings specifically set aside for that purpose," Anne emphasized. "These are the dollars that you are going to live on for the next two years. I call the savings your living expense fund, and they need to be protected."

Anne then tore off the chartboard sheet and hung it on her wall with masking tape.

"Please explain again why it makes sense to put away two years' living expense in a low-return investment?" Joe asked.

Additional recommendations

♦ **Always have some growth opportunities as part of your portfolio.**

♦ **Have a professional money manager handle 80 to 90% of your portfolio.**

♦ **As you require additional income, gradually make the transition from growth investments to growth & income investments.**

♦ **Never borrow to invest and never speculate.**

"The establishment of a living expense fund frees you from most of the market volatility," Anne replied. "Consider that with a portfolio of 50% stocks and 50% bonds (which earned the market average in the past twenty years) there has been only one 2-year period that lost money. With this freedom, regardless of your age, you can diversify and invest at least 40% of your portfolio in growth mutual funds to keep up with inflation. Too often, retirees depend entirely on income-producing investments such as CDs or dividend-paying bonds. Investing too conservatively will inevitably lead to future problems because of inflation.

"Let the professionals manage your money," Anne said, as she reemphasized an old-theme.

"With that information as a background, let's first look at investment styles to better illustrate diversification," Anne said, as she tore off and hung the second chartboard sheet. "*Morningstar* uses a 'style-box' method to display portfolio characteristics and to allow their readers to determine a particular fund's investment objectives. I've borrowed, with their permission, a matrix *Morningstar* uses to display which funds belong in which category," she said, as she illustrated on the chartboard.

Equities Investment Style

"The equities style-box categorizes mutual funds by the size of companies in which each fund invests and the relationship of the price/earnings and the price/book of the stocks in each fund relative to the S&P 500 index,"

	Value	Blend	Growth
Large companies			
Medium-sized companies			
Small companies			

Anne continued. "I often use this matrix to illustrate how to diversify funds properly. I believe a well-diversified portfolio should have a spread of large to small company funds as well as some mix of growth and value. First, let's look at company size. Large company funds invest in companies with capitalization in excess of $5 billion. Medium funds invest in companies with capitalization between $1 billion and $5 billion. Small company funds invest in companies with less than $1 billion capital."

"Why is this important?" Betty asked.

"Because small companies are not as financially sound as larger companies. The market takes this disparity into account when it considers the risk/return relationship," Anne answered. "The risk increases as the size of the company diminishes. Therefore, the return should increase. Value funds are identified as those with low stock prices compared to their earnings and often have a steady dividend-paying record," she continued. "Growth funds invest in companies whose potential earnings are expected to increase faster than the market. Blend funds have a portion of both investment philosophies."

"Why don't you just use the stated objective of the funds: for example, growth, growth and income, aggressive growth etc.—the same way the papers identify them?" Jim asked.

"I decided to follow *Morningstar's* lead, primarily to clearly identify how the fund actually invests," Anne answered. "Consider a fund with 'Value' in its name and a stated objective of growth. The manager says he is sensitive to value, but leans toward companies with significant prospects for earnings growth. *Morningstar* listed this fund as a blend, and I concur. Another fund with 'Capital Growth' in its name, listed under the growth objective, very clearly is value-oriented because its manager is a bargain hunter. The name of the fund doesn't matter, but how its advisors invest does. I hope that explanation helps," Anne noted as she continued with the discussion on diversification.

"Before we continue," Joe interjected, "suppose I wanted a steady stream of income. How would I choose a fund using your method?"

"In that instance," Anne answered, "your matrix would be heavily weighted to the value column. Once we have the large picture in focus we choose those specific funds within the chosen categories. To respond to the need that you identified, we would look for funds with a high dividend payout. In addition, we would look toward bonds, which is our next subject.

"**Bond funds** can also be displayed in a matrix. The quality or credit risk of the bond fund's portfolio is expressed as high, medium or low. The average effective maturity is shown on the horizontal heading, with short being less than four years and long being longer than ten. I normally recommend that a retiree invest in high-quality or medium-quality intermediate corporate or government bond funds. I also recommend funds with an intermediate duration, because these generate a return almost equal to long-term bonds with less risk. This matrix enables an investor to quickly understand how well diversified he or she is in bonds. International equity and bond funds can be displayed in the same fashion," Anne explained.

Bonds Investment Style

	Short maturity	Interme-diate maturity	Long maturity
High quality			
Medium quality			
Low quality			

"To illustrate, let us assume that you desire a 60% stock, 40% bond portfolio with about 10% of each invested internationally.

"Secondly, let us presume that you want the following diversity." Anne wrote the following on the chartboard.

	Stocks		Bonds
30%	large blend funds	20%	medium intermediate
20%	medium growth	10%	low intermediate
10%	international medium blend	10%	international high long

"Using the *Morningstar*-type-style-boxes, your investments would look like the following[4]."

---

[4]Author's note: These allocations are for illustrative purposes only. They do not represent recommendations from Morningstar Inc.

Domestic Stock Funds

	Value	Blend	Growth
Large companies		30%	
Medium-sized companies			20%
Small companies			

Anne continued, "As you move diagonally down the table on the stock matrix, market volatility increases. As you move from left to right on the bond matrix, the impact of interest rate risk increases."

"Why would anyone want to invest in low-quality, long-maturity bonds?" Mary asked.

Domestic Bond Funds

	Short maturity	Intermediate maturity	Long maturity
High quality			
Medium quality		20%	
Low quality		10%	

International Stock Funds

	Value	Blend	Growth
Large companies			
Medium sized companies		10%	
Small companies			

"Because a low- quality long-maturity bond fund could be a high yield fund or a MUNI bond fund," Anne answered. "A low-quality rating doesn't necessarily mean the bond fund invests in bonds of questionable credit quality. A low-quality rating is also given to any non-rated bonds, which includes many high-income MUNI and high-yield corporate bond funds.

International Bond Funds

	Short maturity	Interme-diate maturity	Long maturity
High quality			10%
Medium quality			
Low quality			

"After you are satisfied with the spread of investment percentages in your proposed portfolio," Anne continued, "then begin your research by considering only those funds that meet those criteria. To narrow the list of potential candidates, consider additional specific criteria, such as funds with a greater-than-average return—funds with proven track records. Notice how we go for diversity first before we get mesmerized by the most recent return or by other criteria that funds push to get our attention," she pointed out.

"Now, that I can relate to," Joe said, "but you haven't gotten to the heart of our concern. What types of investments should people have when they retire?"

"For simplicity, I will concentrate on mutual funds only," Anne answered. "What I say about mutual fund categories also applies to the 20% or less I recommend for individual stocks and bonds. How much a person puts into each depends on his or her need for income in the short-term."

On a new chartboard sheet, Anne then listed those investments that she considers acceptable for inclusion in a retiree's portfolio:

♦ Growth and income funds—invest in a mix of blend, value, and growth stocks.
♦ Corporate or government bond funds—invest in government or corporate debt.
♦ International or world equity (stock) funds—invest in a mix of foreign and domestic companies.
♦ Small cap funds—invest in stocks of small companies.
♦ International government bond funds—invest in foreign government bonds.
♦ Growth funds—invest in companies with expected above-average earnings growth.
♦ High-yield bond funds—invest in lower quality or non-rated bonds—usually bonds of small to mid-sized companies.
♦ Municipal bond funds—invest in debt of states, cities and their agencies.
♦ Variable and fixed annuities—investments sold through and backed by an insurance company.

Anne then emphasized. "In my view, 60% or more of a retiree's portfolio should be invested in:

♦ "Growth and income funds,
♦ "Growth funds,
♦ "Corporate or government bond funds,
♦ "Municipal bond funds (if the investor is in a high tax bracket),
♦ "Variable and fixed annuities.

"For short-term parking, until the funds are invested in the above or for protection of principal in the living expense fund, I would recommend the following:

♦ "Treasury notes and bills,
♦ "Money market funds,
♦ "Certificates of deposit.

"The remainder of the funds fall into a more risky category. Retirees should have less than 40% of their total portfolio invested in these more risky funds."

"Anne, you emphasize that a retiree can't recover from a disaster, yet you include high-yield bonds as a recommendation. How come?" Joe asked.

"First of all, you should understand these are mutual bond funds, not just high-yield bonds. I include high-yield mutual funds because they can add a little spice to one's portfolio. They pay a greater dividend because of the risk involved. Because of this added risk, a retiree should have no more than 10% in high-yield bond funds. Keep in mind that a bondholder gets paid off before a stockholder should the company declare bankruptcy. To gauge the safety of a high-yield bond, calculate the monetary safety net in the form of equity value in a company. Multiply the stock price by the number of shares outstanding to determine the equity value. Many companies that issue high-yield bonds have hundreds of millions of dollars of common stock outstanding. That's an awfully large safety net. Furthermore, the risk involved, even though some of the fund's holdings may go bankrupt, is often acceptable because of the higher return that these funds offer. Historically, the higher return more than paid for that small percentage of companies within the fund's portfolio that have gone bankrupt."

Anne finished with a final conceptual discussion on what the retiree should consider in deciding how to invest. "Retirees investment allocations need to be driven by their time horizon and by their need for income and growth. For a married couple the timeframe could easily be thirty years:

"Retirees have to keep in mind the possibility of these long timeframes when they invest. If retirees fail to provide for sufficient growth opportunities in their portfolio, they will undoubtedly suffer a lifestyle decline as their retirement funds diminish. Inflation is insidious. Its cumulative effect over a long period of time totally destroys a non-growth investment."

Age	Time Horizon
70	10 to 25 years
60	20 to 35 years
50	30 to 45 years

"Is the name of the game to avoid using or losing any of your principal?" Jim asked.

"Most retirees will eventually eat into their principal and that's okay," Anne replied. "The name of the game for most retirees is to stretch their money while living at a reasonable comfort level for the rest of their lives—not just the first couple of years after retirement.

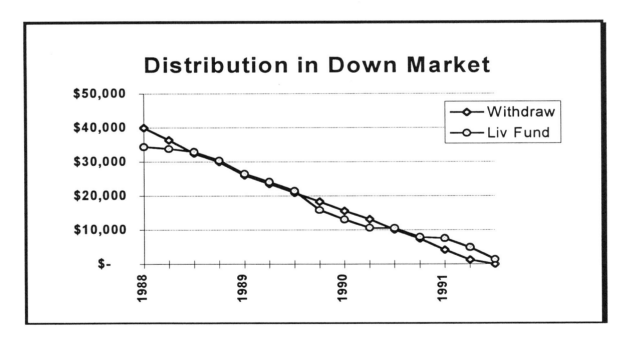

"When we discussed investment risk, I showed you a chart which compared what I call mattress money to taking dollars out of investments in a down market. If you recall, the dollars would have lasted longer by just putting them in a mattress. This chart depicts that same situation showing the with-drawal depleting the funds in less than three years.

However, instead of keeping the money in a mattress, I substituted a living fund concept. Notice that the initial investment is lower because of the dollars put in a living fund. The same original dollar amount lasted longer in the same down market situation because the retiree wasn't forced to withdraw money in periods when the market was down. The ability to 'withdraw or wait' gives the retiree flexibility as well as an added level of control. About the only additional advice that I offer is to compensate for needed income by adjusting your portfolio," Anne continued.

"Gradually, move from growth funds to growth and income funds as you age. As a target, you may wish to consider the following chart.

Age	50-60	60-70	70+
Cash	5%	5%	10%
Growth	60%	50%	30%
Fixed Income	35%	45%	60%

"These figures are not meant to be set in concrete. They only recognize that income becomes more of a concern as one ages," Anne concluded.

"Okay, I understand everything that you discussed and I agree with most of it," Jim said. "However, you still haven't satisfied the question of how I, Jim Keane should, invest?"

"Before we got into your specific case," Anne answered, "I wanted to establish a background in which I could explain my investment philosophy. You and Mary have sufficient resources to retire at a level which is commensurate with your present living standards. You have a medium to high risk tolerance, and you understand the need for growth and the impact that market volatility has on growth shares. You understand the need for and intend to invest for the long-term, which means reinvesting dividends and capital gains. You also intend to utilize the living-expense fund that I have emphasized. Stop me if I'm incorrect in reading your intentions as a couple," Anne said.

"Keep going," both Jim and Mary said. "You seem to be right on the mark."

"Let's utilize the style-boxes and begin to address your specific question—except now we will name the tables."

Anne explained her reasoning for recommending the above diversification[5] of the Keane's portfolio. "These percentages do not include the living expense fund nor do they include your emergency fund. They represent your retirement assets only. For domestic stock, the 10% in a large value, the 30% in a medium blend fund and the 10% small company growth fund fit your medium to high risk tolerance and meet the high return goal that you expressed.

The Keanes' Domestic Stock Funds

	Value	Blend	Growth
Large companies	10%		
Medium-sized companies		30%	
small companies			10%

The Keanes' International Stock Funds

	Value	Blend	Growth
Large companies			
Medium-sized Companies		10%	
Small companies			

"Regarding international stocks, I prefer large company or medium-sized company stocks. Often, I suggest that a person invest up to 20% of his or her portfolio overseas.

---

[5]Author note: The allocation percentages shown are for illustrative purposes only. They do not represent recommendations of Morningstar, Inc.

The Keanes' Domestic Bond Funds

	Short maturity	Intermediate maturity	Long maturity
High quality			
Medium quality		20%	
Low quality			10%

"For domestic bonds, the 20% medium-quality, intermediate-term bond fund provides that solid bond investment that I believe all portfolios need. The 10% low quality, long-term can cover either a high-yield fund or a MUNI fund. The choice is driven either by your need to reduce current income taxation or by your desire to spice up the bond return.

"For international bond funds, I prefer government bond funds only.

"As you can see from these two pie charts (see following page), the capitalization of the world-stock market has changed dramatically over the last decade. It is clear that the long-term investor has a significant investment opportunity overseas.

The Keanes' International Bond Funds

	Short maturity	Intermediate maturity	Long maturity
High quality			10%
Medium quality			
Low quality			

"When you consider this growth opportunity in light of our earlier discussion on diversification—international investing simply makes sense," Anne concluded.

"What are your thoughts about keeping 15% or more in cash that my broker keeps insisting upon?" Jim asked.

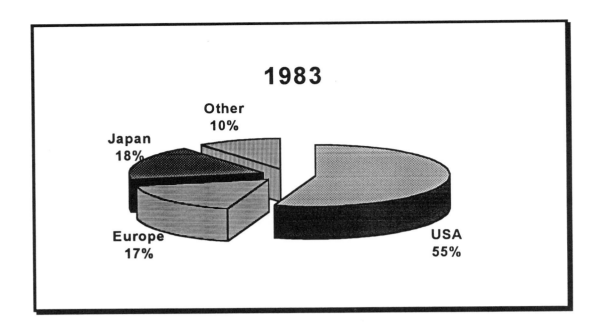

"First consider why you might need the cash. Is it to invest when the market drops? If so, many mutual funds also anticipate such an eventuality and maintain a significant percentage in cash. Other than that, we have provided for your cash needs with an emergency fund and a living-expense fund. I really don't see the sense of keeping a high percentage in cash," Anne responded.

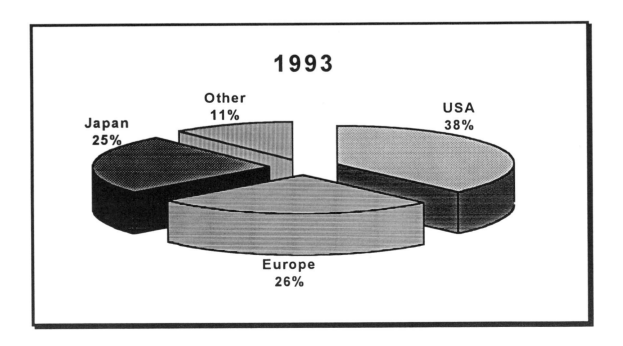

Following that discussion, this portion on financial planning came to a close. Both couples thanked Anne and agreed to having a final session to discuss the issues involved in taking a distribution from a tax-deferred account.

"Would it be possible for us to take some of those chartboard notes and charts," Jim asked.

"You are welcome to all of them," Anne said, as she began to gather up the sheets. "If your calendars permit, let's set up that final session for next week. Betty and Joe, since this doesn't really apply to you for several decades, you really don't have to attend."

Betty begged off, but Joe indicated an interest in attending. Following another series of good-byes, the Keanes and Meehans left for home.

Jim was very happy with a copy of the Keane's investment table in hand. On the way home, he confided to Mary, "We now have a direction in mind."

Chapter 17

Financial decisions on the distribution end

A week later at Anne's office

Joe Meehan picked up Mary and Jim for their final session with Anne Jahn, their financial planner. The session was scheduled to educate the Keanes about taking distributions from qualified retirement plans and tax deferred investments.

"Thank you, Anne. I'm delighted that you have helped to clear up many of our concerns about investments," Jim said, as they began their final informational session.

"As I said at our last session, this topic on distributions is more immediately relevant to the Keanes than to you, Joe," Anne reiterated. "It covers the issues around taking money out of retirement accounts and explores the rules governing such actions. Let me forewarn you. This subject is complex, can be very dry and maybe even boring. However, it is extremely important to your being in control of your tax-deferred funds. The rules for withdrawing money from tax-deferred accounts are quite complex and not very well understood. The tax publication #590, *Individual Retirement Arrangements*, doesn't do the topic justice."

"Why don't we wait until we're taking a distribution to worry about the rules?" Jim asked.

"I am very concerned about elderly retirees making choices at difficult times," Anne answered. "The impact of the distribution decision does not take place at the time the decision is made. It occurs later with an event such as the death of a spouse, which is absolutely the worst time to learn that a wrong choice was made. Believe me—now is the time to think about it, not when you are $70\frac{1}{2}$."

With those comments as a background, Anne went on to discuss how a retiree takes a distribution from a tax-deferred investment, "Think about any qualified retirement savings as being in a box surrounded by regulations. Let me draw you a picture."

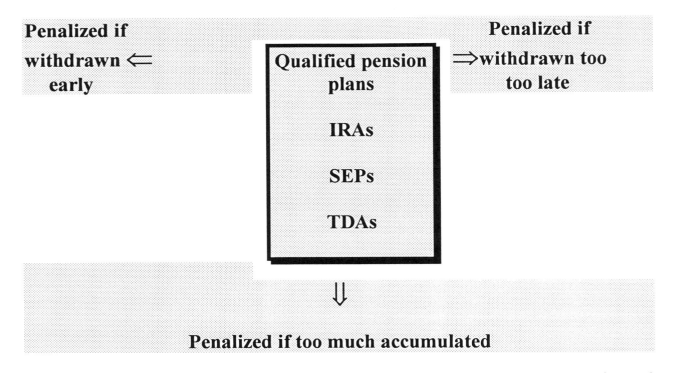

Penalized if withdrawn ⇐ **early**

Qualified pension plans

IRAs

SEPs

TDAs

Penalized if ⇒**withdrawn too too late**

⇓

Penalized if too much accumulated

"As you can see, all the regulations involve a heavy penalty for the unwary. Try to understand that Uncle Sam provides the tax-deferred buildup in order to encourage people to save for retirement. The penalties are to ensure that the savings are de facto used for retirement. Let's take a few minutes and cover these penalties, because it is very important that you understand them," Anne said.

Too early penalty	
Amount withdrawn	**$5,000**
Income tax	**(1,400)**
(assume 28% marginal rate)	
10 % penalty	**(500)**
Net available	**$3,100**

"The 'too early penalty' applies to people under the age of $59\frac{1}{2}$. This 10% penalty is in addition to income taxes paid upon distribution and also applies to ordinary (non-qualified) annuities," Anne then demonstrated the calculation on the chartboard, "Be aware that both the income tax and the penalty apply to the gross amount withdrawn. The penalty does not apply in the case of death, disability or rollovers from a qualified plans to an IRA. Furthermore, it doesn't apply to qualified plans for people over 55 who have been separated from service. Except for IRAs, it applies to payments made under a qualified domestic relations order relating to a divorce.

"There is a method to avoid the early withdrawal penalty on a distribution even from an IRA, when a person is under $59\frac{1}{2}$."

Anne continued. "You can take the withdrawal in the form of an annuity. The law provides this exception if the withdrawal is part of a series of substantially equal periodic payments made for the life of the employee or the joint lives of the employee and his or her beneficiary. Notice, I choose to take the withdrawal from one IRA only." Anne used the chartboard to illustrate how this calculation would work.

> **IRA withdrawal, joint survivors both age 57**
>
> **IRA #1 $100,000**
> **IRA #2 $ 50,000**
>
> **$50,000 ÷ 32.5 = $1,538**

"There are several approved methods to compute this amount. In this instance, I used a table from IRS publication #590 for the life expectancy years of 32.5 for joint life and last survivor. As you can see, it's a simple calculation. I also wanted to demonstrate that you can choose from which IRA you want to take the funds, assuming you have more than one. I caution people to use this technique only if necessary, because it will deplete your retirement account, and it may cause a tax burden should the person obtain another job."

Joe frowned. "Does this mean that if I want to withdraw from my IRA before I'm $59\frac{1}{2}$. I'm stuck with having to take the same amount for the rest of my life?" he asked.

Anne replied with a smile. "I was waiting for that question. No, Joe, because there is an exception within the exception. The taxpayer can change the annuity election after 5 years if he or she has attained age of $59\frac{1}{2}$."

"Let's look at two quick examples. Two taxpayers, ages 50 and 58, have been laid off. 'Permanently restructured' is the expression companies now use. Each needs some additional income in order to survive. Both elect the annuity method to withdraw from their rollover IRAs in order to avoid the 10% penalty. Both must wait at least 5 years before making a change in the amount. The 50-year-old taxpayer has to wait until age $59\frac{1}{2}$ before making any change. The 58–year-old taxpayer must wait until age 63, or 5 years, before making any change."

"Won't that reduce their ability to live during retirement?" Mary asked.

"Yes, it will. That's why retirement funds should only be tapped if they are the last source of funds. But sometimes that's the only choice you have. Perhaps you were just been laid off and need money to live on. Keep in mind, the untouched balance is still compounding, tax-deferred, so this early withdrawal of a portion of your retirement accumulation may not be that severe. A person has to run the numbers and decide if this is the best way to obtain the funds needed. Once they have met the minimum requirement, the amount of their withdrawal can be anything from zero to the total value," she continued. "There are, of course, regulations describing how to calculate the minimum pay-outs at age $70\frac{1}{2}$ which apply to all withdrawals from tax deferred savings except annuities. Withdrawals from non-qualified annuities are not subject to IRS regulations and can be delayed according to the contract with the insurance company until age 80 or age 85."

"Please explain what minimum distribution means and how to calculate it"? Joe asked.

"This distribution refers to the minimum amount that must be withdrawn, and it is often called the 'rule of $70\frac{1}{2}$.' Actually, it takes effect on April 1st of the calendar year following the year that you reach $70\frac{1}{2}$. This first distribution counts toward the preceding year since a second distribution must be taken before December 31st of that same year," Anne said. "Don't you wonder sometimes why the laws have to be so complex? Distributions for each year, after the year the owner becomes $70\frac{1}{2}$, must be made by December 31st of that year," she continued. "After $70\frac{1}{2}$ you are required to begin withdrawing your entire interest on an annual basis over whichever of the following is applicable:

♦ "Your life expectancy,
♦ "Your life expectancy and that of your beneficiary,
♦ "Life expectancy of your beneficiary.

"Even here, the participant is given several choices for distribution. He or she can select a term-certain method or the amount can be recalculated each year. The recalculation stretches out the payments," Anne explained.

"Why?" Mary asked.

"Mortality tables are used to make the calculation," Anne answered. "Mortality tables display the probability of dying at a certain age. The older a person is, the better his chances to live even longer. Therefore, the more we age, the more likely it is that we will need to stretch our retirement assets farther."

"This seems like the best bet," Jim remarked. "Why would anyone choose the term-certain method?" he questioned.

"If only the decision were that simple," Anne commented, as she turned the question over in her mind. "Planners and others disagree over which strategy is best. Many argue that the recalculation method is the best choice, because it spreads out the payment over a longer period, thus making more money available. Using the term-certain method, a couple with the participant, age 70, and a spouse, age 67, would reduce the balance by $\frac{1}{22}$ in year one, $\frac{1}{21}$ in year two, $\frac{1}{20}$ in year three, etc. Let us suppose that the same couple chose the recalculation method. Based on the tables, they can spread their distribution over 22 years and they take $\frac{1}{22}$ of the balance in year one. Then they recalculate in year two based on their age at that time and they take $\frac{1}{21.2}$ of the balance. Mathematically, less money is withdrawn in the early years," Anne explained.

"Slow down, Anne—you are losing us," Joe interjected.

"Perhaps an illustration of the table would help clarify things," Anne said, as she drew the following illustration on the chartboard. "Using the recalculation method, the couple each year divides the balance in their IRA by the figure in the joint life column. Now," Anne suggested, "consider what would happen should the spouse die in two years at age 68? The survivor would have to use a different table, that of a single life expectancy at age 72, in which case the remaining years would drop from 20.3 to just 14.6. Consequently, the amount to be withdrawn increases dramatically. Not only is the balance drawn down quicker, but also any withdrawal is taxable.

"All this bother just to defer a few dollars a while longer?" Anne asked. "I don't think it's worth it, but that choice should be up to the retiree. The retiree needs to understand that if he doesn't make a choice, one is made for him. That's right! The recalculation method is automatic unless the term-certain method is selected before the $70\frac{1}{2}$ distribution begins."

Participant		Spouse	
Age	Single Life	Age	Joint life
70	16	67	22.0
71	15.3	68	21.2
72	14.6	69	20.3
73	13.9	70	19.4
74	13.2	71	18.6

"What happens when the survivor dies?" Mary questioned.

"Under the recalculation method the remaining balance goes to the estate the year following death and is immediately taxable. Under the term-certain method, the money would be paid to the estate over the remaining life, and thus prolong the tax-deferred benefit."

"This stuff really is complicated, isn't it?" Mary remarked.

"Yes, it is," Anne agreed. "That's why the retirees need to understand and make their decision sooner rather than later. And there's more. Failure to begin, and to continue, the minimum distributions can cost 50% of the difference between the required distribution and the actual distribution. That's right—50%! Uncle Sam really is serious," she said for emphasis. The Secretary of the Treasury may waive the tax if the shortfall was due to a reasonable error and steps were taken to remedy the situation. There are other distribution regulations covering the death of an IRA owner, which we will discuss later."

"That 50% penalty is enough to get my attention," Jim quipped.

"It's even harsher when you consider that the penalty is non-deductible and you still have to pay income tax on the distribution," Anne remarked.

"How many other ways can Uncle Sam tax my retirement savings?" asked Jim.

"Well, Jim, there are also excess contribution taxes and excess distribution taxes," Anne answered. "Except for a rollover, there is a non-deductible excise tax of 6% on IRA contributions over the $2,000 limit plus the spousal allowance. However, if you can get it out before the April 15th filing date for that tax year, then you don't pay the excise tax. Also, as I mentioned, there is an excise tax on excess distributions," she continued. "This 15% excise tax is imposed on all distributions received in a taxable year in excess of the *greater* of $150,000 or $112,500 indexed for inflation.

"This is the *too much tax*," Anne explained. "It covers distributions from qualified plans, IRAs, SEPs and 403(b) tax-deferred annuities. This 'too much' tax regulation extends to excess retirement accumulations left in a person's estate, a fact that most people don't realize. To calculate the excess aggregation of the remaining balances, present values are used. The difference between this calculated amount and the retirement amount is also subject to a 15% excise tax." Anne went on with her explanation, "Often people trying to hoard money in tax-deferred accounts overlook this very severe tax. Because this excise tax is non-deductible, income taxes are paid on the full amount of the distribution and estate taxes, if applicable. The 'too much' tax is an excise penalty levied in addition to other taxes," she emphasized. "Often, in these instances, there is little left for the heirs. Between $59\frac{1}{2}$ and $70\frac{1}{2}$, you can withdraw as much as you like, subject to the 'too much' tax limits. This is your window of opportunity to level your IRA balance and avoid the 15% over accumulation excise tax."

"Anne, you mentioned distribution regulations at the time of our deaths. What are these?" Mary asked.

"Let me illustrate these in the form of a matrix," Anne answered. "They are complex since the rules differ depending upon beneficiaries and upon whether distributions have begun.

"These regulations can be confusing," Anne said. "Please take a copy of the matrix. You may find it to be beneficial."

"You talked about income taxes on distributions. How are these calculated for mutual funds?" Joe asked.

"First, let's discuss IRAs and then taxable mutual funds," Anne answered. "Generally, all distributions from IRAs are taxed at the ordinary tax rate. However, you may have contributed amounts on which taxes have already been paid. These are called **nondeductible contributions** and they come back to you tax-free. Uncle Sam treats all individual retirement plans and distributions from those plans as though they were one plan. The total account balance used in any calculations is the sum of all the IRAs owned by an individual at 12/31 of the previous year."

Named beneficiary	Death occurs before distributions start	Death occurs after distributions start
Spouse	◆ Can treat as own IRA ◆ Can be paid over spouse's lifetime ◆ Does not have to start until the decedent would have been 70 1/2	◆ Paid over life expectancy in effect at time of death ◆ Spouse can recalculate life expectancy annually ◆ Or spouse can treat as own IRA
Beneficiary other than spouse	◆ Paid over life-expectancy of beneficiary ◆ Life-expectancy recalculation not permitted ◆ Payments must begin within one year of date of death	◆ Paid over life expectancy in effect at time of death ◆ Life-expectancy recalculation not permitted
Estate	◆ Entire account must be paid within 5 years of death	◆ Paid over period in effect at date of death ◆ Life-expectancy recalculation not permitted

Anne continued. "The nontaxable portion of a distribution is a ratio of the unrecovered, nondeductible contribution to the total account balance, times the amount actually distributed. In simple English, you are allowed to subtract from each annual distribution a portion which represents your nondeductible contribution. The formula looks like this."

$$\frac{\text{Unrecovered nondeductible contributions}}{\text{Total of all IRA balances}} \quad \text{X} \quad \textbf{Annual amount distributed}$$

"Suppose you invested $40,000 in after-tax dollars into your IRA over 20 years ($2,000 annually). Let us also assume that, over this time period, you also paid taxes on an additional $20,000 from dividends and capital gains that you reinvested, which brings your total basis up to

$60,000. At the same time, your IRA appreciated to $100,000. Now you wish to withdraw $15,000. You would calculate the nontaxable portion as follows:"

$$\frac{\$\ 60,000}{\$100,000} = 60\% \text{ times (X) } \$15,000 = \$9,000$$

"You have already paid taxes on $9,000 of your $15,000 distribution. If an owner dies prior to recovering his or her full investment, the unrecovered portion, on which taxes have been previously paid, becomes a deduction on the final year's tax return.

"Now, Joe, I'll answer your question on taxable mutual funds," Anne said. "Taxable mutual funds carry their own level of complexity," she emphasized. "When you make a withdrawal from a taxable mutual fund, you must first establish a cost basis in order to determine the capital gain or loss on your redeemed shares. If you had only one contribution, then that is your cost basis. Most people not only make numerous contributions, but also they reinvest dividends and capital gains income," Anne explained. "Even though these people do not receive a check from the fund, they do receive a 1099-DIV which is reported as taxable income on their annual 1040 return. These reinvested dividends and capital gains add to the cost basis and, unless considered, will result in tax being paid on the same dollars twice. To avoid double taxation, the cost of the newly acquired shares must be added to the cost of the originally purchased shares. Remember, Uncle Sam only keeps records of the contributions and withdrawals, but not of the reinvestments in between. That's up to you," she emphasized. There are three methods of calculating the cost basis for your shares.

"**Average cost**—The total cost of all shares, including reinvested dividends and capital gains, is divided by the total number of shares in the account. If you elect the average share method for a mutual fund, you must continue to use it for that fund. This becomes complicated because of the short-term/long-term nature of some of the shares. IRS publication #564, *Mutual Fund Distributions*, covers this choice in depth.

"**First in, first out (FIFO)**—Shares are deemed sold in the order in which they were purchased, which means the cost bases of the oldest shares still available are used first.

"**Specific share identification**—Under this method, the mutual fund has to confirm your instructions to sell particular shares. This approach is useful if you wish to minimize or maximize the gain or loss by using either the high-cost or low-cost method.

"**High cost**—Shares with the highest cost per share are sold first. This results in the lowest gain or maximum loss.

"**Low cost**—Shares with the lowest cost per share are sold first. This results in a greater gain or minimum loss."

"How in the world is anyone supposed to keep sufficient records to support their cost basis?" Jim asked.

"Most mutual funds, with the exception of money market funds and retirement plans, report this information to you when you redeem or exchange shares, " Anne replied. "However, prior to the year-end that you make a redemption, you have to make a choice of methods, or, in most cases, the average cost method will become the default. Even with this service, I recommend that you keep each year-end statement from each mutual fund as a permanent record just in case.

"To further add to the complexity, a return of capital is a nontaxable distribution and reduces the cost basis. This instance may occur when the fund distributes more income and gains than it has actually earned during its fiscal year. Any return of capital will be reported by the fund. Also, some mutual funds pay taxes to a foreign country," Anne commented. "Those funds with greater than 50% of their assets invested in foreign securities may elect to pass through this tax deduction, thereby giving the investor an opportunity to claim a foreign tax or deduction. Finally," she said, "the IRS requires mutual funds to withhold a percentage if the taxpayer identification is incorrect or missing.

"As you can see, retirees have to face the growing complexity involving distribution from their retirement savings. It pays to keep good records. Often the services of a financial planner or competent tax advisor is required, even for the well-informed," Anne emphasized. "Even professionals may not provide all the answers. Investment laws are extremely complex and few professionals understand them," she stated. "For example, there are some financial planners who advise clients to name their 'estate' as the beneficiary for their IRA or qualified plan. In a community property state such as Washington, this may be courting disaster. If the non-working spouse dies first, the worker may be faced with an estate-tax issue with the funds still locked up in his or her qualified plan. If the plan allows, the worker may borrow the money. If a withdrawal is required, the worker may be faced with the 10% 'too early' tax that we discussed earlier. Keep in mind, the withdrawal is subject to income tax. What a mess!"

"What would happen if we had a living trust? Is it Okay for that to be the beneficiary?" Joe asked.

"I would stay away from naming the living trust as the beneficiary," Anne answered. "Keep in mind that actuarial tables are used to calculate the remaining years of life for the survivor. A living trust has zero-life expectancy. Therefore, with a distribution to a living trust, the funds become immediately subject to income tax. Since the distribution will go immediately to the survivor and not be subject to probate, there is no reason to run them through the trust."

"What should a retiree do?" Mary asked.

"I advise people to name their spouse, if still living, as the beneficiary. Then I recommend that the spouse roll over the dollars into his or her own IRA to protect the tax-deferral advantage."

"What other advice do you have for us regarding distributions from IRAs and qualified plans?" Joe asked.

Anne thought for a few moments. "I think I covered almost everything. Throughout our discussions I used the term 'use a sharp pencil.' That applies here as well."

"I think there is one thing we can all agree on," Jim commented. "The tax laws are too complicated."

"Amen to that," Joe agreed.

"Thank you, Anne," Mary said for all. "We came to gather a little knowledge, and we are leaving with a lot. But don't worry, your efforts were not in vain. Jim and I will be back to use your expertise."

Chapter 18

"Better three hours too soon, than one minute too late."
Shakespeare

Long-term-care insurance issues

Another seminar at the senior center

Once again, while visiting their mother, Joe and Mary attended a seminar at the senior center. Following a delicious lunch, Marie and her two children settled back to listen to the speaker.

"I don't know why we didn't start attending these sooner," Mary remarked to her mother. "The food is excellent and we learn something every time we come. Thank you for inviting us. This subject is very important."

The topic of the day was long-term-care insurance. Gordon Snyder, the speaker, sells long-term-care insurance. Prior to entering the sales field, Gordon had been a consultant on issues involving aging for a number of years.

"Wasn't that lunch great!" Gordon began. "Before I begin my presentation on long-term-care, I just want to take a few minutes and comment on some related topics that I discussed with several of you during lunch.

"For the record, diseases such as Parkinson's and osteoporosis are not normal consequences of aging," Gordon stated. "Aging is not a disease. However, the majority of folks over the age of 65 do have one or more chronic health conditions for which they take medication. Diseases that occur among seniors are typically chronic and drugs are often prescribed to modify their effects," he continued. "The cost of drugs is a tremendous expense for our older generation. Of the $900 billion cost of healthcare, drugs account for only about $75 billion. Nevertheless, this is small comfort to the elderly among the population, because of their high usage of drugs.

"Why do seniors take a disproportionate share of drugs?" Gordon asked, and then answered his own question.

- "To help them deal with chronic diseases.
- "To satisfy the habit of taking drugs for anxiety, sleeplessness, depression. We are a drug-oriented society.
- "To calm the concerns of family members about their loved one's discomforts.
- "To get attention, even to the point of paying for a visit by a nurse to administer a drug.

Gordon continued, "Obviously, people should only take drugs on a regular basis to help with chronic diseases. Today, with the constant influence of advertising, people are taking too much medication. Drugs are not candy and misuse is quite common among older people—who are most likely to experience severe reactions."

"What should we do when our doctors prescribe the drugs?" a participant asked.

"First of all, make certain that your doctor knows what other medications you are taking, who prescribed them and what they were prescribed for," Gordon answered. "A friend of mine, who sells prescription drugs, recently reviewed the medications that his eighty-five year old mother was taking. Several of those drugs counteracted each other. He visited the doctor, along with his mother. After hearing my friend's explanation, the doctor agreed to a trial period where the dosage of several prescriptions was reduced. Today, my friend's mother is taking far fewer prescriptions without any ill effects.

"I didn't mean to get off on a tangent regarding medications, but it is a topic that you should know about. Let me summarize the steps you can take to ensure you are receiving the correct medication and the correct dosage," Gordon said.

1. "Understand what medication, even the over-the-counter kind, you are taking and why you are taking it. Annually, review, with your doctor, all the medications you are taking.

2. "Ask your doctor or pharmacist about the side-affects. Drugs often become toxic or ineffective when used in conjunction with other drugs.

3. "Make sure a prescribed drug is taken on schedule in the proper dosage. For example, if it is prescribed to be taken with meals, then take it with your meals.

4. "Alert family members to follow up with the caregiver about the patient's reaction to any medication administered."

Gordon ended his side-trip discussion with the following admonishment, *"We are responsible for our own health—not our family, not our physician, not our healthcare provider—us!"*

He began his discussion on long-term-care with the following statement, *"The purpose of a long-term-care policy is to protect your assets. If you don't have any assets to protect, then you probably don't need a long-term-care policy."* Gordon continued, "A nationally syndicated columnist, Jane Bryant Quinn, offered the following rules of thumb, which I will paraphrase: *If your estate is below a $100,000, Medicaid will pay when your money runs out. For an estate over $1,000,000, you can afford to pay. Between $100,000 and $1,000,000 you need to consider a long-term-care policy if you wish to preserve an estate for your heirs."*

"Before we go into long-term-care policies, let us spend a little time understanding **Medicaid**," Gordon said. *"Medicaid is different than Medicare.* Medicaid is a program that is partially funded by the federal government and partially by your state. It pays for medical services *including nursing home care.* To be eligible for Medicaid, your income and assets cannot exceed specific levels—this is called a financial means test. In addition, you must need skilled care provided by a skilled-care facility, such as a nursing home. Limits are set by law for both your income and your assets, which are called resources. Assets or resources consist of real estate, bank accounts, stocks, etc. Income includes Social Security, VA benefits, pensions, wages, etc. The limits differ by state, with complex rules regarding the amount of income which can be retained to support the community spouse. The state limits also describe assets or resources which are exempt. These exemptions are far too detailed to go into at this session, but include assets such as your home, if it is occupied by a Medicaid recipient, a spouse, or others under certain circumstances."

"How do we find out about what is payable in our state?" a participant asked.

"Most states provide some type of support for citizens needing to understand their eligibility rights," Gordon answered. "Call your state department of social services or your state insurance commissioner for the correct parties in your state."

"I have friends who have given all their money away in order to qualify for Medicaid. How does this work?" asked another participant.

"There are financial strategies called **spend-downs** which can assist people to qualify for Medicaid," Gordon answered. "Simply stated, the spend-down strategy involves transferring (gifting) your assets, so they will not be available to pay for nursing-home care. This type of planning consists of converting countable resources into exempt resources. For example, cash is a countable resource, while your residence is an exempt resource. Paying off your mortgage with surplus cash will change the status of the asset from available to exempt."

"Is that legal?" asked the same person.

"The laws that apply to this type of planning are constantly changing. The **Omnibus Budget Reconciliation Act of 1993 (OBRA)** did more than just tax the rich. It also made gifts to trusts and other individuals less attractive as a spend-down strategy. States are now required to recover from the Medicaid recipient's *estate* any long-term-care funds paid. Assets that may be recovered by the state include transfers to individuals during the 36 months prior to the receipt of Medicaid. A transfer to a trust has to take place 50 months prior to applying for Medicaid. As you can see, a spend-down strategy needs to be initiated long in advance to be effective. You need competent legal help for the type of financial planning that Medicaid requires. At a minimum, I urge you to look in the Yellow Pages® for attorneys who specialize in **elder law**."

"Suppose I'm one of those people with assets in-between the one hundred thousand and a million that you referred to. What do I do regarding long-term-care," Mary asked.

"Thank you for that question, because it leads into my next topic," Gordon answered. "Those changes in the law that I referred to make long-term-care insurance a more attractive alternative. For the long-term-care (LTC) portion of my talk, I'm going to cover 5 major topics.

1. "Statistics and Facts,
2. "Due diligence on policies,
3. "LTC policy considerations,
4. "What the future may hold for LTC insurance,
5. "Due diligence on facility selection.

"The paper I've passed out covers the definition of terms I use in LTC (appendix 18a)," the speaker explained. "When we speak of LTC we are speaking of a continuum of coverage and costs." Gordon then drew the following on the blackboard.

> ♦ **Home healthcare**
> ♦ **Chore services**
> ♦ **Nutritional services**

Affordable by most

> ♦ **Adult foster homes**
> ♦ **Adult daycare**
> ♦ **Respite care**
> ♦ **Retirement Communities**

Affordable by many

> ♦ **Skilled nursing care**

Affordable by few

"Often we hear concerns about LTC being a financial nightmare for senior citizens," Gordon continued. "These concerns are attributable to the fear of having to enter a skilled nursing facility. It's true that LTC in a nursing home will be a financial nightmare for *some* senior citizens. Please note my emphasis on the word 'some.'

"Statistics from a mid-1980s study[6] compiled by the National Center for Health Statistics (NCHS) tell us that almost one-half of all the people over 65 will enter a nursing home. Further, these studies tell us that the average stay will be about three years," Gordon explained.

"Many opportunistic insurance sales people combine those two pieces of data to convince people to buy their LTC insurance products.

"Rather than concentrate on the population of nursing homes, we should consider the flow through nursing homes," Gordon continued. "About 50% of the people who enter a nursing home reside there less than three months. About 75% of the patients reside for less than a year and only about 10% for periods that substantially exceed three years. Furthermore," he continued, "the percentages representing short stays will increase significantly, because hospitals are using nursing homes as their extended care facilities, due to Medicare's payment schedule.

"From a volatility view point, the statistics tell us that LTC in a nursing home is not going to be a major event for most seniors. However, for those seniors unfortunate enough to spend a significant amount of time in a nursing home, it could be a major financial disaster. Nevertheless, even though our senior population is growing, there will be fewer facilities available on the average. Medicaid is paying most of the cost of nursing homes. Since states pay the bulk of Medicaid, many states, in order to cut costs, have declared a moratorium on issuing licenses for new nursing-home facilities. Other States—particularly those in the west, with tax reducing initiative processes—face even greater constraints. The question that begs to be answered is, '*who* is most likely to need nursing home care?'" Gordon asked for emphasis.

"When we study the current population in nursing homes, we learn that the following are the most likely to require extended stays in a nursing home:

♦ "Elderly, single men and women,
♦ "Women, particularly those over the age of 75,
♦ "People who are chronic substance abusers, and
♦ "Those who are mentally incompetent.

"It seems obvious that LTC insurance will be more useful in the future, if only to enable people to get into a nursing home," Gordon rationalized. "No one can predict his or her need for LTC insurance."

---

[6]*LongTterm-Care Insurance: Who Really Needs It?* R. A. Gilmour, Journal of Financial Planning. p.144, October 1992.

"How can we tell if long-term-care insurance would be appropriate," a participant asked.

Gordon answered. "Ask yourself the following questions to help you make your own decision:

♦ "Are you single and lacking a support system?
♦ "Can you afford the premiums without significantly impacting your quality of life?
♦ "Is it feasible or practical for you to move in with your adult children?
♦ "Is it feasible for an child or grandchild to move in with you and become your caregiver?
♦ "Is there a history of Alzheimer's disease or other debilitating illness in your family?
♦ "Do you have assets that you wish to leave to your beneficiaries?
♦ "Are you the type of person who needs the security of long-term-care insurance?

"When you answer these questions, you are close to an answering the question of whether or not you need long-term insurance," Gordon commented.

"Let us suppose I answer affirmatively to most of those questions. What do I do next?" Mary asked.

"Should you choose to purchase this protection, your next step is to proceed with diligence. **Due diligence** is a term that attorneys and CPAs use referring to the attention and care, expected and required before making decisions of importance. There are many policies on the market and they all vary. You need to study to understand the coverage and cost appropriate for you.

"All policies should:

1. "Guarantee renewability;*
2. "Pay benefits for Alzheimer's, senility and dementia;*
3. "Provide benefits for all care levels; skilled, intermediate, custodial; and benefits should include home health care;
4. "Have inflation protection indexed to the Consumer Price Index;
5. "Have a free look period of at least 30 days;*
6. "Pay illness and accidents on the same basis;* and
7. "Waive premiums and continue coverage while you are collecting benefits."
      *These are required for all policies sold in Washington State and a number of other states.

> **Don't focus solely on cost, decide what coverage you need, then price it out.**

"When you choose a policy, *consider* the following," Gordon said.

♦ "Look at the financial strength of the company. It may be decades before the policy pays off. A company rated as a 'best buy' by a magazine was out of business before the article was even published. Companies such as A.M. Best, Moody's Investor Service, Standard & Poors rate insurance companies according to their financial strength. Their reports may be available at your public library or you may need to pay a small fee to the company for a rating.

◆ "Even though the premium will not increase because you grow older, the premium will increase because of a rise in the costs of the issuing company.

◆ "The inflation protection for some policies is a fixed rate, usually 5% compounded annually. I prefer one that is indexed to the Consumer Price Index (CPI). This enables your policy to maintain its relationship to the level of your spendable dollars that you planned to use for long-term-care.

◆ "Have your premium paid automatically by your bank. This will prevent a policy lapse if you overlook a payment.

◆ "Choose a daily benefit rate that will cover nursing homes and home healthcare in your location. This rate should be based on the *net amount* you need. To calculate the rate, subtract other income—such as Social Security—to arrive at the net amount needed.

◆ "For the maximum number of years, the lifetime benefit is the most costly. Many experts consider a four-year policy as being a safe bet, five years may give you a cushion.

◆ "Be aware of and understand the gatekeepers in your policy. **Gatekeepers** are those provisions which usually begin with 'if or when' statements. They are the restrictions that must be satisfied before the policy will pay out. For example, avoid a policy with a gatekeeper that requires three days' prior hospitalization before it will pay nursing home benefits.

◆ "Remember, if you are married, the policy covers only one person."

"Is there anything else we should consider?" Mary asked.

"Today, there are life insurance policies which prepay death benefits," Gordon answered. "Riders can be written into *universal life policies* to enable the owner and insured to use the benefits while they are alive to pay for nursing home costs. The unused portion of the death benefit will go to the designated beneficiary. You may want to enter into an agreement with some relative—a grandchild perhaps," he continued. "The relative could earn an interest in your residence in exchange for home custodial care. With today's high cost of home ownership, a live-in situation may be a very viable option. For those few couples in the audience in their forties and fifties, I suggest that you add two to three years of nursing home care expense to your retirement planning. Then begin to fund those expenses today."

"What does the *future* hold for governmental assistance?" Joe asked.

"If anyone here is clairvoyant, please come on up and help," Gordon said, with a smile. "Here is my guess! There may be some type of LTC assistance in the future health care reform acts, and it will be very stringent. Any future LTC assistance will probably take the form of tax incentives.

"In addition:

♦ "It will not be entitlement-based, as is Social Security. Therefore, there will be some type of means-test, such as income or resources.

♦ "It will probably cover only those with very severe disabilities.

♦ "It will not cover custodial care.

♦ "The receiver of the benefits will cost-share with the government.

♦ "The use of LTC insurance will be encouraged through tax incentives such as deductibility of premiums and non-taxable benefits.

♦ "Tax credits may be a tool used as an incentive for insurance.

♦ "It may take a decade or longer before these changes become a reality, but I believe they are coming.

"Even today, some states are entering into partnerships with LTC policy owners. The policy covers the basics, the state pays any excess over the policy coverage. I hope that general discussion helps you understand the policies themselves. My final topic deals with selecting a nursing home or assisted living facility," Gordon said, as he changed the subject.

1. "Always visit the facility. Don't merely stop at the office. Go back to the care units. Get a feel of what it's like to live there.

2. "Visit the patients and stay to observe the daily routine. Appreciate the interaction between the patients and the staff. How quickly does the staff respond?

3. "Take part in the structured activities. Are the activities meaningful or just initiated to take up time. Are all patients involved or do many just sit in the hallways?

4. "Check out the facility's state inspection report. This report is available upon request if the facility is Medicaid-qualified. If they refuse to show it to you, be wary.

5. "Check out costs, and ask to see several bills for typical patients. This investigation enables you to come to grips with the extra charges.

6. "Ask the friends and relatives of people who reside in the facility about their experiences.

"That concludes the formal part of the program. I hope it assists those of you who may be interested in long-term insurance and nursing-home issues. Thank you for being so attentive. I'll be around for a while to answer any of your questions," Gordon said, as he concluded his remarks.

"One of the rules of our senior center is to keep these seminars as brief as possible," Marie explained to her children.

Joe and Mary were overwhelmed with the scope of the seminar and the knowledge of the speaker. "Maybe we should join a senior club," Joe whispered to Mary as they took Marie home.

Sometime later on

The next time the Keanes met with Dan Palmer, their insurance professional, Mary asked about long-term-care insurance. Mary explained how she attended a seminar with her mother and what she learned about LTC insurance.

Dan thanked Mary for sharing what she had learned from the seminar.

"Over the last decade, there has been a change in attitude toward long-term-care. This fundamental change has made LTC an extension of healthcare. You can see this in the change in the role of hospitals. Many hospitals own skilled-care facilities. They are run as an extension of the medical care. I believe in a balanced approach to LTC coverage. People are all over the lot on this topic," Dan illustrated his position:

No insurance	**Reasonable and balanced**	**Too much insurance**

"Mary, the speaker at the seminar concentrated on the analytical side of LTC insurance. There is another side that pertains to the emotional needs of people. A friend of mine describes these two positions as those issues decided by the brain and those issues decided by the heart. As people grow older, they often feel a need to know that they will be taken care of without being dependent. Long-term-care can be considered a disability-insurance policy, which, in my opinion, should be part of most people's portfolios. It becomes a question of how much can you afford to spend out of your pocket for long-term-care insurance without sacrificing the financial independence of the healthy spouse. Anything exceeding this amount should be covered by long-term-care insurance. Most people can afford, some out-of-pocket spending toward their own or their spouse's long-term-care. The more they can afford the less LTC insurance is required.

"Let me give you an illustration," Dan said. "A friend's father suffered a stroke several years ago. He did not have any LTC insurance. The stroke cost the family a lot of money, forcing them to cut down on their expenditures. Even though the father recovered physically, to about an 85% level of pre-stroke ability, he never recovered emotionally. This loss of control over the family's living standard led him to a deep depression. In the family's view, he died of depression. Sadly, while taking care of him, his wife began taking complex medications which led to complications resulting in a decline in her own health. These kinds of experiences fuel my belief that even those with a lower-than-average income can afford some type of LTC insurance. It's not just the institutionalized person that suffers financially; it's the whole family."

"I hear you," Jim responded. "Your example illustrated how a major catastrophe can harm people who cannot afford to pay their own way."

"You are absolutely correct," Dan responded. He then communicated his belief that the Keanes had sufficient resources to pay for any LTC that may be required, and therefore, did not recommend that they purchase a policy. When Jim asked about his mother-in-law's need for coverage, Dan explained that the speaker at the seminar was correct when he told the attendees that the purpose of LTC insurance is to preserve assets. "If your mother-in-law doesn't have any assets to preserve, then she doesn't need long-term-care insurance," he said.

"However, as I explained earlier, she may have an emotional reason, such as peace of mind, to have some type of LTC insurance. In my business I come across *four types of people who purchase long-term-care insurance*:

1. "In the first category, I include people who want to minimize any type of risk. These people include LTC insurance in the same category as auto insurance and liability insurance. They think of it as a weapon they want in their arsenal, even if they never use it. It's a peace-of-mind issue. They view it as a blank check which will help pay some of the bills.

2. "The second type is very conservative with their funds. You might call them frugal people who have saved sufficiently for that rainy day and now are afraid to enjoy the fruits of their savings. The protection afforded by a LTC insurance policy often allows them the freedom to enjoy the bounty they have been hoarding.

3. "The third type is similar to the first. They are like business people who feel that insurance is part of the overhead. It's simply good business to have such a policy. This type of person may liken it to a safety valve on a water line. It's something they can't do business without. Long-term-care insurance provides the financial foundation that this type of person depends on.

4. "The fourth type is the analytical person. Perhaps they have some genetic defect in their family, such as Alzheimer's. They compute the odds of it affecting them and compare it to the potential cost of being without LTC insurance.

"The speaker at the seminar seemed to relegate the lower-income people to Medicaid," Dan continued. "Currently, Medicaid will cover long-term-care for people who qualify on an asset and income test. In other words, a person must be poor or considered to be poor to be eligible. This may fit your mother-in-law's situation."

"I hear you, Dan," Jim acknowledged, "but, even if that were the case, I can't believe that Mary will allow her mother to be put into a nursing home as a Medicaid patient. We have heard too many horror stories of the difference in treatment between a full-paying patient and a Medicaid patient."

"You've got that right," Mary said. "We would take my mother in with us before letting her become a Medicaid patient."

Nursing Home Issues

What are the chances that someone will need to enter a nursing home?

Based on 1985 statistics from the U.S. Dept. of Health, about 55% of the residents of nursing homes were females over age 75.

Though 45% of all people over 65 will require nursing home care, only about 10% are in a nursing home over 3 years.

These statistics come from various 1985 National Nursing Home Surveys.[7]

"Many people think the way you do, Mary," Dan commented. "However, they often fail to take into consideration the tremendous responsibility that being a caregiver entails. It can become a major disruption in family life, particularly when the patient's needs are very technical or physically demanding. Furthermore, caregiving can require more time than a family can afford to give. I hear about families that no longer can take a vacation because of the special needs for a live-in relative. When you are in this situation, a nursing home becomes a very attractive alternative.

"While we are on the subject of nursing homes, let us begin with a short explanation of nursing home issues," Dan said, as he turned to write on the chartboard in his office.

Pointing to the chartboard, Dan continued. "We know that your mother-in law is the right sex and in the right age bracket to utilize a nursing home for an extended period of time. However, we must keep in mind that most patients spend less than one year in a nursing home."

"What does a long-term policy cost and what does a nursing home cost?" asked Jim.

"Currently, in this locale, nursing homes cost between $23,000 and $36,000 annually," Dan answered. "LTC policies vary according to the terms and what they include. For a person your mother-in-law's age I have seen LTC policies as low as $3,000 and other policies that range between $8,000 and $15,000 annually. Compare that cost to a policy costing only $2,300 to $3,800 annually to cover both you and Mary. The younger you are when the policy is purchased, the cheaper it will be."

"Since I can afford it, it may be cheaper just to pay the difference between her retirement income and what it would be to buy her a policy," Jim said.

---

[7]*Ibid.*

"Because we have to explain all this to Joe and Betty, if we were to purchase a policy, what should it include?" Mary asked.

Again, writing on the chartboard, Dan listed the LTC coverage considerations.

"These are the minimum requirements that I look for in a long-term-care policy," Dan replied to Mary's question as he wrote down the requirements.

"How about people the age of Joe and Betty. Should they be concerned about purchasing long-term-care insurance?" Mary asked.

Minimum LTC Coverage

1) **Inflation rider**
2) **Benefit period of 3 to 4 years**
3) **Policy with a waiting period of 60 to 90 days**
4) **Coverage to include:**

   - **Skilled**
   - **Intermediate**
   - **Custodial care**

5) **Qualified when unable to perform certain activities of daily living**
6) **A financially strong insurance company**

"Look at LTC insurance as an elevator in a very tall building where the floors correlate with the age of the person getting on the elevator. People can get on at any floor if they are eligible. However, the higher the floor number, the greater the cost and the more crowded the elevator because, the higher the floor, the older the person, the greater the risk. When the elevator becomes too crowded, only the healthy can get on. In my experience, I have found that 15 to 20% of the people who apply for LTC are ineligible. For example, if a person has high blood pressure, that condition has to be controllable."

"What do you suggest?" Jim inquired.

"Get on the elevator while LTC is still affordable," Dan advised. "There are three triggers that impact the cost of LTC insurance. The first is the inability to perform activities of daily living. The second is cognitive impairments, such as Alzheimer's. The third is medical necessity. Though these triggers are not directly related to the aging process, they are more prevalent in older people. People who purchase LTC in their 40s and 50s will pay less over time than if they waited until their 70s. Part of the reason is level premiums. The price of LTC is designed to stay level."

"What about the cost increases that the seminar lecturer spoke of?" Mary asked.

"The person who gave the seminar may have implied that LTC will increase as other costs, e.g. nursing home costs, go up. That's an over-simplification, LTC cost increases often have little relationship to increases in nursing-home costs. If you have a policy that pays $100 a day, it will pay only $100 a day, regardless of the increase in the nursing-home cost. Reasons for cost increases lie in other areas. For example, in Washington, an insurance company has to pay out a prescribed percentage of what it takes in or it has to change the rate that it charges. Sometimes the change makes the rate go up, sometimes down. Let's say the current percentage is 65% for every one dollar of revenue. That means, if the cost of the product over a specific time-frame is less than 65%, then the rate goes down; if greater, the rate goes up. This finding is based on the cost structure for all participants and not based on age. Therefore, the rate for all participants in a class changes at the same time," Dan answered.

"It seems to me that insurance companies still charge too much," Mary complained.

"Almost everyone believes that," Dan said smiling. "But, keep in mind something that I alluded to when I discussed life insurance. The insurance company needs sufficient reserves to provide benefits for all those insured. Think of it as a buffet luncheon at a fancy wedding. To be a quality affair, the last person served should have the same variety of selection as the first person. An insurance company cannot afford to spend all its reserves on the first people who need long-term-care, leaving little or none for those policyholders who come later. How each company does this is called **underwriting**, the process by which a company accepts applications for insurance."

"Dan, once again, you have given us more information than we can handle. Just tell me. Should Joe and Betty get long-term-care insurance now?" Jim asked, then continued. "They want to wait until the current political process has cleared. At that time, they believe they will have a better picture of how LTC fits into the national health care system."

"Though Joe and Betty have time on their side, I would recommend they stop in and get an estimate of the cost of LTC at their respective ages. Then they can make their decision using facts and data and not just emotion," Dan answered. "Both of them should consider getting a policy. It's not like the old life insurance days where the husband was the only person insured. Like many professionals, I recommend that an average male consider a coverage of three years, while a female should consider five-year coverage. A person's current health is the single most important element of LTC cost. A person's health is variable and accidents do happen even to the young. As we age, we are often affected by our past lifestyles, such as by old sports injuries suffered when we were young. Being young and healthy is a real asset, but people have to understand that the elevator is always going up," Dan counseled. "People often overlook the delay in getting coverage," he continued. "For example, consider a recovering alcoholic. This health impediment may delay his receiving coverage for up to five years, depending on the underwriting guidelines of the company."

"What happens if a person uses up all his LTC insurance?" Mary questioned.

"Today, many policies have a restoration of benefits clause with no limit to the number of restorations," Dan answered. "Benefits are restored to their original level if the person sufficiently recovers and no longer needs LTC. For example, a client is now covered for a second stroke, which hasn't always been the case. These policy improvements are responses to the emphasis on healthcare issues. Policies have changed for the better in the past few years."

"Is one company's policy better than another?" Jim asked.

"Most company's policies are similar in a quality sense. Competition and a better-educated public, plus the advocacy of state insurance commissioners, drive them to improve their product. The differences lie more in the desires of the buyer."

"As a businessman, I am always looking for a means to lower the cost. What are some of the means to do this with LTC insurance?" Jim demanded.

"We discussed earlier the tradeoffs of coverage versus costs," Dan answered. "These tradeoffs are still valid. The quantitative decisions, as with any other insurance policy, all have an impact on the cost.

- ◆ "Should the applicant take a higher deductible to lower the cost?
- ◆ "Should he insure for the institutional portion only and anticipate paying for homecare on his own?
- ◆ "Should he pay for a set amount and finance inflation out of his own pocket?

"To get information regarding what type of policy a person may want to purchase, he needs to compare the variety of options offered."

"Doesn't everyone need inflation protection?" Jim asked.

"I would take into consideration the person's age," Dan answered. "It may take up to 10 years for the value of the protection to offset the cost. If that's the case, let's look at some rules of thumb. A person acquiring a policy before age 65 should consider compound inflation protection indexed by the Consumer Price Index (CPI). From age 65 to about 73, think about deferring your option. By deferring your option, you wait until the company offers a window of opportunity to add inflation protection, then make a decision. At age 74, a fixed interest rate may suffice and, after age 78, I would not bother with inflation protection. I offer these guidelines because CPI inflation protection is priced at the attained age. Older people run the risk of being priced out of the policy eventually. As I said earlier, look for a reasonable balance."

"I suppose that you will even argue about having your premium automatically paid by a bank?" Mary said with a smile.

"Where would you get that idea? I never argue," Dan answered with a smile. "I merely point out options. Generally, payment by a bank entails monthly premiums, which is more expensive than annual premium payments. Insurance companies often will reinstate policies, even if they have lapsed, if the reason is due to oversight on the part of older policyholders. Speaking of options, being an old life insurance salesperson, I know of some life insurance products that will pay the face value over a period of time, usually five years, should one enter a nursing home. If one needs to use the proceeds for LTC, they are available. If not, it's still a life insurance policy. Furthermore, any balance not paid as a nursing home cost will still be paid to the beneficiaries in the form of life insurance. Before you jump in and purchase one of these policies, you should first determine if you need any life insurance and you should understand any 'gatekeepers' inherent in the policy."

Mary and Jim thanked Dan for his candid advice. Their knowledge of how to cope with the future had been expanded again.

On the ride home

"I hope you took a lot of notes, because it was more than I could handle let alone explain to Joe," Jim remarked to Mary as they drove home.

"It seems to me that we have heard two sides of the same issue," Mary answered. "The seminar speaker, Gordon, took an analytical approach, while Dan, in my view, took a more pragmatic approach. You and I will have to sort out the issues and decide what is best for us. A good professional like Dan will be able to help us mold a product that is reasonable and balanced for Mom. We'll explain the issues to Joe and Betty as best we can and let them make their own decision."

Chapter 19

"Trusting that the legal process will take care of you is the worst assumption you can make. But you can emerge from divorce with your fair share."
Kathleen Miller, author of
Fair Share Divorce for Women

Issues for the divorced and single person

On a ride home from Marie's house

After another visit with their Mother, Mary and Joe were driving home toward Tacoma on Interstate I-5. During the ride they discussed how content their mother seemed to be as a single person.

"When I contrast her to my sister-in-law, Joyce, I see how fortunate Mom really is," Mary remarked.

Joyce Reagan is Jim Keane's younger sister. Joyce has been divorced for several years, and lives alone. Unfortunately, Joyce's husband suffered a series of business losses during the time of their separation and subsequent divorce. Joyce had to return to the work force in her late fifties. Her degree in fine arts was no help in finding employment at this stage of her life. Her financial outlook is bleak, and she needs to stay gainfully employed for the remainder of her life.

"Joyce is about 59, isn't she?" Joe inquired, but he continued on not allowing Mary a chance to respond. "She is just a little too young to begin receiving Social Security, but she is lucky that she was married for over 10 years. That qualifies her for Social Security based on George's earnings whether or not he retires. Don't forget to tell her not to remarry until she is past 62, or she will lose out on getting the distribution based on George's earnings."

"After the experience that Joyce went through, I doubt that a second marriage is on her mind," Mary responded.

"I've heard you and Jim talking on occasion about Joyce's problems, but what did happen?" Joe asked.

"Some very strange things took place," Mary answered. "As you may recall, George was employed by the Power Company for years before he decided he could make more money in his own business. The marital problems were long-standing, but came to a head about the time he went off on his own. They went through a long separation, and it took two or three years before the divorce was final. Unfortunately, during this time, George's business went from bad to worse. His capital was tied up in non-liquid real estate which decreased in value causing him to plough in more money to salvage what he could. Don't misunderstand, George wasn't a bad person. He simply got in over his head, and Joyce suffered as a result."

"I always liked George," Joe confessed. "But what effect did George's business have on Joyce?"

"For starters, he could not pay his income taxes. He and Joyce had continued filing a joint return during the time they were separated. The Internal Revenue Service (IRS) has now come after Joyce to collect. It's a real mess. Apparently, a spouse is jointly and severally liable for any taxes owed plus the interest and penalties. That means she is liable for taxes owed by her spouse, if the spouse can't pay. Joyce had George sign an indemnification agreement before she agreed to sign a joint return. Even that document didn't cut any ice with the IRS. Joyce's only recourse was to hire an attorney and sue George, which, of course, she couldn't afford. But, that's all water over the dam now," Mary sighed. "The message for all the Joyces of the world, whose marriages may be in trouble, is not to sign any joint tax returns unless they understand the full consequences."

She continued. "That's the not only mess with the IRS that George got himself into. George didn't pay the capital gains on the house, because he intended to purchase another house within two years. Unfortunately, about four years passed between the time he moved out and the time he purchased another house. Good old George didn't realize that a section of the tax code states that he must have the right to reside in the house in order to qualify. I think it says that he must *physically occupy and live* in the dwelling. He moved out when they separated. Even though he continued paying the mortgage, that didn't count with the IRS. So he owes taxes, plus interest and penalty for not paying the capital gains tax when due."

"Wasn't George old enough to qualify for the **Internal Revenue Code section 121**, $125,000 one-time exclusion of gain on the sale of the house?" Joe asked.

"He had to be, because Joyce qualified," Mary answered. "I really don't know the whole story, but George served as his own counsel and you know the trouble that can cause."

"The war stories on the use of the capital gains exclusion are horrendous," Joe agreed. "One of the guys I work with has really gotten worked over by the IRS. This guy had sold his house and, along with his spouse, filed the form to indicate that they intended to purchase a new house within two years. Subsequent to that, they got divorced. He later purchased a new residence while his former spouse did not. Now he owes the IRS for taxes on one-half of the gain recognized by his former spouse, plus interest and penalties."

"I don't understand that. Why should he have to pay her share of the taxes?" Mary asked.

"It's that 'joint and several' liability that you were talking about. You see, it works both ways," Joe stated. "Women aren't the only ones to get hurt in a divorce. Enough about capital gains; it's a mess and only an expert tax authority can understand it. Let's get back to Joyce's problems."

"Joyce's problems only got worse," Mary said. "George not only didn't have the money to pay the IRS, he didn't have the money to pay Joyce's **maintenance** (sometimes called **alimony**) either. She was getting a guaranteed minimum income that would disappear if she earned above a set amount which she has yet to reach. George is now considering bankruptcy."

"I understand, from listening to the guys at work, that a new law, **The Bankruptcy Reform Act of 1994**, would allow maintenance to continue during bankruptcy and even have a greater priority than past due taxes," Joe said. "By the way, did you realize that less than 5% of divorce cases today provide some sort of alimony or maintenance."

"That's a lot less than I thought," Mary answered. "In Joyce's case, because she was married so long and since she didn't have an outside career, she had to get some alimony just to survive. Where I work, the biggest discussion on alimony concerns the tax deduction. Did you realize that alimony or maintenance is deductible by the payer and taxable to the recipient?" Mary asked, then continued. "One of my co-workers forgot to take the tax impact into account when she made settlement and had to reduce her standard of living. I learned from that incident to always calculate the after-tax consequences. This co-worker was also ticked off when she learned that the alimony payments must stop should she die. Now she tells everyone that her 'ex' is praying for her demise to reduce his obligation. Divorce can be a real learning experience."

Mary then returned to the discussion to Joyce's problems. "Not only was the capital gains exclusion a problem, but so was George's defined contribution pension plan. By the time of the divorce settlement, the underlying assets of the plan had significantly decreased in value. Joyce's attorney wisely provided in the agreement that Joyce receive a fixed percent of the pension. In addition, her attorney also got George to agree to a dollar amount below which Joyce's share could not fall. George had to make up the difference between the plan's decrease in value and the agreed amount. It's been over two years, and he still owes on that portion."

"Joyce is very fortunate to have a brother who could afford to help her out or she would be in deep trouble," Joe said. "Could Joyce roll over her share of the pension?" he asked.

"Yes, she could, and she did," Mary answered. "Even though Joyce was less than $59\frac{1}{2}$ at the time, the law allows a one-time opportunity to take a cash distribution without a 10% penalty. Income taxes would have been due immediately, so she decided to direct-transfer roll-over the distribution into an IRA. However, she soon learned, that in order to survive, she had to take a distribution from her IRA."

"Since she disclaimed her one-time opportunity, did she have to pay the 10% penalty in addition to income taxes?" Joe asked.

"Since she was still under $59\frac{1}{2}$, she took the distribution in the form of an annuity to avoid the 10% penalty," Mary answered. "Now she has to continue receiving the distribution until at least five years are up, whether she needs it or not."

"Did you learn all this just from Joyce's experiences?" Joe asked.

"Most of it. It's surprising how much you delve into things when one of your own is involved. I also learned a lot from the women that I work with. Did you know that unless you get a **QDRO**, that's a **qualified domestic relations order,** the working spouse can deal directly with his or her pension administrators without the other spouse's involvement. That happened to a friend at work. Theirs was a bitterly contested divorce. My friend never knew where she stood until the divorce was final. Fortunately, for her, the law would not allow her husband to change her beneficiary status without her signing off and having her signature notarized," Mary emphasized.

"Are divorce settlements the major topic of conversation at your work?" Joe asked jokingly.

"It seems that way," Mary answered. "Over half the women in my office have gone through a divorce, and many are living on their own. They all tell me how their asset valuation and distribution can be really complex. A person would think that when living in a community property state, such as Washington, all assets would be cut down the middle. However, it's not done that way. Assets are not distributed equally, they are distributed equitably."

"What's the difference?" Joe asked.

"It seems assets are distributed using an equitable standard for which there is no legal definition," Mary answered. "It's all up to courts, case law, precedents and the skills of your attorney to determine exactly what this means. If a person has to go to court, then the burden of proof is on each spouse to present the relevant facts. An experienced attorney can obtain additional value for his or her client. For example, a business license, an advanced degree, or a potential high income may be shared with the wife if she helped her spouse attain it. The length of the marriage, the age of the spouse, their standard of living during marriage, even the health of the spouse are all relevant factors to be considered."

"What advice do you offer all these women when they ask you about your experiences?" Joe quipped.

"Very funny! I don't offer advice, I just listen. There are some serious issues here," Mary stated. "For example, how do you value the homemaker role? The chores of raising the children, running the household, worrying about the health and nutrition of the family all on an allowance from the husband. I remember how Jim's mom viewed her job as a money-saver. As Jim tells it, the loose change in the cookie jar was all that kept the family from going hungry. The biggest crime, in my opinion, is that women work all those years in the home and don't even wind up with a pension."

"I agree that women are hurt more than men when a marriage breaks up. However, they are not the only ones hurt," Joe said. "A fellow I work with went through a divorce several years ago. He seems to have fared pretty well, but he still hurts, financially as well as emotionally. His income has increased, but only because he took on more work, including a part-time job. He has traded time for dollars. He no longer feels as financially secure as he did during his marriage. Consequently, all his major purchases, such as a car, have to last him a long time. He once planned to retire in his fifties, now he thinks it will be 65 or older. I like his comment, 'When you divide the whole, it is not equal to its parts.'"

"If people who have relatively amicable divorces have difficulties, how do people with difficult situations work through the issues of divorce?" Mary asked.

"My co-worker used an uncommon process called **mediation**," Joe answered. "In this process, a trained and neutral third party helps the parties reach their own resolutions by:

♦ "Identifying the issues.

♦ "Identifying the differences between the couple.

♦ "Reviewing all pertinent information, including any legal documents.

♦ "Developing a quantitative and qualitative agreement.

♦ "Presenting the agreement to the couple for their acceptance."

"The mediation approach is confidential and not binding, which seems to me to be an objective way to settle the financial issues involved in divorce," Joe said.

"How do you know if the mediator is unbiased or if the spouse is honest in describing his assets?" Mary asked. "I recall reading recently where a husband lied, on the stand, about the value of a payment he received for a piece of land. He got caught in the lie, but there must be plenty of husbands who get away with it."

"One can never be certain about any person's bias, however, the mediator should be an expert and either a financial planner or a person with a strong financial background," Joe answered, ignoring the implication that husbands are the ones always at fault. "Organizations such as the **American Arbitration Association**, a non-profit organization, train people to be mediators. As a professional, a mediator ought to be unbiased. If there is an issue, then he or she should back out of the case immediately. Many experts suggest that even the agreement from the mediation should be taken to an outside attorney before signing."

Joe tried to change the subject. "Enough with the divorce stuff. What other issues affect single women, and why is it tougher on them than on single men?"

"There is little difference between individual men and women who are both in the same economic circumstances," Mary conceded. "Overall, it's tougher on females because there are significantly more women than men in economic trouble. It's not a problem. It's a crisis. I read where women over the age of sixty-five have only 60% of the income level of men. Only half as many women receive pensions as men and those pensions, on average, are 50% less. Did you realize that Social Security is the only source of income for most older women?"

"Please believe me I'm not against women. I have a wife and a daughter, not to mention a darling sister," Joe responded with a smile. "I just want to point out that your statistics represent history. Things are different now!"

"I agree that things seem to be changing," Mary conceded. "But even if they are, did you stop and consider that it will take over half a century before the scales even begin to come into balance. Think about all the women you have met:

♦ "Who have low-paying jobs.
♦ "Who change jobs frequently.
♦ "Who take time off to care for children.
♦ "Who don't know a thing about their family finances.

"For all of these reasons, it will take a long time to wash through the system," Mary continued. "The tax law maybe neutral, but the impact isn't. Pension plans, in large companies such as mine and even medium-sized companies like yours, are designed to reward the long-term workers. Women are not long-term workers. Many women, housewives in particular, don't even know how their husband's pension plan works or even if they have one."

"If it were in your power to correct all this, what would you propose?" Joe asked.

"I just wish that all married people and single ones as well put together a financial plan, similar to the plans both our families developed," Mary answered. "Just developing a statement of financial position and a cash flow budget will increase their ability to understand finances one thousand percent. I also wish that, when couples suspect a marriage is in trouble, they get professional help. Unfortunately professional advice is really only available if you have money— that's the dilemma. Joyce would have avoided a lot of trauma had she received professional advice."

"What do you recommend for issues other than divorce?" Joe asked.

"Just the other day, we discussed this at work," Mary answered. "The first thing we agreed upon is that women, in particular, need financial education.

1. "Make money management a part of the primary education system. People, especially women, need to grow up learning how to handle their finances and how the stock market works.

2. "Make all pension plans portable. Allow people to take their benefits with them from job to job and have the ability to invest those benefits while they take a break from their working career.

3. "Lower the vesting schedule. Make all employees fully vested following their first anniversary date. That way, more people will save for their retirement.

4. "Broaden the coverage. Following their first anniversary, include all part-time workers and older workers who are now excluded."

"I can't argue with those suggestions, particularly about part-time workers. Two of my employees already job-share," Joe acknowledged. "When one of them is out on vacation or sick, the other works a longer week. The company benefits, because there is always an experienced person on the desk. I agree—even though they are part-time—that each of them should get a pension based on their income. In relative terms, it won't cost the company any more than having one person on the job. Furthermore, I think job-sharing will be the wave of the future. As I've been trying to point out on this entire trip, there are issues here other than gender," he continued. "The same problems affect either spouse. Both spouses need the solutions that you stated and more. Education in and of itself isn't sufficient unless it answers specific needs. For example, a divorcee may have to make a decision on whether to keep the house or sell it. We talked earlier about the complexity of the capital gains exclusion on that decision. In addition, a divorcee needs to be able to calculate the impact of the mortgage, property taxes and maintenance of a home on a single salary. Should he or she take the house or sell it and take the proceeds? It's a major decision either way."

"There are lots of other issues as well," Mary interjected. "Do divorcees realize that they should change their *wills* and *durable powers of attorney*? Do divorcees realize that they should check to see who is the beneficiary on their *life insurance policies*? Do divorcees realize that both parties are responsible for debt on jointly-owned credit cards? And furthermore, do they realize if one defaults, creditors will try to collect from the other? In the end, both will get black marks on their credit."

"If we keep going, we will have solved all the problems of the divorcee," Joe said smiling, as he interrupted. "I agree that, overall, single women face a greater financial crisis than single men. However, whether male or female, married or single, people need to gain control. The first step in the process of gaining control involves education."

"I'm glad that I finally convinced you," Mary said. "Can we change the subject? Did you realize that..."

The conversation turned to a lighter subject for the remainder of the trip.

Chapter 20

*"Your estate assets will be distributed
either according to your wishes or
according to the laws of your state.
The choice is up to you."*

The basics of distributing estate assets

At the Meehans

Over breakfast, about a week after the seminar on long-term care at Marie's senior center, Joe mumbled to Betty. "I forgot to tell you. Tomorrow, I'm going with Jim and Mary to see their new attorney. They are going to discuss their will and other estate issues. I'm sorry that you have to work and won't be able to join us."

"Don't feel sorry for me. I don't like talking about estates. Furthermore, I don't understand why they need a new attorney," Betty remarked. "Why don't they just use the attorneys from Jim's business?"

"They wanted someone who specializes in wills, trusts and estate planning. This guy comes highly recommended, and you know Jim and Mary. They want nothing but the best. I'm only attending in order to be another pair of eyes and ears."

Tom Vincent, the attorney, was a specialist in wills, trusts and estate planning and a partner at Moots, Craft, Waples, and McGinty, one of the largest law firms in Tacoma, and near where both the Meehans and Keanes live. In addition to being an attorney, Tom has a masters degree in taxation and is a CPA. He had taught both law and tax courses at the University of Puget Sound, a local university, and is considered to be an expert in his field.

At office of Moots, Craft, Waples and McGinty

Tom welcomed the Keanes and Joe. He offered them coffee, as he invited them into his conference room. Tom's downtown office overlooked lower Puget Sound. On this day, the snow-covered, jagged peaks of the Olympic Mountains were framed between the blue waters of the sound and the cloudless sky. Joe wondered how a person could get any work done with this view.

"Thank you, Jim, for sending over your current will. You are absolutely correct. It does need to be revised, considering it was drafted prior to 1982. Because of the antiquated wording, you and Mary would not have been able to take full advantage of the **unified tax credit**, which I will explain momentarily. As a rule of thumb, people should have their wills reviewed about every five years."

At this point, Mary set the parameters for the visit. "Both Jim and I, as well as Joe and his wife, have been in the process of trying to understand all we can about our financial planning. Please don't limit yourself to just a will. Explain all about estate planning so we can feel comfortable about our decisions."

"Thank you, Mary. That's a good point. Let me start out at the big picture level and then digress to the details. Estate planning has three specific purposes or phases. For estate planning to be successful, many of the strategies that we will discuss have to be implemented while the person is competent and still alive. There are some elections that a personal representative can take after the death of the estate owner, but these are limited. Let's look at the three phases:

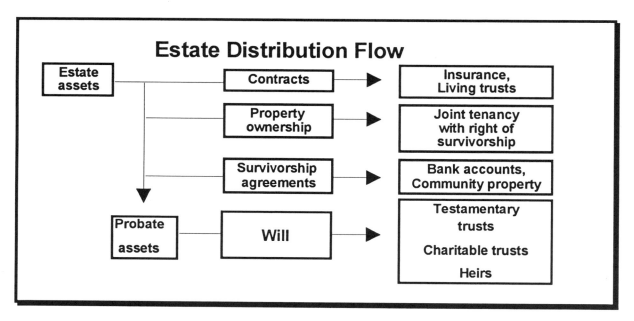

1. "Asset Distribution—The intent of this phase is to insure that the decedent's assets are in a legal condition to be distributed according to his or her wishes.

2. "Estate Taxation—The intent of this phase is to minimize the estate taxes payable.

3. "Liquidity—In this phase we determine if the estate has sufficient liquidity to pay the taxes due as well as other expenses.

"This chart is an illustration of the process flow for the asset distribution. Think of it as a diagram depicting the flow through time. When someone dies, the first impact on their assets comes from any contracts or survivorship agreements. As you can see from the flow chart, the transfer of this type of asset takes place before probate; therefore, they are not included as part of the probate assets."

"Why isn't there a phase about avoiding probate?" asked Jim, "I know I don't want to go through probate and pay all those taxes."

"Let's first understand the probate process," Tom answered. "Then we'll tackle the tax issue." Beginning with the probate process, Tom explained the asset distribution phase of estate planning. "**Probate** is a legal process to validate and carry out the instructions in your will. Probate has nothing to do with estate taxation. The court first assures itself that your will is valid. Then your personal representative, called an executor, is appointed to do the following:

♦ "Inventory and value your assets,
♦ "Notify your creditors,
♦ "Pay your bills, including your final tax returns, and
♦ "Distribute the remainder of your estate, according to your wishes.

"When you think about it, all of these functions need be performed," Tom pointed out. "The State of Washington doesn't know Jim Keane from Joe Meehan, nor can it know Jim's final wishes. It needs a method to determine if Jim Keane's will represents Jim's final wishes. Probate is that legal method.

"Many horror stories abound about the probate process," Tom continued. "Often you will hear about some famous person who had to pay a lot of estate taxes because of probate. These are examples from other states and sometimes from generations ago. The people relating these stories most probably want to sell you a product, such as a living trust, which we will cover later. Remember, probate has nothing to do with how much estate tax you will pay."

> **Probate has nothing to do with estate taxation.**

"You folks are very fortunate because you reside in Washington State. Washington State is one of the more enlightened states regarding probate. Our state has an innovative, non-intervention process. This means that your executor, once appointed, can complete the process before having to go back to court. In some instances, the entire process can be accomplished by mail."

"But what about the cost and the lengthy process?" countered Jim.

"The cost of probate depends upon your state of residence. In California and some other states, the attorney's fees are based on a percentage (%) of the total estate assets. On the other hand, in states such as Washington, attorneys charge by the hour. The law in these states requires fair and reasonable compensation for services supplied."

"Let us consider a concept I call the *hard costs of probate*. The hard costs are the costs associated directly with the probate process itself. In a survey of **estate attorneys**[8] conducted here in Tacoma, Washington, the consensus was that the hard costs of probate are in the neighborhood of $1,000. Costs other than the hard costs of probate depend on the complexity of the estate that's being probated. Items such as filing a federal and state estate tax return or the sale and distribution of assets add to the final bill. However, these costs are incurred whether or not an estate is probated.

"Since you currently reside in a state in which attorneys charge by the hour, you can significantly reduce the costs of administrating a will by keeping good records. I am delighted to see how well you are prepared. The record keeping tool, *Thoughtful Suggestions for My Loved Ones* (Appendix 1b), will save you considerable attorney's time, and time costs money.

"Regarding the *length of time involved in probate*, the process itself, without any complications, takes about four months. Other factors cause the delay, most notably:

♦ "Selling assets.

♦ "Paying off creditors.

♦ "Awaiting the approval of IRS on the final tax returns. This event may be the most lengthy of the entire process. The executor or the trustee may be held *personally* responsible to pay any excess of estate taxes that exceed the remaining assets, if they have distributed any assets. Therefore, even an estate utilizing a living trust should await this approval before distributing all of the assets.

♦ "Keeping poor records."

"Do we have to wait until all that takes place before we get any money out of the estate?" Mary asked.

"That depends on the tax and creditor circumstances," Tom said. "As we saw on our chart, a number of items avoid probate and go directly to the beneficiaries. These items include insurance policies, tax-deferred retirement plans and assets held as joint tenancy with right of survivorship and, of course, assets under a community property agreement. We will discuss all of these in some detail. In addition to the above items, an executor, at his or her discretion, can begin to release assets as early as day two."

"That's a relief," said Mary.

At this point Joe asked. "Can't people go down to probate court and look up your records? I've read where competitors can learn all about your debts, bank accounts and everything."

---

[8]James F. Smith, *Who Will You Trust*, Financial Planning Bulletin, Issue #2, 1993.

"On the first point you are correct," Tom answered. "Probate is a public process, and people can review your files. What a probate court requires depends on the laws of that particular state. For example, in the State of Washington, inventories of estate assets with dollar values need not be filed in court. Consequently, the values of probate assets need not be found in your public files. Furthermore, they require only a slight degree of disclosure. If you were to look at some of the probate files, you will find such vague descriptions as bank accounts, stock and bonds and other assets describing one asset type. Not very revealing, is it?"

"Doesn't probate invite **will contests**?" Joe asked.

"That's a question that I hear often," Tom replied. "Probate doesn't invite will contests. Disgruntled heirs contest wills. Will contests are messy. However, they are rare and they rarely succeed. Significant burdens must be overcome to overturn a will. Generally, the court will try to resolve the issue at the first hearing. The openness of the probate process does makes it easier to contest a will than to initiate a court action against a trust. But, in reality, both a will and a living trust can be challenged. If you purposely wish to disinherit someone, work with your attorney to structure your will or trust to minimize a successful court challenge. Always obtain professional legal advice from an attorney who is competent."

"Are there any advantages to probate? In other words, why would anyone want to go through it if he or she didn't have to?" Mary asked.

"There are several advantages, and the most important involves creditors' claims," Tom stated. "If creditors fail to respond within a specified time after notification has been published, their claims are barred forever. This could be critical for the heirs of someone like a surgeon, who has the potential of being sued years after an operation has been performed. Some attorneys consider it to be malpractice if such a vulnerable estate is not probated.

"Think of how your heirs may feel if someone files a claim against your estate years after it has been settled. Now, consider how they would feel if the claim is found to be valid. Not a pleasant thought," Tom remarked.

"I would feel more comfortable if our estate went through probate," Mary whispered to Jim.

"The second advantage involves the safeguards offered by an open court forum. I recall the case of a professional businessman who returned to his hometown for his mother's funeral. During this period of grief, he found out that his elderly mother's caregiver was the trustee for her living trust. This caregiver stripped the trust of all the assets. The businessman currently has a court case pending, which will probably take years. When the assets are distributed the involvement of knowledgeable professionals can be a significant advantage.

"Finally, many people with living trusts do not fully fund the trust by *assigning all of their assets* to the trust. A **pourover will** is a necessary addition to a living trust to cover this type of contingency. Triggering the pourover will, of course, leads to probate—which is the very thing that the living trust was established to avoid. Keep in mind that assets can flow into an estate after a person dies. Consider a case where the person dies as a result of an auto accident which pays off after death. A person should plan for all contingencies.

"A **living trust** offers an advantage in that the assets in the trust avoid probate. A living trust is established during a person's lifetime and generally can be amended or revoked. To be effective, the trust must be funded. That is, assets must be titled in the name of the trust. As a major advantage, in my estimation, a living trust offers the capability to have the trust's assets managed should the owner become incompetent," Tom continued. "For example, the assets may include stocks and bonds which need to be traded. Initially, most people serve as their own trustees and manage the assets of the trust. A successor trustee is named in the agreement to serve when the grantors become incompetent or die. Even a professional trustee, such as a bank trust department which charges for their services, can be named. Furthermore," he said, "living trusts are useful devices when a person owns real estate in another state. Having the trust may save the cost of an ancillary probate in that state and may save the need for an attorney in that state, as well.

"The assets in these living trusts *avoid probate*—providing some confidentiality," Tom continued.

"Finally, assets can be transferred very readily into a living trust, making it an excellent vehicle to transfer control of your assets. A living trust may be just the solution for a widow or widower without any immediate family," Tom pointed out. "On the down side, setting up a living trust can be more expensive than a will, even if you include the hard costs of two probates. As I said earlier, this is dependent on the state of residence." He continued, "Normally, I recommend a living trust only to people as they enter their later years. At this stage of their lives, their assets are ordinarily set and rarely change. Waiting until your twilight years often avoids the nuisance of titling assets in the name of the trust which are subsequently sold or exchanged. It takes a good bit of discipline to ensure that *all assets* are transferred and recorded in the name of the trust. If you fail to do this, portions of your estate will end up in probate anyhow."

"Aren't there ways to *avoid probate* other than having a living trust?" Joe asked.

In answering Joe's question, Tom again pointed to the illustrative drawing that he had made earlier. "Let us return to the asset distribution flow process. If you recall, I said that contracts, titling of property, and survivorship agreements avoid probate. They take precedence over wills because they are enacted before the probate process begins.

"A *life insurance policy* is an example of a contract—an agreement between the insurance company and the policy owner. The insurance company agrees to pay the face amount to the beneficiaries named in the policy in the event of the death of the insured. If the *estate* of the insured is named beneficiary, then the proceeds may become involved in the probate process."

"I want to draw a distinction between **probate assets** and **taxable estate assets**," Tom said. "Life insurance may be part of the asset base used to calculate estate taxes

> **Assets that avoid probate may still be taxable under estate tax laws.**

even though it avoids probate. We will cover this in greater depth when we talk about estate taxes.

"IRA proceeds, annuities and benefits from retirement plans are other examples of assets passing by contract.

"How you title your assets is very important," Tom advised.

"**Joint tenants with right of survivorship (JTw/ROS)** means that the property is owned jointly. Each tenant has an undivided interest in the entire property. When one tenant dies, the ownership passes by operation of law to the surviving tenants. The interest of the decedent is not a probatable asset. Often the principal residence is titled as jtw/ros. Non-spouses can also own property as jtw/ros. This can be an effective method of passing title to heirs. However, since the entire property is owned by both parties, any legal problems of one party can impact the ownership of the non-involved tenant. For example, a divorce proceeding concerning one of the owners of a firm can get awfully messy for the other owners."

"How about a joint bank account?" Mary asked. "I have one of those with my mother."

Tom answered. "It could depend on the particular state's law. Often these accounts are recognized as convenience accounts and not true joint tenancies. If there is a good and trusting relationship between the parent and his or her children, I strongly recommend them."

"I'm confused about the community property agreement on the illustration. Don't we live in a community property state? What good is the agreement?" Jim asked.

"Washington is one of nine states whose property law originates from Spanish Law. The remaining states, called separate property states, base their property laws on the old English Common Law. A state favoring the Spanish version is called a community property state where basically one-half of the property is deemed to belong to each spouse and can be bequeathed in their will. Some property, such as gifts and inheritances can be maintained as separate property. Bear in mind, many community property decisions are based on case law rather than statute, and vary from state to state. In addition to being a community property state, which applies to the ownership issue, Washington State recognizes a community property agreement.

"The community property agreement generally provides for the transfer of all separate and community property to the surviving spouse. That is why I call it a **survivorship agreement**. The transfer generally includes property received both before and after the agreement is signed. For example, it will include an inheritance received subsequently. The agreement takes precedence over the terms of your will and enables that property to avoid the first probate. *Now here's a caution*. If you desire a specific asset, a potential inheritance, for example, to go to a specific person other than your surviving spouse, the community property agreement will impede your wishes. You may have to change the title to a jtw/ros or gift it directly after obtaining your spouse's consent in each case."

"How can I provide for Mary and still assure that my property gets distributed the way I want? What happens if Mary doesn't go along with my wishes and gives the property to someone else?" Jim asked. "In other words, how do I keep control?"

"That's a great question," Tom answered. "Any assets that are probated are distributed according to the terms of your will. Therefore, if you will your assets to Mary and Mary survives you, it is now her choice to distribute those assets according to her wishes. However, thanks to **testamentary trusts** you can have your cake and eat it too. A testamentary trust is activated upon your death under the terms of your will. Let's discuss several.

"One type of testamentary trust is the **bypass trust**, often called a **credit trust** or a **B trust**. A bypass trust can provide a lifetime income to your surviving spouse, if needed. The income can also be allowed to accumulate. If necessary, the principal, called the corpus, can be invaded and used for maintenance of your spouse. After the death of your spouse, the remainder in the trust is distributed as you directed.

"A second type of trust often used is called a **qualified terminable interest trust,** or **QTIP** for short. This trust gives the surviving spouse the right to all the income from the trust for life. After the death of your spouse, the remainder in the trust will be distributed as you directed. Thus, control over the distribution of assets can continue even beyond the grave.

"My throat's getting a little dry. Let us take a break before we continue with the estate tax implications. Would any of you like some more coffee?" Tom asked.

Chapter 21

*"Two weeks of solid work on his estate may
be worth more to an executive than his
financial gains of the past 10 to 15 years."*
Joseph D. Coughlan
Price Waterhouse Review, Autumn 1966

How to preserve what you have accumulated

At Tom Vincent's office following a short break

After the group reassembled following the break, Tom continued with his explanation of estate planning and the Keanes, along with Joe Meehan, listened attentively.

"**Estate taxation** can be extremely expensive and most people need solid financial advice to avoid the many traps that exist," Tom cautioned. "Quite often, people would pay far less in estate taxes if they could visualize the tax savings offered by the various strategies."

"Why don't their attorneys explain the strategies when they prepare their wills?" asked Joe Meehan.

"There could be several reasons," Tom answered. "First of all, the attorney may not be a specialist in wills & trusts. Therefore, he or she may not be aware of some of the strategies. Secondly, the parties to the will may be unable or unwilling to tell their attorney the actual value of their estate. Remember, many people go to attorneys with whom they socialize and wish to keep such matters confidential. In other instances, they just never take the time to figure out how much they are worth and underestimate the amount when questioned. Also, additional wealth may have been accumulated after the will and estate plan were drawn up. As I said earlier to Jim and Mary, the law has changed since their will was drawn up. Should they die before getting it revised, they will lose an opportunity to save a considerable amount in estate taxes."

Tom continued. "Let us begin by understanding the nature of estate taxation. Beginning in 1977, the tax liability for lifetime gifts and distributions from estates has been governed under the **unified system**. A transfer during life falls under the gift tax provisions. Following death, the transfer falls under the estate tax provisions. In effect, the government said, 'It doesn't matter whether you give your estate away while you are still alive, or dispose of it at your death. The tax consequences will be the same.'

"Estate taxes begin at 37% of every dollar over $600,000 in your estate, and it very quickly gets progressively higher until the tax reaches 55% (see appendix 21a). As you can see, without proper planning, a sizable portion of what you worked all of your lives to accumulate will disappear in a flash. Remember, your estate assets consist of everything that you own at the time of your death. Since you reside in a **community property state**, this includes one-half of all community property. Estate assets consist of everything in which you have retained a legal interest."

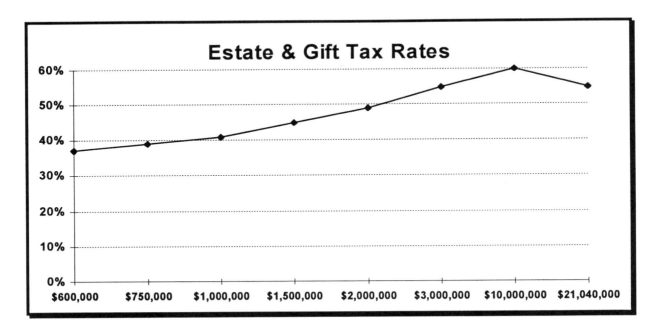

Tom continued. "For example, the total gross estate assets include the fair market value of:

♦ "Assets in a revocable living trust or other revocable trusts where you have the right to alter or amend terms or timing.

♦ "Revisionary property or property that can revert back to the owner should certain circumstances occur.

♦ "Life insurance in which you retain incidents of ownership. These incidents include life insurance gifted within 3 years of owner's death and the right to revoke or change the beneficiary.

♦ "Assets owned in joint tenancy of any type.

♦ "Assets owned outright, as separate property.

♦ "Outstanding accounts receivable, judgments or promissory notes which are owed at the time of death.

♦ "Wages owed to the decedent, vested rights in retirement plans, IRAs.

♦ "QTIP assets remaining in the estate of the second spouse to die, since these qualified for the marital deduction at the time of the first death."

Jim immediately jumped in. "Let me get this straight. Are you telling me that almost half of my estate can be taken away in taxes?"

"Yes," Tom answered. "Without proper planning, it can."

"Well, keep going, you've got my attention," Jim said.

"How is the estate tax calculated?" Joe asked.

"That's a question few people ask," Tom replied. "Here is a worksheet (appendix 21b) which will assist you in calculating your own estate tax. The first line of defense against excessive estate taxes is the **marital deduction**. Of course, you have to be married to take advantage of it," he said smiling. "The **Economic Recovery Act of 1981** allowed an unlimited marital deduction. This means that any property can be transferred or gifted, during life or via a will, to a spouse without any gift tax or estate tax liability."

"Are you telling us that all we have to do is give everything to our spouses to avoid estate taxes?" Joe asked.

"That approach, often called an *I-love-you-will*, avoids taxes only at the first death. At the second death, without a spouse, the tax comes due, unless the surviving spouse remarries and gifts everything to the new spouse. Furthermore, the tax bill may be higher since it is cumulative on the remaining estate. Remember what I illustrated about estate taxes being progressive?"

"Okay, I understand the marital deduction only delays paying the tax. It doesn't avoid it," Jim said.

"That's true for all estates over $600,000 in the current law," Tom added. "Let me describe how the **unified tax credit (UTC)** works. Each person, and that means each spouse, is entitled to shield from estate taxation an estate value of $600,000. They can do this during their life or at the time of their death."

"How can I shield my $600,000 if I should die first?" Mary asked. "Don't get your hopes up Jim—This is just a hypothetical question," she added with a smile.

"The by-pass trust is the simplest method you can use to ensure that both unified tax credits are utilized. We covered this trust during our discussion on asset distribution," Tom answered. "A by-pass trust, sometimes called a credit trust, is funded with property of the decedent up to the amount of the unified tax credit, which is currently $600,000. These trusts are usually set up testamentarily, which means they become effective upon your death and are triggered either by a will or by a living trust."

Jim jumped in. "I thought you told us that a living trust doesn't save on estate taxes?"

"This question is a point of confusion with many people. I said that probate has nothing to do with estate taxation. However, a by-pass trust can be embedded into either a will or a living trust. The by-pass trust not the living trust itself, helps reduce the estate tax. Income and growth of the assets in the by-pass trust can be either accumulated to be passed on to the heirs or used to support the spouse during his or her lifetime. This decision should be left to the discretion of the trustee and not made mandatory."

"Let me understand how this works," Jim said. "Do you mean that Mary could be the trustee and still get income from the trust?"

"Yes, that's a very distinct possibility," Tom said. "Mary can be the trustee and receive not only the income, but also the principal if necessary. However, to keep the trust assets out of her estate when she dies, the authority to distribute from the trust must be subject to what is termed an **ascertainable standard**. IRS recognizes the words *'to provide for the surviving spouse's health maintenance and support'* as an ascertainable standard. Earlier, we discussed how people quite often would pay far less in estate taxes if they could visualize the tax savings offered by the various strategies. Unfortunately, many wealthy people utilize the by-pass trust as their *only* estate-tax strategy. Earlier, we covered some of the reasons why this happens. It is important to remember that the by-pass trust will save the average wealthy person only about $250,000. While this is sizable, it is a savings of only 25% if the total tax is $1,000,000. Most wealthy people need to include additional strategies or they risk paying more estate taxes that they can legally and morally avoid."

"Before we go on to another topic, assuming your estate exceeds $600,000, is there an advantage to either gifting during life or waiting until you die before you distribute your assets?" Joe asked.

"Keep in mind that you are trying to minimize the over-all impact of estate taxes," Tom answered. "When you gift to someone other than your spouse during your lifetime, you avoid the estate tax on the gift and on any future appreciation of the gift."

"How does the **step-up in basis** impact whether you gift during life or through your will?" Joe asked.

"You've been doing some reading. That's a good point," Tom answered. "The basis of an asset is its original cost and any modifications to that cost. For example, deducting the depreciation of a business asset reduces its cost basis for income tax purposes. A step-up in basis on appreciated property to the current fair market value occurs at the date of death. In a community property state, a step-up in basis is received on the entire property. This situation is different from property owned jointly by a husband and wife in a separate property state where the step-up is received only for half the property."

Joe pressed on. "Shouldn't we wait until we die to take advantage of the step-up in basis?" he asked.

"You are correct in that a step-up in basis is applicable only to capital gains on property which is included in a person's estate assets for federal *estate tax* purposes," Tom answered. "This means that an *estate tax* may have to be paid on the property even if capital gains are avoided. A person needs to calculate the advantage of either paying a **capital gains tax** (currently 28%) and probably using a portion of their UTC early or avoiding the capital gains tax but paying estate taxes," he continued. "A second advantage of utilizing the UTC early, involves the giving away of assets which will appreciate. Not only is the estate tax saved on the UTC, it is also saved on the appreciation of the asset. This occurs because the asset is no longer included as an estate asset. There is no clear cut answer as to when a UTC should be used. You just have to use a sharp pencil," Tom concluded.

"I touched on using your **unified tax credit (UTC)** early, but there's another way to gift without impacting your unified tax credit. Each person is entitled to gift up to $10,000 annually to each person of his or her choice. A married couple, therefore, can gift $20,000 annually to each person. Jim, you and Mary have 3 children and 4 grandchildren. **Annual gifting** enables you to move $140,000 out of your estate each year without affecting your UTC. I do want to caution you about unintentional gifting. Earlier, Mary asked about a joint bank account. These accounts are not normally considered gifts. However, they could become gifts if the non-depositor makes withdrawals without the need to account to the depositor. A second example involves a joint tenancy with right of survivorship arrangement with a non-spouse. The death of one of the owners may trigger a taxable gift."

"How about **charitable gifts**? Do they work the same way?" Mary asked.

"Charitable gifts are similar in some respects to the unlimited marital deduction," Tom answered, "in that a charitable gift is not limited to a cap, such as the $10,000 amount. Any charitable gifts, whether distributed during life or in testament avoid estate taxes. There are also some current income tax advantages to consider. Not only does a current charitable gift avoid a future estate tax, it also is eligible for deduction against income taxes. The amount which qualifies for deduction varies depending upon whether the charity is a public or private charity. If you are contemplating a charitable gift, I recommend that you run it by your tax advisor.

"A **charitable remainder trust (CRT)** may enable you to have your cake and eat it too. In the correct circumstances it can be a very valuable tool to reduce both income and estate taxes. Let me illustrate how this type of trust works," Tom said. "A charitable remainder trust normally works best when:
1. "A person owns an asset with a low basis (original cost), which has significantly appreciated. The sale of this asset would normally trigger a capital gains tax, currently at a 28% tax rate. Stocks which were purchased at a low price but which have grown in value would be an example. Stock which cost $20 per share, and was held for at least a year, and is now worth $100 would have a capital gain of $80. The capital gains tax would be over $22 per share.

2. "The asset has a low current yield, and the owner(s) need current income. In our example, the stock may pay a low, or even no, dividend.
3. "The owners have an opportunity to invest in a stock of similar risk and growth characteristics which pays a higher dividend.
4. "The owners(s) are charitably minded.

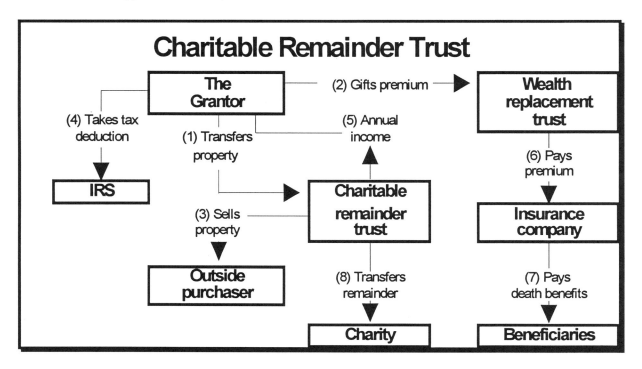

"To summarize what I have just said a charitable remainder trust (CRT) calls for the following characteristics. Owners with a valuable low basis asset, with a need for current income and with a charitable outlook. However, before you consider this approach, I strongly recommend that you use the services of a local attorney who specializes in such transactions."

"Which, of course, you are," Joe quipped.

"Of course," Tom said, smiling as he answered. Then he drew the flow diagram on the chartboard.

"Once the trust is established, the owner transfers the asset to the trust. Assets are transferred by changing the title to name the trust as the owner. When the assets are transferred, the owners receive a deduction on their current income tax return. Since it is a charitable trust, the trust can sell the asset and avoid the capital gain. The trust then invests the full value into something with a greater current income. The owner(s) receive the income for either life or for the term of the trust, while the remainder goes to the charity. Because the remainder goes to charity, it avoids any estate tax. In summary," Tom concluded. "A CRT avoids any capital gains tax, may provide higher current income, can provide a current tax deduction, can avoid estate tax and can help your favorite charity. Depending on how long the people live, they could conceivably recoup in income an amount significantly greater than their original contribution."

"What is this box called the **wealth replacement trust?**" Joe asked.

"That's just a fancy name for a life insurance trust," Tom answered. "I will explain this type of trust more fully when we cover liquidity. Basically, it's a trust set up to own one or more life insurance policies. The grantors—in this case, the asset owners—gift to the trust an amount to cover the premiums. Upon the death of the owners, the insurance company pays the face amount of the policy(ies) to the named beneficiaries. It is a mechanism to add back to the estate the amount it lost by virtue of the charitable gift, hence the name 'wealth replacement trust.' By the way, if it's set up correctly, the insurance proceeds also avoid the estate tax.

"There are other types of charitable trusts, such as a **charitable lead trust,**" Tom explained. "Here the process works in the reverse of a CRT. The annual income goes to the charity, and the remainder reverts back to the owner or estate, depending upon the terms of the trust. This is useful when the owner wants a particular asset to remain in the family, but also has a charitable bent. A charitable lead trust can be very complex. Therefore, it requires an attorney experienced in these structures."

"I hate to ask this question, since my mind can only hold so much, but are there any other ways to minimize estate taxes?" Mary asked.

"I agree with you, Mary—the mind can absorb only so much at a sitting. Let's take a short coffee break," Tom answered. "Then we will explore a few other options."

The group took a short break

Upon their return, Tom continued. "The simplest option is to spend the money. Then there is no estate to worry about. A second way to transfer wealth is to give away assets that have the potential to appreciate. The added appreciation, as well as the original value, are no longer in your estate, but only the original costs count as a gift. It make sense to use your UTC early.

"Often a person's residence is one of his or her most valuable assets. The concern that the residence may lack liquidity is another problem, but we will save that for later. Is there a way to use our residence while we are living and still remove its value from our estate at a reasonable cost?" Tom asked, and then answered. "One method of use involves a **grantor retained interest trust (GRIT).** The residence is transferred into the trust. The parents live in the residence for the term of the trust. Only a fraction of the value, which is calculated using a revisionary interest table published by IRS, is used to represent the value of the gift. Neither the value of the residence nor any appreciation from the time of the transfer is included as an estate asset."

"What happens if I live longer than the term of the trust?" Jim Keane asked.

"Let us look at both alternatives," Tom answered. "If you should die before the term of the trust expires, then the asset reverts to your estate. You have gained nothing. On the other hand, you have lost nothing. Should you outlive the term of the trust, the house then becomes the property of whomever you named in the trust document. You then have the choice to either move or rent from the new owners."

"How about if I change my mind and want to sell the house before I die?" Jim asked.

"The residential GRIT is often called the most revocable of irrevocable trusts," Tom answered. "First, you can use the proceeds to purchase another house and leave the new residence in the trust. Or, if you wish, you can leave the proceeds in the trust in some other form, such as an investment in stocks and bonds. And finally, you can change your mind and not put the proceeds back into the trust. You must realize, that if properly structured, the trust covers the residence. If the residence no longer exists, then the reason for the trust can disappear as well. Should you choose this action, you lose the opportunity to reduce your estate taxes."

"How about our grandkids? Can we gift to them?" Mary asked.

"There are several considerations when gifting to grandchildren," Tom answered. "The first concerns their present age, and the second involves when you want them to have access to the funds. If they are minors, they may not be able to legally own the property. Trusts are used to overcome this impediment, but, in some cases, guardianships accomplish this need."

Tom explained further. "Gifts to minors under the **Uniform Gifts to Minors Act (UGMA)** or the **Uniform Transfer to Minors Act (UTMA)** provide convenient and inexpensive methods to reduce a grantors tax liability. These two acts are similar, with UTMA providing more flexibility. The UTMA is not available in all states. Transfers under either of these acts qualify for the annual gift tax exclusion. However, per the regulations the assets must be distributed when the minor reaches age 21.

"The income from another type of trust, the **2503(b) trust**, must be distributed annually—often to a UGMA or UTMA account. The income is taxed at the minor's income tax rate. Distribution of the assets to the minor is in accordance to the terms of the trust agreement, which need not be at age 21. Other trusts, such as a 2503(c), can accumulate the income rather than distribute it annually, though recent tax law changes make this a very expensive habit.

"Often trusts for children use a **Crummey power** to preserve the annual gift exclusion for gifts to a trust," Tom emphasized. "Under a Crummey power, the beneficiaries are given a non-cumulative right to demand current distribution of limited amounts. The trustee notifies the beneficiary annually regarding his or her right to withdraw a specified sum. Should the beneficiary choose not to withdraw, the amount can be accumulated within the trust and still qualify for the annual $10,000 gift tax exclusion. Gifting to a minor can be done in a variety of ways," he continued, "but some work has to be done to determine which method best meets the criteria of the donor.

"There is one other aspect of gifting to grandchildren that we should touch upon, and that's the **generation skipping transfer tax**. We attorneys often tell how the Texas millionaire, whose children were well off, decided to leave his estate of about $30 million to his grandchildren. The grandkids received less than $3 million. I don't know if the story is true, but the math works out.

"The Generation Skipping Transfer Tax (GSTT) is an additional tax. The tax was passed to ensure that each generation pays its fair share of estate taxes. To get your attention, the tax is imposed at the highest estate tax rate, which is currently 55%. The use of a trust is not effective in avoiding this tax since the distribution from the trust will be to the grandchildren.

"However, $1,000,000 per person ($2,000,000 per couple) is exempt for gifts made during a lifetime or at death. As it applies to estate taxes, all future appreciation of the asset, after it has been gifted during a person's lifetime, will be excluded—in addition to the million dollar exemption. Furthermore, you can also avoid this tax by making use of the annual gift tax exemption of $10,000 or $20,000 if split by the grandparents. You can also directly pay your grandchildren's educational or medical expenses, which does not count toward the generation skipping tax.

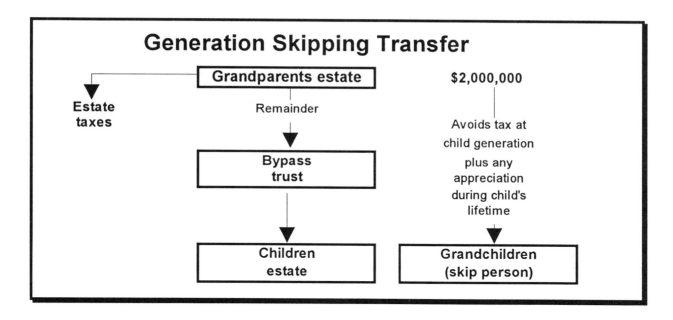

"This seems like a good time to take another break," Tom said. "Then we will discuss the need for liquidity in estate planning. But before we do, there is one thing that you should recognize. We have covered a lot of concepts about estate planning to assist you in understanding your options. However, estate planning is not for the do-it-yourselfers. A competent attorney is very necessary to ensure that the employed strategies work."

During the break, Mary asked Jim if they had any assets that he would be willing to transfer to a charitable remainder trust. "You are always complaining about that airline stock and the low dividend it pays, think about it."

Chapter 22

*"The lack of liquid assets to pay estate taxes
and other expenses is the most overlooked
aspect of the estate planning process."*

Estate liquidity and healthcare directives

Still at Tom Vincent's office

After a short break, Tom continued on with his discussion regarding estate planning.

"The third aspect of the estate planning process is liquidity which simply means having sufficient cash, or assets that can be easily converted to cash, to pay the estate tax bill, final income tax, funeral costs and other legal/administration expenses.

"People should be concerned about receiving less than fair value when they need to unload assets in a hurry," Tom advised. "An estate tax return form #706, with the taxes due, must be filed nine months following the date of death. Only one extension for six months can be obtained, which doesn't leave a whole lot of time to sell illiquid property."

Tom continued, "Also, bear in mind that your pension plans, even if you roll over to an IRA, will be reduced by income taxes when the funds are distributed. You may not have as much liquidity as you think. Take a sharp pencil and get down to the net numbers."

"Isn't this the problem that the owners of the Miami Dolphins ran into when they had to sell part of the team?" Joe asked.

> ◆ The value of your business
> ◆ Your residence
> ◆ That vacant lot in Arizona
> ◆ Your vacation home
> ◆ The value of your autos and personal property
> ◆ Possibly your investment in MUNIs

"Exactly," Tom answered. "The Robbie family offered 34% of the team for sale. They needed money to pay the estate tax that was due on the death of the founder, Joe Robbie. If you have a sizable estate, you can minimize estate taxes, but you will have to pay some estate taxes.

"Jim and Mary, let us take a quick look at your assets which may fall into the non-liquid category," Tom said. He then wrote the examples on the chartboard.

"These possessions represent a fair share of your estate assets," Tom said.

"I can understand about the business and the houses, but why would my investment in MUNIs be illiquid?" Jim asked.

"I recently had a client who ran into a non-liquid situation with MUNIs," Tom answered. "MUNI bonds are what the market calls *thinly traded*. My broker told me such trading is caused by the sheer size of the market. There are approximately 40 times more MUNI bond issues outstanding than corporate bonds. With this large a selection, most of these bonds do not trade actively. In addition, there are no central exchanges for MUNIs. Daily prices are available on only about 100 large issues. Consequently, when you go to sell MUNIs before maturity, as often happens with an estate sale, they may fetch a lower value or be very difficult to unload."

"What can be done about making our estate more liquid?" Mary asked.

"There are basically four ways to obtain liquidity," Tom answered.

1. "You can save.
2. "You can borrow.
3. "You can liquidate, which means to sell, assets.
4. "You can purchase life insurance.

"The easiest, and often the least expensive, source of liquidity is insurance. Of course, you need to discuss this with a financial planner or with an insurance professional to quantify your needs. We lawyers only draw up the legal documents," Tom said, with a smile.

"Aren't we too old to purchase insurance?" Jim asked.

"Every day I learn about new and different products offered by the insurance industry," Tom answered. "Let's discuss one type of policy that may be beneficial, a **second-to-die policy**. This is a policy that insures both of your lives and pays off when the last person dies. It is most often used to provide liquidity to pay estate taxes. Sometimes people use it to replace retirement assets which have been decreased by income taxes. Because it covers more than one life, it is less expensive than purchasing the same level of insurance for both of you. Furthermore, you can usually obtain coverage even if one of you is not insurable."

"Doesn't that add to the estate assets and, in fact, become taxable as well?" Joe asked.

"That depends on how you structure the ownership of the policy," Tom answered. "The cleanest and simplest way is to have the policies purchased and owned by the beneficiaries—in this case the children of Jim and Mary. Jim and Mary would gift sufficient funds to the children to pay the premiums when they become due. At the second death, the children could lend the proceeds to the estate or purchase assets from the estate. Either way, the estate receives liquid cash to pay the estate taxes."

"If that's such a great idea, why doesn't everybody do it?" Jim asked.

"There are issues with every strategy, as there are with this one," Tom answered. "'What happens if my child gets a divorce?' is one concern I hear often," Tom continued. "The answer is that the strategy may end up in a mess. The same is true should one child die and his or her heirs end up with the policy. The heirs may not be inclined to continue the payments on the policy."

"But, of course, you know a way around these issues," Joe said with a smile.

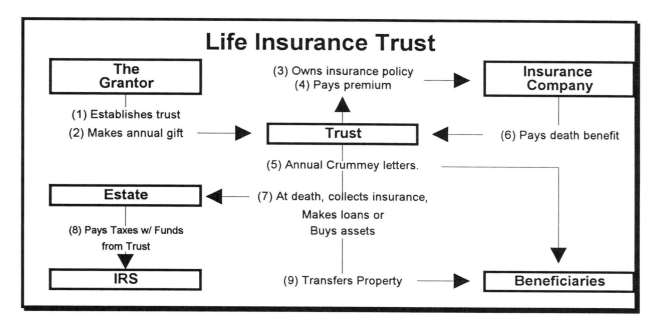

"That's what attorneys are for," Tom explained, "which brings us to the topic of the irrevocable **insurance trust**. With this strategy, you set up a trust which purchases and owns the insurance policy. Jim and Mary would annually gift funds to the trust. The trustee, at his or her option, would use some of the funds to pay premiums on the insurance policy."

"Is this trust the same as a **wealth replacement trust** that people keep trying to sell me?" Jim asked.

"It is exactly the same type of trust," Tom answered. "The only difference is the purpose for which the trust is set up. In our example, the trust is to provide liquidity, upon the second death, to pay estate taxes. The typical wealth replacement trust is intended to leverage the premium paid for an insurance policy in order to increase the wealth in the estate. To preserve the annual gift tax exclusion, the use of a *Crummey power* is also required for this type of trust. You remember, we discussed this approach when we covered trusts for minors. The beneficiaries must be given an opportunity to withdraw the annual gift from the trust in order for it to qualify."

"How much control will we have over this trust?" Jim asked.

"In my opinion, you should have virtually no control," Tom responded. "That means you should not be allowed to alter, amend or revoke the trust. Further, you should not be allowed to change trustees, or even order the trustee to purchase the insurance policy. What's more, you can't even be certain that the proceeds will be used to pay the estate taxes."

"That's a lot of "can't do's," Jim said.

"The purpose of an insurance trust is to provide liquidity at the time that estate taxes are payable, without having the proceeds included in the estate of the insured. If the trust were revocable in any sense of the word, the proceeds would revert to the estate and be taxable. A trust is revocable when the grantor can dictate the terms. To go to all the effort to set up a trust and then have it fail because of procedures is an awful waste of time and money," Tom emphasized. "Furthermore, as you can understand from the discussion, choosing the correct trustee is vital. You need someone who understands your wishes, agrees that they make sense and will carry them out on his or her own authority."

"We already have insurance. Can't we just transfer it to the trust?" Mary asked.

"Yes, you can and I would recommend that you do that," Tom replied. "But there is one hitch called the three-year-look back rule. The proceeds will be included in your estate if you transfer an insurance policy to another person within three years of your death. IRS doesn't want you to transfer a policy at the last minute, just to avoid estate taxes."

"Why, then, do you recommend the transfer?" Mary asked.

"Nothing ventured, nothing gained," Tom answered. "In your case, you will pay estate taxes on the insurance that you already own as it is presently structured. If you transfer it, there is a possibility that it will escape estate taxes. You just have to live three years after the transfer. If you don't, you are no worse off."

"I'll try to do that. I'll try live at least three years," Mary said, with a smile.

Tom continued the discussion. "Regardless of age, losing a parent is usually a traumatic experience. I guess it reflects on our own mortality. Because of this loss, I often suggest that, when a parent dies, some gesture of inheritance ought to go to the children. It doesn't take the place of the lost parent, but it helps the children to know that they were remembered by that parent."

"Won't they know they'll get the inheritance?" asked Jim.

"Yes," Tom answered. "However, estates are often structured with by-pass and QTIP trusts which often don't pay out to the heirs until the second death. For many, this is a long wait."

"I am all for providing something early to the kids. Is there an easy way to accomplish this without draining the estate?" asked Jim.

"As I said earlier, if you have a problem, some insurance company has a product which will provide a solution," Tom said. "Not only do insurance companies have second-to-die policies, they also have **first-to-die policies**. These policies are similar, but work in reverse. Both spouses are insured under the same policy, but the policy pays off on the first death and provides some funds for the children, or other needs, upon that death. For example, if the departing spouse is a business owner, it would provide funds at a time when they are usually needed. Of course, to avoid estate taxes, this policy also has to be either owned by the children or owned by a trust.

"The selection of an estate executor, also called the **personal representative**, is extremely important. The executor is the person who values the estate property, pays off the creditors, files the tax returns and distributes the remainder of the estate. I believe it would be useful for you to understand a few options that are available to the **executor**," Tom said. "These options are often called post-mortem strategies, because they can be executed following one's death. Choose the executor carefully and if possible avoid the following," he advised.

♦ "Avoid appointing people who live in other states or some distance from the decedent.
♦ "Avoid appointing people who do not have the knowledge, time or ability to handle the financial affairs of the deceased.

"It often is wise to name co-executors to compensate for the lack of experience of the person that you really want to handle your affairs.

"Only the executor has the authority to make the *QTIP election* to qualify property transferring into that trust for the marital deduction. It is fortunate that all of you are U.S. citizens. To prevent a *non-U.S. citizen* from just taking the money and returning to his native land, property, left to a spouse who is a non-U.S. citizen, does not qualify for the marital deduction. In this circumstance, to qualify for the marital deduction, a **qualified domestic trust** has to be established and has to have at least one U.S. citizen as a trustee at all times.

"The executor has a certain amount of discretion. For example, a date six months following the date of death, called an **alternative valuation date**, can be selected for valuing the estate assets. This selection is helpful when there is a significant decrease in the value of the assets. For example, the stock market may take a downturn.

"The decedent's estate is considered as a taxpayer and must file a **fiduciary income tax return**, and if the estate is large enough, it must file an estate tax return as well. Decisions need to be made as to which return will take certain deductions. For example, the estate administration expenses can be deducted from either return. As a guide, the executor uses the higher of the income tax marginal rate or the estate tax marginal rate. The final income tax return can be filed as a joint return if one spouse survives.

"A **qualified disclaimer** can be an effective device to maintain flexibility to distribute property in the most tax efficient manner.

"Normally, when an heir disclaims what is naturally his or hers and it goes to a *third party*, the third party has received a taxable gift. However, if certain IRS requirements are satisfied, the disclaimer is *qualified* and no gift tax is imposed. Among the requirements are:

- "The disclaimant cannot accept the property or any interest in it.
- "The disclaimer must be in writing, irrevocable and made within nine months of the date of death.
- "The disclaimant cannot direct the disposition of the bequest."

"What does all that mean?" Jim asked.

"A disclaimer is a means for the recipient of the bequest to walk away from it if he or she doesn't need it. The bequest then goes to the next beneficiary in line.

"Let me give you an example," Tom continued. "Suppose, in your will, you leave everything to your spouse. This action qualifies those assets for the **marital deduction**. In addition, suppose your will contains a disclaimer trust. Your spouse can disclaim all or part of the bequest, allowing the property to pass on to a credit trust—which then enables the property to qualify for *your* **unified tax credit** and reduce estate taxes at the time of your spouse's death."

"Why would a beneficiary want to use this technique?" Joe asked.

"This approach is often used for estates which may or may not meet the greater-than-$600,000 threshold at the time of the first death," Tom answered. "It gives the beneficiary added flexibility at that time. If the surviving spouse needs the funds, he or she simply ignores the disclaimer feature. If, at that time, the surviving spouse has sufficient assets, he or she then disclaims the property. There is also the **family settlement**. In this instance, the family redistributes the estate assets and then gets court approval. Courts are said to favor this approach.

"This explanation covers the highlights of actions that can be taken by the executor and family after a person's death," Tom concluded. "There is one more topic that will be useful to you, but it is lengthy and needs to be rescheduled for another time. It involves a number of strategies that could assist small business owners. I would appreciate it if we could set up another session to cover this topic. But before you go," Tom added. "let us talk briefly about a **healthcare directive** often called a **living will** and a **healthcare power of attorney**."

"I bring these up because of a situation that happened in my daughter's family last summer. Her father-in-law, retired from the army, was diagnosed as terminally ill due to cancer. The father-in-law did not want to burden his children with making medical decisions for him when he became incapable of doing so. Observing how well that very trying situation was handled made me a believer. I think that every person should have a document that helps him control his own destiny.

"There are two documents that perform different functions relating to long-term health planning:

1. **"Healthcare directive (living will)**—This document is operational only when a person is terminally ill. In it, the person states his or her desires as instructions to the health care provider. Issues, such as whether or not the terminally ill person be given nutrition or hydration to sustain his or her life, should be included in this document.

2. **"Healthcare power of attorney**—This document, which should be durable, empowers another person (a third party) with the authority to make healthcare decisions for the grantor. This can be invaluable to a person's family when the grantor is suffering from an illnesses such as Alzheimer's disease. In some states, this authority can be incorporated into the financial **durable power of attorney**.

"Though there are 'off-the-shelf documents' to ensure that the person's wishes can be carried out completely, I strongly advise everyone to use an attorney," Tom said. "I further advise that you explain your intentions to your physician(s) and to your family and that you keep a copy of the documents with your binder containing *Thoughtful Suggestions for My Loved Ones* (appendix 1b)."

Jim and Mary made another appointment with Tom, for the following week. With this appointment, they were to begin implementing some of the lessons they had learned in their quest for a financial plan. On their way home, they also agreed to set up appointments with Anne Jahn, Dan Palmer and Brian Larkin.

Chapter 23

"The closely-held-business owner needs education on the perils of inadequately dealing with succession planning. Succession planning, liquidity and estate planning are the three challenges for the small business owner for the 90s."
Timothy J. McDevitt, Attorney

Some tips for the small business owner

The following week at Tom Vincent's office

As the secretary escorted the Keanes into the inner office, Jim greeted their estate attorney. "Hi, Tom, it's us again. Are you getting tired of meeting with us?"

"Not a bit," Tom answered smiling. "After all, I have the timeclock running now."

As Jim and his wife Mary got settled, Tom instructed his secretary to hold all his calls.

"The reason for this session," Tom began, "is to cover some opportunities that are advantageous to the owners of a small business, like yourselves. I'm going to cover a multitude of topics to respond to your request at our first session when you told me you wanted to learn about the broad picture. If that's okay with you, we will continue in that direction. If you want me to put together an estate strategy that meets all your specific objectives, I will need to work with your financial planner and other professionals."

"That's exactly what we want, so let's get to it," Jim replied.

"We will begin by discussing the concepts of ownership, control and value," Tom said. "Most often in a small business, these are all vested in the owner or owners. Let me write these concepts on the chartboard.

"Can these interrelationships be spread among different people? Of course they can," Tom said, answering his own question.

"Look at how a corporation is structured. The stockholders are the owners, the board of directors has control, and there may be many people who receive value. For example, bondholders receive interest for lending money to the corporation. Therefore, they receive value. In my experience, I have found that many small business owners don't like to give up control of their business even after they retire. Why do you suppose that is?" Tom asked for emphasis.

"Speaking for Jim, the business is his identity," Mary answered. "When we go out, people will introduce me as Jim's wife, you know, the owner of Keanes Tool and Die Company."

"Oh, come now," Jim said. "That doesn't happen all that often. Besides, there are other reasons to want to continue controlling a business. For instance:

♦ "The owner could want a source of continuing income after retirement.

♦ "He could want to have some say in the conduct of the business, to prevent it from making bad decisions and taking incorrect actions.

Chart board Notes:

♦ **Ownership rests with the people who have legal title to the assets.**

♦ **Control rests with the people who make the decisions regarding the acquisition, disposal or use of the assets.**

♦ **Value rests with the people who receive the benefits of the assets.**

♦ "He could want a place to hang his hat and still feel a part of the business that he built."

"You are both correct," Tom agreed. "Survey after survey indicates that business owners enjoy the control aspect as well as the ability to increase the value of their assets. That is why they often fail to plan for their own transition. They never picture themselves as a retiree. Let me ask you another question. How do your children fit into the business?" Tom asked.

"They do and they don't," Jim answered. "Joe, our oldest, is the sales manager, while Mike runs production. Maryellen is married and teaches school in California."

"Do you want to treat all of your children equally and fairly?" Tom asked.

"Of course we do," Mary answered. "We want to treat them equally. But what do you mean by fairly?"

"You can treat your children equally by giving each of them one-third of the ownership of the business. But would that be fair to the children who work in the business?"

"Touché," Mary said.

"Let us sit back and look at the objectives that we just discussed," Tom said, as he listed the objectives on the chartboard. "Does that capture the essence of what you are trying to accomplish?"

Objectives

1. **Keep the business in the family, by transferring it to the children.**

2. **Retain some control, particularly the ability to step in if things look like they are going sour.**

3. **Treat all of the children both equally and fairly.**

4. **Begin the process of transitioning out of the business.**

5. **Retain some of the income for your retirement.**

6. **Minimize any capital gains tax in transferring the value of the business.**

7. **Minimize your estate taxes to retain more of the capital that you helped to build.**

"That pretty well sums it up," Jim replied.

"To accomplish many of the above objectives, we often have to separate the three intrinsic issues of *ownership*, *value*, and *control*," Tom continued. One strategy is to form a **family limited partnership (FLP)**. We will first discuss the structure, then we will cover the benefits.

"A family limited partnership," Tom continued, "consists of general partners and limited partners. The general partners are the managers of the assets in the partnership and normally have complete control. Because they have this level of control, they have unlimited liability. That means a creditor can go after their personal assets as well as the business assets. The limited partners are usually liable only to the extent of their partnership value. The parents are the general partners, and the children become the limited partners."

"You mean that we parents keep all the liability," Jim kidded.

"As general partners, you would be in no worse shape, since you have all the liability now," Tom replied.

"Doesn't our C-corporation status protect us from liability?" Jim asked. "If it doesn't, should we retain that type of corporation?"

"Any business which has employees, and deals with the public, should be incorporated," Tom answered. "The liability provided by incorporating protects you from the acts of people that you employ. However, a corporate structure does not protect you from acts that you personally perform or torts that you personally commit. There is a new organization type called a 'limited liability company' which affords liability protection similar to a C-corporation and the flexibility of a partnership."

"Why don't we just go to that form?" Jim asked.

"The limited liability corporation is a relatively new concept and is not legal in all states," Tom answered. "Furthermore, the concept has not been court-tested. However, the process that we will discuss is similar with either a limited liability corporation or a family limited partnership."

Tom guided the conversation back to the limited partnership structure. "To begin the process, either business or personal assets are transferred into the newly formed partnership. Because of a change in the tax law in 1992, we recommend a 10% general partner share and 90% limited partner share arrangement. Let's presume that your business is worth $3,000,000 and 1000 shares are issued. The 100 general shares are then worth $3,000 each and $300,000 in total. The 900 limited shares cover the remanding value. Initially, the parents own both the general and limited shares. At this point no ownership transfer has transpired. Since the parents own the trust, they also still own all the assets transferred into the trust. A picture of the entities involved may help explain this strategy. The illustration separates the operating assets from the business building and other property which I will describe in a few moments," Tom said.

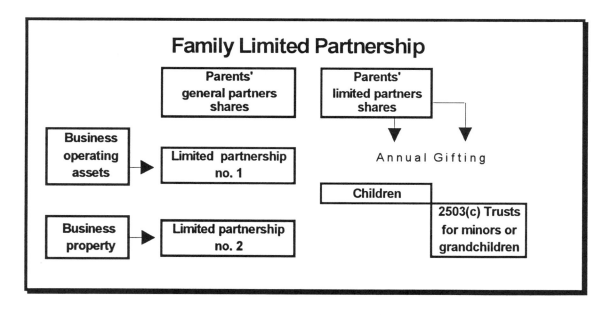

"Now we can examine how the structure will assist us in accomplishing your objectives.

"First of all, the assets of your business are transferred into the limited partnership. It is fortunate that your company is a C-corporation, since a limited partnership is not qualified to own the shares of a Subchapter S corporation.

"After the transfer, the assets are owned by the partnership(s). The general partners control the partnership, which means they can buy and sell assets, distribute any cash income, etc. The general partners retain pretty much the same control as that which Jim presently exerts in his business. This accomplishes objective #2, retention of some control. To meet objective #1, the transfer of the business, you begin to gift limited partner's shares to your children and, if you desire, to your grandchildren. Since the grandchildren are still minors, I indicated on the chart that their gifts can go to a 2503(c) trust. I covered this type of trust during an earlier session.

"Value in a family limited partnership is transferred by gifting limited partnership shares," Tom continued. "The key is to gift these shares in a manner which does not create a gift tax. To accomplish this tax-free transfer, you can utilize your **unified tax credit (UTC)** of $600,000, which, combined for both of you, totals $1,200,000. The UTC can be used while you live. In addition, you can transfer, gift-tax-free, up to $10,000 from each of you to your children and grandchildren. With three children and four grandchildren, you can gift $140,000 annually. All of this can be transferred without incurring any gift tax or income tax. Each transfer helps you to reduce your estate taxes, objective #7.

"There are additional gifting benefits. Most often, the gift can be discounted by as much as 25% to 40%. On an annual basis, you are capable of reducing your estate assets by $12,500 to $14,000 for each $10,000 annual gift. How is this possible?" Tom asked. "It's the inverse of control," he answered. "The limited partners cannot market their shares; they cannot declare a cash distribution; and they have no voice in the buying and selling of the assets. What they really own is a right to the income earned by the partnership, *if and when it is distributed.* In effect the $10,000 value isn't worth $10,000. It's worth less, because it lacks real control. These examples of lack of control are called minority interest and lack of marketability discounts. IRS recognizes that these conditions exist. Therefore, they allow a discount on the value of the share transferred. Consequently, more shares can be gifted to bring the true value up to the annual $10,000 exemption. Many experts place the discount in the 25 to 40% range."

"Now, Tom, this may avoid gift taxes and reduce estate taxes, but experience tells me it doesn't come without pain," Jim said.

"Jim, the process is relatively pain-free," Tom answered. "But you need to adhere to one rule. Any income earned by the assets has to be shared proportionately with the limited partners. IRS is looking to be certain that the partners are de facto. Therefore, if they own 10% of the shares, 10% of the income belongs to them as well. It is always wise to provide sufficient cash to at least pay for the income taxes the limited partners will incur. Income taxes will be owed whether the income is distributed as cash or not retained in the partnership. Otherwise you may have some very unhappy children. In addition, the family limited partnership structure enables you to shift income from your high tax bracket to the lower tax brackets of your children. A heck of a deal."

"How about objective #3, treating all the children equally and fairly?" Mary asked. "I want to be certain that Maryellen is taken care of, since both of our sons draw salaries."

"Knowing the tyrant that Jim is, I bet they earn those salaries," Tom answered, smiling. "I separated the buildings from the operating assets to emphasize that point," Tom continued. "It would be unfair to your sons, who will operate the business, to eventually have the outsider, Maryellen, in a position to dictate company policy. One way around this dilemma is to transfer fixed assets, such as the building, to the non-involved children. The business can then lease the building and similar assets at a fair market price under a long- term contract. This setup will provide both assets and income to Maryellen without having her and her heirs directly involved in managing the company."

"Now let us consider objective #5, retaining some income for your retirement. You control the number of shares that you gift. Just remember that when you gift, the proportionate income goes with the gift."

"I really like your suggestions on how to help Maryellen, without causing controversy with Mike and Joe," Mary said. "You have given us some food for thought on all our objectives except for #6, minimizing the capital gains tax."

"Mary, I should have known that you would keep track," Tom responded with a smile. "As you may begin to appreciate, there are tradeoffs in everything. The capital gains tax can be avoided by holding onto the stock until your deaths. Then you can take advantage of the step-up in basis that we discussed earlier. That means the stock will pass on to your heirs at the fair market value rather than at the cost basis."

"Wouldn't that be worth waiting for?" Mary asked.

"Probably not, because we are trading off capital gains tax savings for estate taxes," Tom replied. "The marginal estate tax in your case may run as high as 55%. It doesn't make sense to tax the value of the business at 55% when it's transferred, just to save taxes for some future generation. Keep in mind that capital gains tax is currently 28% and there is talk of the percentage being reduced." Tom explained further, "Bear in mind, the concern with a C-corporation is double taxation. The difference between the cost basis and fair market value is taxed to the corporation when the gain is recognized. There is a second tax to the owner when the dollars are distributed in the form of dividends. To avoid this double tax, you can change the status of the corporation to an S-corporation. This change still provides the liability protection plus, as a pass-through entity, it avoids the double tax liability inherent in a C-corporation. There is a ten year waiting period before the built-in gains can fully escape the capital gains tax. However, following the S-corporation election, any future appreciation of those assets is only taxed once. Furthermore, there is a drawback to the S-corporation involving the type of shareholder. An S-corporation cannot be transferred to a family limited partnership, or, for that matter, to a **charitable remainder trust,** without disqualifying its S-status. That's what I mean by trade-offs."

"Each business owner must first establish his or her goals, Tom continued. "What does he or she want to accomplish with the transfer of the business? What method or structure may best serve his or her needs?"

Tom returned to the chartboard and wrote a series of questions.

"Do you intend to give your business to your children, or will they buy it from you?" Tom asked, then continued on. "If the children are buying the business—with profits generated by the business—payments must come in the form of after-tax dollars. Often, the business is not sufficiently profitable to provide the new owners a living wage while the old owners are paid for the value they built up.

"A small business owner needs to answer these types of questions early on," Tom counseled. "It often takes years to implement a strategy, and far too often, in my experience, the owner waits until it's too late to accomplish anything meaningful."

Chartboard notes

♦ **Does the owner anticipate being compensated for the value of the business?**

♦ **Where will the new owners get the funds to purchase the business?**

♦ **Can this compensation be accomplished with before-tax dollars?**

On their way home from Tom's office, Jim and Mary acknowledged that they may have waited too long to do their financial planning. They decided not to wait any longer.

Chapter 24

*"People need to look back to see
how far they have come."*

What have we learned?

Breakfast at the Keanes several years later

Jim was still poaching the salmon, and Mary was preparing the cucumber dill sauce as Joe and Betty Meehan arrived.

"Come on in and help yourselves to your first latte'. Jim is a little slow this morning," Mary called from the kitchen.

"I'm not slow," Jim remarked with a laugh. "It's just that this recipe is more complex and time-consuming than I realized."

"This should keep us occupied until the master chef gets finished," Mary said, entering the recreation room with a tray full of hors d'oeuvres.

"How are the world travelers getting over their jet lag," Betty asked.

"That cruise was the best ever," Mary answered. "In Sri Lanka, we met a woman working for the Peace Corps. She was 74 years old and enjoying every minute of her teaching. Who says growing old can't be fun? Travel has been a godsend for us. Since Jim's lumbar disc acted up and made golfing all but a dream, the ability to travel has saved our marriage—let alone our retirement. It keeps us involved mentally and physically. We really feel stimulated on a trip."

After the breakfast discussion covering the Keane's latest trip, the conversation turned to how Marie was doing.

"We haven't seen her since we got home," Mary said, feeling somewhat guilty.

"No one expected you to just get home and run down there," Joe remarked in a comforting tone.

Joe continued. "Mom is doing great since she moved to that retirement community. She wishes now that she and Dad had made the move years before. After her eyesight began to get worse, she felt that she was becoming isolated, since all her friends lived in another part of town and she could no longer drive."

"I feel relieved that she finally made that decision," Mary said. "Particularly since her vision became impaired. I know that giving up driving has concerned her. But I, for one, am relieved."

"Driving is no longer a concern for Mom," Betty said. "She is close enough to safely walk to everything she needs. The community library is full of large-print books. You know how Marie always liked those romantic novels. She also goes on group tours, run by the retirement community, with her new friends. Now she is even thinking of joining a drama club. Imagine that! Though it's tougher to become involved as you get older, Mom seems to have overcome that problem."

"It's just too bad that we spent all that time and effort on redoing the old home," Joe said. "Even though the remodeling added value and we got our money out of it, a lot of effort went into it."

"No sense worrying about it," Jim said. "It was the best decision at the time. How are you guys making out with your retirement plans."

"We are both delighted that we formulated a plan when we did," Joe answered. "It's always easier to look back with satisfaction than to look forward with concern. The savings aren't growing as rapidly as we would like, but they are growing. Among other things, in the last year we purchased a new car and replaced our roof."

"Not only that, we decided to put in an alarm system after two of our neighbors' homes were broken into," Betty said. "We also took out a long-term-care policy."

"I thought you were going to wait on that," Mary said.

"It was on our list to do and the clock was ticking. The longer we waited, the more expensive it would be," Joe answered. "However, the issue that pushed us over the edge was something that happened to a co-worker of Betty's. This woman's elderly parents got seriously ill and the co-worker had to quit her job to become the caregiver. Betty and I decided that we did not want to be a burden to our kids, so we bought two long-term-care insurance policies."

"Why is it that the woman is the one that has to quit her job to become the caregiver?" Mary wondered aloud.

"Other than that, we are pretty much on schedule," Joe continued, ignoring Mary's remark. "In fact, now that Betty's Simplified Employee Retirement Plan (SEP) is in place, we are saving more than we had planned. With Social Security becoming such a political issue, we feel that we cannot depend on it. You two are lucky that you had the opportunity to take early retirement. I read recently that the number of people taking early retirement had risen from 2% in 1956 to 68% today. At that rate, the Social Security Fund will run out of money even quicker."

"I agree. I'm concerned as well," Jim replied. "It seems that every time a politician offers a constructive recommendation to solve the Social Security and Medicare dilemma, he or she is immediately cut off at the knees by a political opponent. I hope someone comes up with a workable solution soon."

"Enough about us, how are you guys faring?" Betty asked.

"You still keep involved with your golfing buddies and still consult at work, don't you?" Joe asked Jim.

"My golfing days are over, I'm afraid," Jim answered. "I still go down to the club occasionally. Unfortunately, my friends are discussing shots they recently hit, while all I can do is offer golf stories from years ago. That becomes old in a hurry. My old business is still going strong. I only drop in once every couple of weeks."

"Did you ever set up one of those family limited partnerships that Tom suggested?" Joe asked.

"We set up something very similar called a **limited liability company**. This type of corporation has recently been legalized in this state. Annually, we transfer non-voting shares to the boys. Maryellen also gets shares from a different family limited partnership to keep our gifting in balance."

"Looking back, how was the transition?" Joe asked.

"As you know, retirement did not work out as I had planned," Jim answered. "Golf and business had been my life and it was a tough transition, particularly the golf. I had counted on that to smooth things over. However, I have you and Betty to thank for getting us started planning our retirement. The simple fact that we set goals made the transition a whole lot better. The Elderhostel courses that Mary and I take stimulate me as much as travel does her. I feel young again, because I realize that I can still learn. I'm still exercising my brain. 'Use it or lose it,' they say. But, best of all, I get pleasure from what I am now learning. For example, my painting is becoming very good. The kids have one picture hanging in the plant's reception area that's getting pretty good reviews."

"Has your retirement lived up to your expectations?" Betty asked Mary.

"Just wonderful. Unlike Jim, I'm doing everything that I planned. Travel and the grandkids top the list. Concerning volunteering, I just got nominated to the Board of Directors at the Andersen Foundation. They are a little-known, but very generous, endowment fund. Now I can combine volunteering with my work skills. Did I tell you about..."

The Meehans and Keanes continued on The Path to enjoy Successful Retirements.

Appendices
Table of Contents

Assets (Things you own)

Cash Accounts (Checking, savings, money market funds...)

	$

Securities (Totals for stocks and bonds by broker or mutual fund

Company/security	# shares	Cost (if available)	Current Value
		$	$

Retirement Accounts (Pension plans, 401(k), IRAs, TSAs, deferred compensation...)

Type	Current Value	Annual Contribution	Annual Growth %	Owner	Beneficiary
	$	$			

Life Insurance Type (Whole Life = W, Universal = U, Term = T, Other = O [e.g.mortgage])

Company	Type	Owner	Beneficiary	Face Amount	Cash Value	Policy loans	Annual Premium
				$	$		$

Other Property (Exclude residence)

Description (Personal, autos, vacation home...)	Fair Market Value
	$

Liabilities (exclude home mortgage)

Description	Current Balance	Interest
	$	%

Residence $_____

Remaining Yrs _____

Mortgage Bal. $ _____   Rate_____ %

Other Real Estate $_____

Remaining Yrs _____

Mortgage Bal. $ _____   Rate_____ %

Thoughtful Suggestions for My Loved Ones

From _____

Dated _____

Table of Contents

Thoughtful Suggestions

This booklet was developed to help the surviving spouse and other loved ones through a very stressful period. While the death of a loved one is an immense emotional loss, it also involves a number of urgent financial and legal matters. In particular, surviving partners must face important decisions as they begin to look forward to the future. During this time of sorrow, there are many necessary details that cannot be ignored.

♦ You will need several copies of the official death certificate for filing insurance, Social Security claims, retitling joint assets, etc.

♦ Avoid (if circumstances allow) making any major financial or life-changing decisions in the early stages of grief. Financial decisions including whether to sell a home or how to manage assets should be postponed for at least six months.

♦ Avoid taking any financial actions that you don't completely understand or that make you feel uncomfortable. Ask your financial advisor to explain any costs, and how any recommendations fit into your personal financial needs.

♦ Cancel extra credit cards or convert them to your name. You can cancel any club memberships or subscriptions that you don't want or need.

♦ The location of the important papers and the steps that you will need to take are described in the appropriate sections of this booklet.

Your heirs and executor should be aware that they have the right to choose their own advisors, including the estate attorney. Before they engage anyone, they should develop a clear understanding regarding what these professionals will do and how much they will charge.

PERSONAL INFORMATION

Name _____   Spouse's name _____

Birthdate _____   Birthdate _____

Occupation _____   Occupation _____

Social Security no. _____   Social Security no. _____

Mother's maiden name _____   Mother's maiden name _____

Residence Address

_____

Children, descendants and relatives:

Name	Address	Phone
_____	_____	_____
_____	_____	_____
_____	_____	_____
_____	_____	_____
_____	_____	_____

Family Tree

Children	Grandchildren	Husband's siblings	Wife's siblings
_____	_____	_____	_____
_____	_____	_____	_____
_____	_____	_____	_____
_____	_____	_____	_____
_____	_____	_____	_____

If currently married: date of marriage _____   Years residence in current state (   )

Years residence in other states _____(   ) _____(   )

Community property agreement is located at _____ Recorded at _____

Other property agreements _____

Prior Marriages (if any)

When? _____ Where? _____

_____ _____

Extent of liability for alimony or support obligations

_____

_____

WILLS

(My/our) will(s) are located at _____ , and last updated

_____ .

The personal representative [executor(trix)] who is designated to carry out the provisions of

my (name _____) will is _____ . If he\she declines or

cannot serve, the alternative representative is _____ .

The personal representative [executor(trix)] who is designated to carry out the provisions of

my (name _____) will is _____ . If he\she declines or

cannot serve, the alternative representative is _____ .

(My/our) estate attorney is _____ located at

_____ , phone _____ .

(My/our) accountant (tax preparer) is _____ located at

_____ , phone _____ .

Addresses of friends or charities named in the will.

_____   _____

_____   _____

_____   _____

TRUSTS

Information on all trusts that (I/we) have created or have any rights to, or responsibilities for:

1) This trust (is/is not) in my will.

Trustee: _____

Assets in the trust:

_____

_____

_____

(See trust agreement located at _____ e.g. attorney's office for details.)

2) This trust (is/is not) in my will.

Trustee: _____

Assets in the trust:

_____

_____

_____

(See trust agreement located at _____ e.g. attorney's office for details.)

Unresolved estates for which (I/we) have any rights or responsibilities:

_____

_____

DOCUMENTS

Safe Deposit Box

(My/our) safe deposit box is located at _____

People with access _____

The **deed** of the home is located _____ and is registered in the

  following manner _____

The mortgage (if any) is placed with _____

The files which pertain to the home, such as cost of purchase, improvements, original closing,

  etc. are marked _____ and are located at _____

Other important documents and their locations: (Insert N/A if not applicable)

Automobile titles/registrations _____

Birth certificate _____

Federal tax records _____

Keys_____

Naturalization/Citizenship papers _____

Patents and copyrights _____

Title Insurance _____

Passport_____

Boat ownership registration _____

Marriage License _____

Cemetery deed _____

Health care directive _____

Durable power of attorney _____

BANKING

Checking Account(s)
Name of Institution _____

Account Number _____

Information relating to these accounts (e.g. co-signer)

_____

Name of Institution _____

   Account Number _____

Information relating to these accounts (e.g. co-signer)

_____

Checkbooks may be found _____

Bank statements may be found   _____

Savings Account(s) and CDs
Name of Institution _____

   Account Number _____

Information relating to these accounts (e.g. co-signer)

_____

 Name of Institution _____

Account Number _____

Information relating to these accounts (e.g. co-signer)

_____

Statements may be found _____

INSURANCE

♦ Call (my/our) agent _____ at _____
to help you, or obtain assistance from your financial advisor or attorney. If you write the insurance company(s) directly enclose a copy of the death certificate with the claims form.

♦ Contact Social Security to file for benefits and instructions for any uncashed checks.

Life insurance policies

Company _____   Company _____

Policy No. _____   Policy No. _____

Face Amount $ _____   Face Amount $ _____

Loan Balance (if any) _____   Loan Balance (if any) _____
      Current beneficiaries: Current Beneficiaries:

_____   _____

_____   _____

♦ If we no longer have any dependents, you may choose to drop your life insurance altogether. However, if you still have dependents, you may need to increase your insurance. If you are still working, you may need to acquire disability insurance.

Homeowners Policy with _____

The policy is located _____

Automobile insurance is with _____

The policy is located _____

Medical insurance is with _____

The policy is located _____

♦ Medigap policies for medical expenses not covered by Medicare could provide an extra measure of security when you are sixty-five.

INVESTMENTS

(My/our) Financial Planner is _____

      Phone (   )_____

(My/our) Stockbroker is _____

      Phone (   )_____

◆ Notify the above advisors of my death so the records can be changed.

◆ A complete list of (my/our) stock, bonds and other investments as of _____ is attached. This list and values often change.

Location of any stock or bond certificates issued _____

My Military History

Service Number _____

Branch of Service _____

Length of Service _____

From _____ to _____

Rank _____

I (do/do not) _____ have a service-connected disability.

Location of special papers:

Document	Location
_____	_____
_____	_____

◆ Notify the Veterans Administration to apply for any applicable benefits.

Veterans Administration Information _____

MY EMPLOYMENT RECORD

Name of Employer   Dates (From-To)

_____   _____

_____   _____

_____   _____

SPOUSE EMPLOYMENT RECORD

Name of Employer   Dates (From-To)

_____   _____

_____   _____

_____   _____

- ◆ Contact my employer; ask for _____. Discuss any final or deferred compensation you may be entitled to, as well as life insurance, pension and profit sharing benefits. If appropriate, you may be entitled to accidental death insurance.

- ◆ Check with my employer to see if my group health insurance will be continued and if you may convert to an individual policy when the coverage ends.

Fraternal Organizations:

_____   _____

_____   _____

The organization marked with an (*) has life or travel insurance which may be applicable.

BUSINESS INTERESTS

Business information: Proprietorship, Partnership, Corporation

Description   Share of Ownership

_____   _____

_____   _____

_____   _____

◆ The following persons can help you with the business matters:

_____   _____
(Name)   (Phone)

_____   _____
(Name)   (Phone)

_____   _____
(Name)   (Phone)

Financial papers, buy/sell agreements, business tax returns and other important papers are located at _____

DEBTS OWED TO (ME\US)*

Description	Terms	Balance	Location of Documents

DEBTS (I\WE) OWE*

Description	Terms	Balance	Location of Documents

*These are long-term obligations which may not have been part of my monthly budget:

OTHER ASSETS AND REAL ESTATE (I \WE) OWN

Location	Nature of Title	Mortgage Holder	Date of Purchase	Cost
_____	_____	_____	_____	_____
_____	_____	_____	_____	_____
_____	_____	_____	_____	_____

♦ If some of this property is located in another state, (I /we) may owe estate taxes in both states. Please check with (my/our) attorney on how to handle this.

An inventory of our household furnishings and their approximate values is located at

_____

Unusual or high value assets   Location of documents

_____ $ _____

_____ $ _____

Inheritances received or large gifts contributed

_____ $_____

_____ $_____
Are any of these separate property?

CASH FLOW

♦ In order to make realistic plans for the future, it's essential to know how much money you have to spend and what you spend it on. I have completed the following worksheet detailing (my/our) current income and spending pattern to provide a basis for projections.

What's coming in each month?

Gross salary $_____

Income from other sources (i.e., investments, partnerships etc.):

_____ $_____   _____

_____   _____   _____

_____   _____

Total Cash Inflow $ _____

What is going out each month?

1) Rent or mortgage payments/ins. $_____   12) Savings $_____
2) Food   _____   13) Federal Income taxes   _____
3) Clothing/household exp.   _____   14) Social Security taxes   _____
4) Utilities   _____   15) Other taxes   _____
5) Recreation, entertainment, vac. _____   16) Donations   _____
6) Other debt reduction   _____   17) Life insurance prem.   _____
7) Gas, oil, auto repairs/ins. _____   18) Car payments   _____
8) Personal expenses   _____   19) Other insurance   _____
9) Tuition, daycare   _____   20) Medical expenses/ins   _____
10) Credit card & other interest _____   21) Household exp.   _____
11) Phone   _____   22) Other   _____

Total cash outflow $_____

Monthly cash inflow _____ (minus) Monthly cash outflow _____ = $_____

FUNERAL ARRANGEMENTS

Funeral Home _____   Address _____

Phone (   )_____

Special funeral arrangement instructions

_____

_____

_____

_____

I would like the following to be included in my obituary:

_____

_____

_____

_____

_____

I would like to donate my organs to the following organization:

Name   _____

Address   _____

City/State _____ , _____ ZIP _____

Phone   (_____) _____ - _____

CASH FLOW

◆   It's essential to know how much money you have to spend and what you spend it on. Complete the following worksheet. Try to use current numbers, be reasonably accurate, but don't worry about being too precise.

What's coming in each month?

Gross salary $_____

Income from other sources (i.e., investments, partnerships etc.):

_____ $_____   _____

_____   _____   _____

_____   _____

Total Cash Inflow $ _____

What is going out each month?

1) Rent or mortgage payments/ins. $_____	12) Savings $_____
2) Food _____	13) Federal Income taxes _____
3) Clothing/household exp. _____	14) Social Security taxes _____
4) Utilities _____	15) Other taxes _____
5) Recreation, entertainment, vac. _____	16) Donations _____
6) Other debt reduction _____	17) Life insurance prem. _____
7) Gas, oil, auto repairs/ins. _____	18) Car payments _____
8) Personal expenses _____	19) Other insurance _____
9) Tuition, daycare _____	20) Medical expenses/ins _____
10) Credit card & other interest _____	21) Household exp. _____
11) Phone _____	22) Other _____

Total cash outflow $_____

Monthly cash inflow _____ (minus) Monthly cash outflow _____ = $_____

Do you plan to make any major purchases or changes in your living style during the next three years that will have a major impact on the above figures? If so, the amounts should be adjusted to reflect these major purchases.

Retirement Projection

Use to estimate the savings needed to retire at your current living style.

1) Determine how much after-tax annual income you will need at retirement. Most studies now say that amount is 75 to 80% of your current income.

Calculation:

75 to 80% of current income $ _____ [less] Social Security $ _____ [less] pension or

other fixed income $ _____ [equals] income needed in today's dollars $_____(a)

2) Determine how much current income you will need at the time you retire.

Calculation:

Age at retirement _____ [less] current age _____ [equals] years to retirement _____

What do you think the average future inflation rate will be? I recommend using 5%.

Yrs to retirement →	1	3	5	7	10	12	15
4%	1.04	1.12	1.22	1.31	1.48	1.60	1.80
5%	1.05	1.16	1.28	1.41	1.63	1.80	2.08
6%	1.06	1.19	1.34	1.50	1.79	2.01	2.39

Multiply answer from step 1 by factor selected. (a) $_____ [x] factor \_\_\_\_\_ [=]$ _____ (b)

3) Calculate the lump sum retirement asset dollars needed at retirement to support inflation-adjusted annual income level (b) from step 2. It's a good idea to plan until age 90.

Calculation:

Determine number of retirements years: <u>Age 90</u> [less] age at retirement _____ [equals] _____
Select the appropriate factor based on the return you expect less inflation (e.g. 7% return - 5% inflation = 2%)

	Yrs, in Retirement →	15	20	25	28	30	33	35
Return you expect, less inflation	1%	13.90	18.12	22.13	24.45	25.95	28.16	29.60
	2%	12.98	16.56	19.83	21.65	22.81	24.46	25.52
	4%	11.30	13.87	16.00	17.10	17.78	18.70	19.25
	5%	10.58	12.77	14.50	15.37	15.88	16.57	16.98
	7%	9.34	10.93	12.08	12.62	12.92	13.30	13.53
	10%	7.86	8.86	9.49	9.76	9.89	10.06	10.15

Multiply answer from step 2 by factor selected. (b) $_____ x factor _____ [=] $ _____(c)

4) Determine how much your current retirement assets will be worth when you retire.

Calculation:

What is the current value of your retirement assets? $ _____ (c)

Age at retirement _____ [less] current age _____ [equals] years to retirement _____

What do you think your average pre-tax return on investments will be?

	Yrs. to retirement →	1	3	5	7	10	12	15
Pre-tax return you expect	5%	1.05	1.16	1.28	1.41	1.63	1.80	2.08
	6%	1.06	1.19	1.34	1.50	1.79	2.01	2.40
	8%	1.08	1.26	1.47	1.71	2.15	2.52	3.17
	10%	1.10	1.33	1.61	1.95	2.59	3.14	4.18

Multiply current assets by factor selected. (c) $_____ [x] factor _____ [=] $ _____ (d)

5) Determine the *additional* retirement assets needed at the time of retirement.

Calculation:

Lump sum retirement assets needed from step 3. $_____ (c)

[less] Value of current retirement assets at time of retirement step 4. $_____ (d)

[equals] additional savings needed at retirement in future dollars $_____ (e)

6) Deflate, to remove inflation factor, the answer from step 5 to determine the amount that must be saved, valued in today's dollars.

Calculation:

Age at retirement _____ [less] current age _____ [equals] years to retirement _____

What do you think the average future inflation rate will be? 4%, 5%, 6%.
Select the appropriate factor from the table and multiple by (e) from step 5.

Yrs to retirement	1	3	5	7	10	12	15
4%	.96	.89	.82	.76	.68	.62	.56
5%	.95	.86	.78	.71	.61	.56	.48
6%	.94	.84	.75	.67	.56	.50	.42

Multiply answer from step 5 by factor selected. (e) $_____[x] factor ___ [=]$ _____ (f)

7) Determine the after-inflation amount that you have to save within the next year.

Calculation:

Age at retirement _____ [less] current age _____ [equals] years to retirement _____

Select the appropriate factor based on the return you expect less inflation (e.g., 7% return - 5% inflation = 2%)

Yrs. to retirement	1	3	5	7	10	12	15
1%	.010	.029	.049	.067	.095	.113	.139
2%	.010	.029	.047	.065	.090	.107	.130
4%	.010	.028	.045	.061	.082	.095	.113
5%	.009	.027	.044	.058	.078	.090	.106
7%	.009	.026	.041	.055	.071	.081	.093
10%	.009	.025	.038	.050	.063	.070	.079

Multiply answer from step 6 by factor selected. (f) $_____ x factor _____ [=] $ _____ (g)

8) Determine the amount that you will have to save each succeeding year by multiplying the answer from step 7 by the appropriate inflation rate factor.

Calculation:

Age at retirement _____ [less] current age _____ [equals] years to retirement _____
What do you think the average future inflation rate will be? 4%, 5%, 6%.

Yrs to retirement	1	3	5	7	10	12	15
4%	1.04	1.12	1.22	1.31	1.48	1.60	1.80
5%	1.05	1.16	1.28	1.41	1.63	1.80	2.08
6%	1.06	1.19	1.34	1.50	1.79	2.01	2.39

Select the appropriate row from the table and multiply (g) from step 8 by each factor in the selected row. e.g., @ 5% inflation year 1 = (g) x 1.05, year 3 = (g) x 1.16 etc. Fill in appropriate row in table below to estimate inflated savings required for each year until retirement.

Annual savings needed in the specific year.	1	3	5	7	10	12	15
(g) [x] factor in 4% row =	$	$	$	$	$	$	$
(g) [x] factor in 5% row =	$	$	$	$	$	$	$
(g) [x] factor in 6% row =	$	$	$	$	$	$	$

Note: If the year in the table does not match your retirement goals, you may need to interpolate. For example you wish to retire in year 9, however, only years 7 and 10 are in the table. Subtract the difference between the factors of years 7 and 10, divide by three (the difference in the years) and add 2 times this amount to year 7. This will approximate the factor for year 9.

Example: A married couple is currently age 55 and plans to retire at age 65. Their current gross income is $50,000 annually and they anticipate $15,000 Social Security.

Step 1 $50,000 x 80% = $40,000 - $15,000 (Social Security) = $25,000 needed in today's dollars.

Step 2   65 - 55 = 10 years until retirement—$25,000 x 1.63 = $40,750 income required at time of retirement.

Step 3   90-65=25 retirement years—$40,750 x 16.00 = $652,000 lumpsum asset dollars required

Step 4 $150,000 current retirement assets available—$150,000 x 2.37 (interpolated) =$355,500
value of assets at retirement

Step 5 $652,000-$355,500 = $296,500 (valued in future dollars)

Step 6 $296,500 x .61 = $180,865 (valued in current dollars)

Step 7 $180,865 x .082 = $14,831 (Amount to be saved during the next year)

Step 8   Inflates the above amount annually to show the retiree the impact of inflation on retirement savings.

Relocation Checklist

Often retirees desire to relocate to a different climate following their retirement or rethink their current situation. This checklist is designed to assist them in making that decision. Retirees need to think of their situations in terms of 10 years from now, 20 years from now.

Choosing a location

How do your spouse, children, other family member feel about your pulling up roots?

Is there anyone who depends on your living nearby?

Have you seasoned yourself to the area in which your are planning to relocate?
♦   Have you lived there during all the different seasons?
♦   Have you lived there for at least three months at a stretch?
♦   Have you considered leasing for a while before you commit to a permanent move?

Is the weather suitable for you?

Is the neighborhood/area stable?

Are property values increasing or decreasing?

Will the new location allow pets?

Is the residence of a sufficient size or is it too large or too small?
♦   Is there sufficient storage space?
♦   Is there space for gardening?
♦   Is there space for parking an RV?
♦   Can you cook out?

Is the area prone to natural disasters?

Have you considered earthquake insurance, flood insurance?

Have you looked at the residence through the eyes of a senior citizen?

Are there too many stairs?
Can ramps be easily installed?
Can hand rails, grab bars be easily installed?
Can the residence be easily maintained?
What jobs need to be done to prevent major expenses in the future?
♦   De-limb or top trees? Clean or replace roof?
♦   Update electrical service? Clean the chimney?
Are there bathroom or laundry facilities installed on the first floor
Will it fit your needs 15 years from now?

Have you considered health and safety issues?

Do you feel safe in the neighborhood or area?
Is the police and fire protection adequate and easily accessible?
Do you require a home alarm system?
Is emergency medical care easily accessible?
Are hospitals easily accessible?
Are the healthcare providers competent and easily accessible?
Is public transportation available? Accessible?

How do the support and social groups stack up to your present location?

Are professional consultants, such as financial planners, attorneys, competent? Accessible?

Are the following available?, Easily accessible?

Recreation facilities	Libraries
Places of worship	Volunteer opportunities
Shopping	Cultural actives
Community clubs	Restaurants
Senior citizen programs	Travel accommodations
Family members	TV / Cable reception
Friends or social networking opportunities	
Neighbors who are compatible with your age, outlook	
Various kinds of support groups	

Are community services available?

Meals-on wheels   Chore services   Senior services

Can you afford it on a retirement income?

Have you considered an apartment, a condo, an RV campground or a retirement community (assisted living)?

Should you buy, or should you rent? Will the mortgage payments or rent exceed your capabilities?

Is there a senior citizen discount or limit on property taxes?

What will it cost to maintain? How about the utilities?

Can you shut off rooms to save costs?

Is there an income tax or sales tax in the state?

Have you taken advantage of the $125,000 one time exemption for capital gains on the sale of your prior residence?

Have you considered utilizing a reverse mortgage to provide living funds in retirement?

Does the state have an inheritance tax?

Is it a high-cost-of-probate state?

How to evaluate a prospectus

A prospectus is a legal document which describes *what you should know before investing in a mutual fund or a variable annuity.* There are stiff penalties for any misstatements or omissions in a prospectus.

A prospectus can be confusing. Knowing what to look for takes some of the mystery out of reading one. The following are the items that I look for, at first, when I review a prospectus.

Date. Be sure that you have the most recent edition. Every prospectus must be updated at least once annually.

Minimum Investment. This is the dollar amount required to open an account.

Investment Objective. All funds have investment objectives which describe what the fund is trying to do. **Equity funds** may have objectives such as aggressive growth, income, growth or growth and income. **Fixed income funds'** objectives generally define the debt instrument in which they invest, e.g., corporate bond, high quality government bond, treasury bond, municipal bond insured. Hybrid funds, which could include a mix of equity and fixed income investments, generally describe their investment approach.

Performance. This is the condensed financial information. If the performance is not provided, you can estimate the total return by the following formula. ((End Net Asset Value [Minus] Beginning Net Asset Value) [Plus] (Dividend and Net Realized Distributions) [Divided by] Beginning Net Asset Value. I personally don't use the "ratio of net investment to average net assets" which is required information. A fund which pays most of its income out as a distribution (e.g., a Bond Fund) will have a greater ratio than one that doesn't.

Investment Policy.   This describes the personality of the fund.

Risk. This is the *core of the prospectus.* You should review carefully what types of risks to expect with this fund.

Fee Table. This describes the types of fees, front-end sales charges, back-end charges, management fees, etc.

All other things being equal, the fund with the lower fees will have the best return on your investment. Rarely are all other things equal.

The prospectus also includes information on such topics as "how to redeem shares," description of the Investment Advisor, the Transfer Agent, etc. which you may find of value.

Keep in mind that historical earnings are not intended to indicate future performance.

Living arrangements for elderly retirees

Adult day care. Provides supervised care for frail and disabled adults in a group setting. Services, in addition to nutrition and social contact, may include therapy and counseling.

Chore services. In-home assistance by volunteers or paid professionals to help with household tasks and home repairs.

Nursing homes. Up to three levels of care maybe provided:
  Skilled. 24 hour medical supervision.
  Intermediate. Assistance for daily living and some nursing supervision.
  Custodial. Personal care and other activities of daily living without nursing supervision.

Nutritional services. Programs, such as meals-on-wheels provide nutrition to home bound seniors.

Respite care. Similar to adult daycare facilities, but dedicated to temporarily relieving family members and other in-home care providers. Services may extend to overnight or longer stays in nursing homes or hospitals.

Retirement communities (Multi-level care facilities). These facilities offer a variety of living arrangements. Often they include the three levels of skilled care, intermediate care and custodial care. Furthermore, they offer group activities and independent living arrangements in apartments or cottages. Meals may be provided in a communal setting.

Shared residences. Older people living with their adult children or grandchildren is the most common illustration. Communities are now changing their zoning laws to allow shared residences of non-related elderly. These are often called adult family or adult boarding homes. The issues for the elderly involve the availability of professional caregivers, such as doctors, nurses and physical therapists.

Long-term care insurance definitions

Activities of daily living. Certification by a caregiver professional that the patient is unable to perform the activities of daily living such as walking, eating, dressing, taking medication, bathing, et al.

Benefits. The maximum daily or monthly amount the policy will pay.

Coverage. Explains the level of coverage for the policy. Policy may include some or all of the following levels:
- Skilled care
- Intermediate care

- ◆ Custodial care at an approved facility
- ◆ Custodial care at home
- ◆ Respite care

Due diligence. The process of reviewing the long-term-care needs as compared to those provided by the policy.

Gatekeepers (also see restrictions). Provisions in the policy, such as three-day prior hospitalization, before the policy will payout. Some policies require a nursing home stay before they will provide home care.

Inflation rider. Policy benefits increase annually based on some index, such as the Consumer Price Index (CPI) in order to keep up with inflation.

Renewability. Many states now require guaranteed renewability. Renewability is the right to continue coverage providing the premiums are paid. The insurance company has the right to change the premium, but only if it is changed for all persons in a particular class.

Restrictions. Policy may not pay for some mental illnesses, such as Alzheimer's disease. Policy may not provide for home care or specific professional services are required before payment made.

Waiting period. This is the period of time before policy payments begin. Usually this is expressed in number of days (e.g., 100 days). The longer the waiting period, the lower the premium.

Unified Federal Gift and Estate Tax Rates

Taxable Estate	Estate or Gift Tax	Tax on excess of Taxable Estate
*$600,000	$0	37%
$750,000	$248,300	39%
$1,000,000	$345,800	41%
$1,250,000	$448,300	43%
$1,500,000	$555,800	45%
$2,000,000	$780,800	49%
$2,500,000	$1,025,800	53%
$3,000,000	$1,290,800	55%

*Note: Because the unified credit amount is deducted as an absolute dollar amount (see appendix 21b), estate taxes, for all practical purposes, begin at the 37% level.

Federal Estate Tax Worksheet
To estimate federal estate taxes due

Total Gross Estate	$ _____	◆ **Total of all assets owned, including insurance policies with rights of ownership**

Less:

Estate administrative and funeral expenses	($ _____)	
Estate debts	($ _____)	
Marital Deduction	($ _____)	◆ **Include mortgages**
Charitable Deduction	($ _____)	

Equals:

Taxable Estate	$ _____

Multiply:

Taxable estate by tax rate	(X) _____ %	◆ **Multiply taxable estate by rates listed in appendix 21a to approximate tentative tax for estates over $600,000**

Equals:

Tentative Estate Tax	$ _____

Less:

Unified Tax Credit	($ _____192,800_____)

Plus: (If applicable)

Excess retirement accumulation tax	$ _____	◆ **15% excise tax for excess accumulation of tax deferred retirement**
Generation-skipping tax	$ _____	◆ **55% tax on generation skipping transfers**

Equals:

Total Estate Tax due:	$ _____

Resource References

Personal Finances & Financial Planning

Cotton, Kathleen L. *Spend Your Way to Wealth*. Boston Books, 1992.

Hall & McDonald. *The Pros and Cons of Mortgage Prepayments*. Personal Financial Planning, July/August 1993, pp31-36.

Leimberg Satinsky, LeClair and Doyle. *The Tools and Techniques of Financial Planning*. National Underwriter, 1993.

Pond, Jonathan D. *Personal Financial Planning Handbook*. Warren, Gorham & Lamont, 1992.

Insurance

Daily, Glenn S. *Does Life Insurance Add Value?* Journal of Financial Planning, October 1993, pp. 154-159.

Gilmour, Robert A. *Long-Term-Care Insurance: Who Really Needs It?* Journal of Financial Planning, October 1992, pp. 144-149.

Leimberg, Satinsky, LeClair and Doyle. *Life Insurance Planning*. National Underwriter, 1993.

Veres, Robert N. *Long-Term Care Complexity*. CFP Today, April 1992, pp. 9-16.

Risk and Investments

Bogle, John C. *Bogel on Mutual Funds*. Richard D. Irwin Inc., 1994.

Bogle, John C. *A Crystal Ball Look at U.S. Markets in the 1990s*. Journal of Financial Planning, January 1993, pp.10-19.

Gibson, Roger C. *Asset Allocation, Balancing Financial Risk*. Richard D. Irwin Inc., 1990.

Hogan Stephen. *Do Variable Annuities Make More Sense After 93 Tax Hike?* Journal of Financial Planning, July 1994, pp. 131-136.

Malkiel, Burton G. *A Random Walk Down Wall Street*. W. W. Norton Company, 1990.

Mittra, Sid. *Investment Strategies for Fixed-Income Securities.* Journal of Financial Planning, October 1993, pp166-174.

Stine & Lewis. *Guidelines for Rebalancing Passive-Investment Portfolios.* Journal of Financial Planning, April 1992, pp. 80-86.

Retirement Planning

Comberiate, Leonard B. *IRA Minimum Distributions: Pitfalls and Sand Traps.* Journal of Financial Planning, October 1993, pp. 160-165.

Estate Planning

Currie, David R. *Planning for Generation-Skipping Transfers.* Journal of Financial Planning, April 1991, pp. 93-99.

Drake & Whiteley. *Estate Planning for the Calhouns: A Case Study.* Journal of Financial Planning, July 1994, pp116-123.

Hopewell, Lynn. *Advantages of Revocable Trusts.* Journal of Financial Planning, April 1994,   pp.87-91.

Leimberg, Satinsky, LeClair and Doyle. *Estate Planning.* National Underwriter, 1993.

Plaintalk Program 81. *Revocable Living Trusts.* Planning Focus Inc, 1993.

Plaintalk Program 88. *Estate Planning: The Common Mistakes.* Planning Focus Inc., 1994.

Schumacher, Vickie and Jim. *Understanding Living Trusts.* Schumacher and Company, 1992.

Lifestyle Issues

Barbara M. O'Neill. *Till Debt Do Us Part: Financial Consequences of Divorce.* Journal of Financial Planning, October 1992, pp. 159-165.

Chapman, Elwood N. *Comfort Zones.* Crisp Publications Inc., 1990.

Chenn, Connie S. P. *The Financial Planner as Mediator, Parts 1 & 2.* Personal Financial Planning, July/August 1993, pp. 3-7 and September/October 1993, pp. 3-6.

Maton, Cicly Carson. *Who Gets What? Distributing Marital Property.* Journal of Financial Planning, April 1993, pp. 72-77.

Miller, Kathleen, CFP, MBA. *Fair Share Divorce for Women.* Miller, Bird Advisors, Inc. 1995.

Plaintalk Program 80. *Second Marriage Planning.* Planning Focus Inc., 1993.

Plaintalk Program 87. *Planning for Incompetency: 48 Ideas.* Planning Focus Inc., 1994.

Social Programs

Landis, Andy. *Social Security, The Inside Story.* Mount Vernon Press, 1993.

Thompson, Dussault and Bleck. *Elder Law and Medicaid Planning Issues in Washington.* PESI, 1992.

Walsh, Janet L. *Plugging the Gaps with Medigap.* Journal of Financial Planning, April 1993, pp. 68-71.

Planning for the Small Business Owner

Fisher & Jones. *Estate Planning for the Family Business, Parts 1 & 2.* Personal Financial Planning, July/August 1992, pp. 17-21, and September/October 1992, pp. 30-35.

Plaintalk Program 79. *Family Businesses: The Inside/Outside Children Conflict.* Planning Focus Inc. 1994.

Smith, James F. *Financial Planning for the Small Business Owner.* Personal Financial Planning, January/February, 1993, pp30-35.

Stanley R. Byrd, *J.D., C.F.P. Asset Protection: The key to keeping what you own.* Seattle, 1994.

Wiggins, Joseph A. Jr. *Preserving Assets Through Family Limited Partnerships.* Personal Financial Planning, September/October, 1993, pp. 28-32.

Glossary

adjusted gross income: The amount shown on line 31 of IRS form 1040 resulting from adjusting gross income by specific allowances.

alimony: *See maintenance.*

alternative minimum tax : A secondary tax calculation designed to insure that everyone pays his or her *fair-share* of taxes.

American Arbitration Association: A non-profit organization which trains people to be divorce mediators.

annual gifting: Each individual is entitled to gift up to $10,000 of present interest value to one or more individuals annually without paying a gift tax.

annuity: A stream of payments at specific intervals for a specified period.

asset allocation: A top-down approach which uses asset diversification to match the long-term risk and return goals of the investor.

assets: Things you own recorded at fair market value.

average cost: A method to value distributions from IRAs.

back-end load (Class B share): A commission expense incurred when class B shares are redeemed before a specified time.

balance sheet: A financial statement which summarizes by category all assets and liabilities and presents them at fair market value.

Bankruptcy Reform Act of 1994: The act that enables maintenance to be paid to divorced spouses during bankruptcy.

bankruptcy risk: The possibility of a company's liabilities exceeding its assets by such an extent that a court has to intervene between the company and its creditors.

beta (β) systematic risk: Measures the change in the stock market as a whole, often called market volatility.

board of trustees: A committee elected by the shareholders of a mutual fund to manage the fund.

bonds: Promissory notes issued either by corporations or government agencies which carry a fixed rate of return.

brokerage costs: The cost to buy and sell securities.

bunko schemes: *See con games.*

by-pass trust (Credit or B trust): A trust set-up to protect the unified tax credit of the deceased.

capital gains tax exclusion section 121: *See Internal Revenue Code (IRC) section 121.*

capital gain: The difference between the cost, as adjusted, and the selling price.

cash expense: The use of cash to pay for expenses.

cash flow statement: A financial statement which summarizes cash inflow (consisting of gross income) less cash outflow (consisting of amounts used) to pay expenses.

cash value: The amount available to the policy owner at the cancellation of the insurance contract.

certificate of deposit (CD): A money market instrument issued by a bank which pays a fixed interest rate for a specified period of time.

certified financial planner (CFP): A person certified by the *International Board of Standards and Practices for Certified Financial Planners (ICBFP)*, *and*. maintains the license by meeting post-certification requirements, e.g., continuing education, and abides by the established code of ethics.

certified public accountant (CPA): A person licensed by his or her state, who has passed a certification test, met educational standards and satisfied specified experience requirements.

charitable gifts: Gifts to a public or private charity.

charitable lead trust (CLT): A charitable trust whereby the charity receives income from the gift for a stated period of time, following which the gift is transferred to the beneficiary named in the trust document.

charitable remainder trust (CRT): A charitable trust whereby the grantor receives income from the gifted assets for a stated period of time, which could be for life, following which the gift is transferred to the charity.

collateralized mortgage obligation (CMO): A cash-flow bond in which payments from the underlying mortgage pools pay principal and interest to the CMO bondholders.

commission expense: The compensation paid for investment advice.

common stock (equities): Certificates which provide evidence of partial ownership of a corporation. Stocks may pay a dividend and, when traded in the stock market, may appreciate in value.

community property agreement (survivorship agreement): A legal contract in the State of Washington whereby a person can transfer all separate and community property to his or her spouse and avoid the probate process.

community property state: A state whose property law follows the Spanish law, whereby a spouse owns 50% of the married couples' property with certain exceptions.

con-games/bunko schemes: Various types of schemes to defraud people. The elderly are prime targets.

consumer price index (CPI): An index which measures the change in the cost of goods purchased by a typical wage-earner when compared to a base-period index.

contingent deferred sales charge (CDCS): The commission paid on most insurance products should the investor terminate the contract early.

cost of living adjustments (COLA): Automatic adjustments based on an inflation index, usually the Consumer Price Index.

Crummey powers: An annual $10,000 gift tax exclusion is available—provided the donee has the right to the immediate use of the gift. The beneficiaries must be notified regarding their capability of withdrawing gifts from the trust.

defined benefit plan: A qualified pension plan which requires mandatory contributions by the employer and pays out a pre-determined benefit based on the employees, age, years of service and compensation.

defined contribution plan: A qualified pension plan which allows an employer contribution, as well as allowing the employee to contribute pre-tax dollars. The amount available for pensions is based on the growth of the investment.

Department of Labor (DOL): An agency of the U.S. government which administers pension plans under the Employee Retirement Income Security Act (ERISA).

direct transfer rollover: A direct transfer of a distribution from a qualified plan to an IRA or other qualified plan.

discretionary cash: The amount remaining after all necessary expenses have been paid.

diversification: An investment strategy which determines the percentage of specific an investor holds, securities to minimize market volatility risk and bankruptcy risk.

divorce mediation: A negotiation between the parties to a divorce overseen by a trained, impartial mediator.

dollar cost averaging: The continuous investing of the same dollar amount at fixed intervals—regardless of market volatility.

durable power of attorney (DPA): A legal document which will enable a party of one's choice to step in and handle that person's affairs should he or she become incapacitated.

early withdrawal penalty: A 10% penalty imposed, except under prescribed circumstances, on distributions from IRAs and qualified plans before age $59\frac{1}{2}$.

emergency fund: A fund of liquid assets maintained to meet low-level emergencies.

Employee Retirement Income Security Act 1974 (ERISA): A law designed to protect the interests of workers and their beneficiaries in qualified plans.

equities: *See common stock.*

estate attorneys: Attorneys who specialize in wills, estate planning and probate.

estate taxation: The federal estate tax due on net estate assets which exceed the unified tax credit, which is currently $600,000. Taxes by states on estate assets are called inheritance taxes.

estate: The gross fair market value of all assets owned or deemed to be owned at the time of a person's death.

excess accumulation tax: A 15% penalty imposed on distributions exceeding $112,500 indexed for inflation from IRAs and qualified plans. Also, a 15% penalty is imposed on excessive accumulations in addition to regular estate taxes.

executor (personal representative): A person appointed by the court to inventory and value assets, notify creditors, pay bills and distribute the remainder of an estate according to the will's provisions.

expense: A financial outlay to obtain some benefit, e.g., a utility bill is an expense.

fair market value: The price at which an independent willing seller and an independent willing buyer would exchange an asset.

family limited partnership (FLP): An association of family members created to manage partnership assets, which provides limited liability to certain partners. The partnership also provides the opportunity to transfer worth at less than fair market value.

Federal Deposit Insurance Corporation (FDIC): An agency of the U.S. government which oversees and guarantees bank deposits up $100,000 per account.

Federal Reserve System Board of Governors (FED): A committee of seven governors appointed by the President to independently manage the nation's monetary growth and credit to meet the needs of the economy and to control inflation.

fee only planners: Financial planners who charge a fee for developing a financial plan, but do charge a commission for any products purchased as a result of the plan.

50% joint annuity: This pension annuity is reduced by 50% should the non-working spouse survive the retiree.

financial survival risk: *See bankruptcy risk.*

first in, first out (FIFO): A method to value distributions from IRAs.

first-to-die insurance policy: An insurance policy covering a married couple, which pays proceeds at the time of the first death.

fixed annuity: An insurance product which pays fixed amounts during the annuity period.

fixed option of 401(k): The allocation of the contribution which guarantees a fixed return. *See guaranteed investment contract (GIC).*

401(k) plan: A qualified profit-sharing plan named after a section of the internal revenue code. Contributions are not taxed until distributed.

front-end load (Class A share): A commission paid immediately after investing in a mutual fund selling Class A shares.

general obligation bond: A type of MUNI bond which bears the full faith and credit of the taxing authority in case of default.

generation skipping tax: An additional tax imposed at the highest level estate tax rate, currently 55%, on transfers which skip ageneration.

grantor retained interest trust (GRIT): A trust most often used with a primary or secondary residence to transfer the value out of the estate at a bargain value. The grantor must outlive the terms of the trust for it to be effective.

guaranteed investment contract (GIC): A investment of pension funds with an insurance company which guarantees a fixed return.

health maintenance organizations (HMOs): Health organizations which provide members comprehensive medical care.

healthcare directive (living will): Signed instructions to the healthcare provider regarding the use of artificial means including hydration and nutrition to sustain life.

healthcare durable power of attorney: A document which empowers a third-party to make healthcare decisions should the grantor become incompacitated.

high cost: A method to value distributions from IRAs.

high-yield bond fund: A mutual fund which invests in high-yield bonds.

income: A benefit gained by utilizing labor or investing capital. There is a difference between cash inflow (actual dollars received) and income.

individual retirement account (IRA): A tax-deferred personal retirement savings plan of both deductible and non-deductible contributions invested with a custodian, such as a mutual fund. Non-working spouses can contribute up to $2,000.

inflation: A measure of the change of the cost to purchase the same item from period to period. Caused by too many dollars chasing too few goods.

inheritance taxes: *See estate taxation.*

insurance guaranty funds: Arrangements between state insurance commissions and a pool of licensed insurance companies to pay off any life insurance policies in default due to bankruptcy of a member company.

insurance trust (wealth replacement): A trust set up to purchase insurance for the grantor. The use of Crummey powers facilitates the use of the annual gift tax exclusion.

inter vivos (living) trust: A trust established during a person's lifetime.

interest rate change: A change in the rate of interest paid for U.S. government debt obligations—usually as a result of a move by the FED to control inflation or to spur the economy. This usually results in a change in interest rates of all debt instruments.

Internal Revenue Code (IRC) section 121: That section of the code that deals with the one-time exclusion of capital gains on the sale of a house for people age 55 and over.

investment advisors: Professional investors for mutual funds, insurance companies and other types of money managers.

investment strategy: A method to achieve an investment goal.

joint annuity: Pension annuity based on the joint lives of the retiree and his or her spouse. This is automatic for a married couple unless the non-working spouse agrees in writing to a variation.

joint tenancy with right of survivorship: Property held by two or more people which transfers in its entirety to the survivor.

level load (Class C share): An annual commission expense levied on the total value of a class C mutual fund holding.

liquidity: The ability to convert the value of a security or other asset into cash.

living trust: *See inter vivos trust.*

loads: *See commission expense.*

long-term care insurance (LTC): An insurance policy designed to provide health-care, including nursing home and custodial care, due to prolonged illness or disability.

low cost: A method to value distributions from IRAs.

lump sum distribution: The total distribution of the account from a qualified plan within one calendar year.

magic of compounding: The extraordinary power to build wealth by reinvesting earnings to gain further earnings.

maintenance: An allowance paid as a result of a legal separation or divorce.

management fee: A fee deducted by a mutual fund from the fund's earnings for portfolio supervision.

marital deduction: The right under the Economic Recovery Act of 1981 to transfer all assets to a spouse without incurring either a gift tax or an estate tax.

market timing: An investment strategy where the investor or investment advisor attempts to exit the market before a downturn and enter the market before an upturn.

market volatility: *See beta.*

marketability: The ability to sell when desired.

mediation: A negotiation process between the divorcing spouses under the auspices of a trained divorce mediator.

Medicaid: A federal program that provides healthcare for the poor.

Medicare approved/accepted charge: The amount Medicare will pay to participating physicians.

Medicare enrollment period: A six-month window time to enroll in Medicare. Failure to enroll during this time requires the enrollee to wait for a specified annual period before enrolling.

Medicare special enrollment: A special enrollment period for people who wish to work past age sixty-five and are covered by their employers' health insurance.

Medicare: The health insurance program from Social Security for people over age sixty-five. Both employers and employees contribute to this program.

Medicare, Part A: That portion of Medicare that covers hospital bills, skilled nursing facilities and hospice.

Medicare, Part B: That portion of Medicare that covers doctor bills and many medical services not covered by Part A. Enrollees pay a portion of these costs.

Medicare/Medicaid Assistance Program (MMAP): A service provided by American Association of Retired People (AARP) to counsel enrollees in Medicare and Medicaid.

medigap insurance: Health insurance sold by private companies to supplement Medicare. Ten standard policies cover such needs as eye and dental care not provided by Medicare.

minimum distributions at age $70\frac{1}{2}$: A requirement to begin taking a portion of funds saved in IRAs and qualified plans. Failure to begin distributions could result a penalty of 50% of the required distribution.

money market funds (MMF): Investments in short term government debt, and commercial paper.

monthly pension: The distribution of a pension in the form of an annuity.

Morningstar: A publication and independent reviewer of mutual fund and variable annuities.

MUNI bond fund: A mutual fund which invests in municipal bonds.

municipal bond (MUNI): A debt issue by a state or municipality on which the interest paid is usually federal income tax free.

mutual funds: Investment companies which sell shares and invest the proceeds in the securities market. The shareholders own their portion of the underlying assets and vote for the board of trustees.

National Association of Securities Dealers Automated Quotation System (NASDAQ): A self-regulatory organization established by law to oversee the over-the-counter securities market.

net worth: The fair market value of what a person owns after deducting all liabilities.

no-load: A mutual fund sold without any commission expense.

100% joint annuity: This pension annuity maintains the amount paid to both spouses should the spouse survive the retiree.

opportunity costs: The cost of accepting a lower return than similar funds with similar risk characteristics.

other mutual fund expenses: Fees paid to compensate for the cost of recordkeeping, auditing, and other shareholder services.

Pension Guarantee Board: An agency of the U.S. Government which administers qualified pension plans and guarantees their solvency.

pourover will: A will used in conjunction with a living trust to provide for assets not transferred into the trust. Any asset distributed via a pourover will is subject to probate.

present value (PV): A mathematical method to discount future case inflows and outflows to a present dollar value.

private activity municipal securities: A type of MUNI which invests in private activities, such as housing projects— the interest of which is subject to the alternative minimum tax.

probate: A legal process to validate and carry out the instructions in a will.

probate assets: Assets that, because of their nature, must go through the probate process.

prospectus: A legal document that describes the investment objectives of a mutual fund, its investment techniques, financial results, organization, and other information which should be known before a purchase is made.

qualified disclaimer: A provision in a will which enables the primary inheritor to disclaim the inheritance, thereby allowing it to go to the next person in line.

qualified domestic relations order (QDRO): A written divorce decree.

qualified pension plan: A plan which meets specific requirements to be qualified for tax-deferred contributions.

qualified terminal interest trust (QTIP): A type of trust eligible for the marital deduction which still enables the grantor to have the remainder distributed according to his or her wishes.

reinvestment risk: A risk resulting from a change in interest rates, which could result in a lower return when funds are reinvested after a current debt investment matures.

Request for Earnings and Benefits Estimate Statement: A form used to request a record of Social Security earnings and an estimate of Social Security benefits payable at ages sixty-two and sixty-five.

return on investment: The income earned from the activity of investing capital expressed as a percentage of the amount invested.

revenue bond: A type of MUNI bond which repays the principal and interest from the revenues of the project for which the bonds were floated.

risk/return relationship: An investment theory which presumes that a knowledgeable investor will require a greater return for assuming a greater risk.

salary reduction-simplified employee pension plan (SAR-SEP): A SEP to which an employee can contribute. New SAR-SEPs cannot be established after 1996.

Savings Incentive Match Plan for Employees (Simple plan) Either an IRA or a 401(k) type for companies of 100 employees or less, which avoids some of the testing and top heavy rules.

second to die insurance policy: An insurance policy covering a married couple which pays the proceeds upon the death of the second spouse.

Securities and Exchange Commission (SEC): A federal agency which enforces the Investment Advisors Act and similar statutes by regulating the securities market.

shareholders: Owners of shares of corporations and mutual funds.

short-term debt: Liabilities due and payable within one year.

simplified employee pension plan (SEP): An individual retirement account set up through an employer which allows an greater rate of contribution than a normal IRA.

single life annuity: A pension annuity based on the life of the pensioner only which will cease with his or her death.

Social Security: A U.S. government program established to protect the individual against the hazards of old age and disability. Social Security also provides survivorship insurance for minors and health insurance for people over age 65. Both employers and employees contribute to this fund.

Social Security disabilities: The types of disabilities covered under the Social Security program.

standard deviation: A statistical approach which measures the range of return for a particular investment or portfolio.

step-up in basis: A change in the value of an asset from its adjusted cost to its fair market value.

subchapter S corporation: A type of corporation which limits liabilities and facilitates the flow-through of income to the owner for tax-reporting purposes.

systematic risk: *See beta.*

T-bills: Direct obligations of the U.S. government initially sold at auction, discounted at the auction rate.

tax deferral: The act of deferring payment of federal income tax on earnings of qualified investments until funds are withdrawn or distributed.

tax-deferred (sheltered) annuities (TDA): An arrangement whereby an employee of a public school or a tax-exempt organization can save tax-deferred earnings for retirement. Also known as a 403(b) plan.

tax-forward averaging: A federal income tax reduction election for a lump sum distribution if employees meet specified criteria. The 5 year option no longer applies after 1999.

taxable estate assets: Estate assets used in calculating estate taxes.

term insurance: Insurance purchased for a specific period of time without any remaining value should the insured survive the period covered.

testamentary trusts: Trusts that come into being following a person's death.

too-early penalty: A 10% penalty assessed against distributions from IRAs and qualified plans taken by people who are under the age of $59\frac{1}{2}$ except under certain conditions.

too-much-accumulated penalty: *See excess accumulation penalty.*

12b-1 distribution expense: A separate charge for advertising, marketing and distribution services.

2503(b) trust: A trust set up for minors whereby the income must be distributed annually.

U.S. dollar value change: The investment risk associated with the relationship of the U.S. dollar to foreign currencies.

unified tax credit (UTC): An exemption of net estate asset value from federal estate taxes. Currently the UTC is $600,000.

Uniform Gifts to Minors Act (UGMA): An arrangement which enables gifts to minors to qualify for the annual gift tax exclusion and still be managed by a custodian until the minor reaches an age specified by state law.

Uniform Transfers to Minors Act (UTMA): A less restricted custodial arrangement than UGMA, adopted by most states.

universal life insurance: Insurance with flexible premiums and adjustable death benefits, the cash value of which changes as current interest rates change.

variable annuity: An insurance product allowing tax-deferral for the net premiums allocated to investment choices available under the contract.

variable life insurance: Insurance where the death benefit varies depending upon the change in the market value of the underlying investments in equities and bonds. Similar to a mutual fund.

vesting: The right to nonforfeiture of pension benefits, usually gained over a period of time.

wealth replacement trust: *See insurance trust.*

whole life insurance: Insurance providing protection for the life of the insured until age 95.

will: A legal document which expresses the wishes of an individual as to the disposal of his or her property.

will contest: A court action to change the bequests in a person's will.

wrap-fee accounts: An account with an annual commission paid to a money manager for on-going management of the investor's portfolio.

Index

For Additional Copies of

The Path to a Successful Retirement

Everyone knows someone they care for, who can benefit from this book.

To order additional copies please send this page and $19.95 ea. plus $4.00 for shipping and handling to:

Sligo Publishing Company
Box #14
1115 Regents Blvd.
Fircrest, WA 98466

(Washington residents, please add $1.58 per book for the 7.9% Sales Tax due)

Ship to:

Name _____

Address _____

City/St./Zip _____

Phone number (_____) _____-_____

Method of Payment:

☐ Check enclosed ☐ Mastercard ☐ Visa

Account # _____

Expiration date _____ 19____

Signature _____

Larger quantity discounts are available - Please call (206) 564-5980